PART OF LIFE ITSELF

The War Diary of Lieutenant
Leslie H. Miller, CEF

THE CANADIAN EXPERIENCE OF WAR

Series Editor: Kevin Spooner

This series of monographs, essay collections, and edited primary sources illuminates connections between war and society in Canada, focusing on military operations as well as the experience of civilians and non-combatants. It is supported by funding from the Laurier Centre for the Study of Canada at Wilfrid Laurier University.

LESLIE HOWARD MILLER

Part of Life Itself

*The War Diary of Lieutenant
Leslie H. Miller, CEF*

EDITED BY GRAHAM BROAD

UNIVERSITY OF TORONTO PRESS
Toronto Buffalo London

ISBN 978-1-4875-0386-4 (cloth)
ISBN 978-1-4875-2294-0 (paper)
ISBN 978-1-4875-1895-0 (EPUB)
ISBN 978-1-4875-1894-3 (PDF)

Library and Archives Canada Cataloguing in Publication

Title: Part of life itself : the war diary of Lieutenant Leslie Howard Miller,
CEF / Leslie Howard Miller; edited by Graham Broad.
Other titles: War diary of Lieutenant Leslie Howard Miller, CEF
Names: Miller, Leslie H., 1889–1979, author. | Broad, Graham, 1970–, editor.
Series: Canadian experience of war.
Description: Series statement: The Canadian experience of war |
Includes bibliographical references and index.
Identifiers: Canadiana (print) 20230220738 | Canadiana (ebook) 20230220754 |
ISBN 9781487503864 (cloth) | ISBN 9781487522940 (paper) |
ISBN 9781487518950 (EPUB) | ISBN 9781487518943 (PDF)
Subjects: LCSH: Miller, Leslie H., 1889–1979 – Diaries. | LCSH: Canada. Canadian
Army. Canadian Expeditionary Force – History. | LCSH: World War, 1914–1918 –
Personal narratives, Canadian.
Classification: LCC D640.M55 2023 | DDC 940.4/8171–dc23

Cover design: Lara Minja
Cover image: Ivor Castle, "Comfort and Safety," June 1917, Canada. Based on
Dept. of National Defence/Library and Archives Canada/PA-001478.

We wish to acknowledge the land on which the University of Toronto Press
operates. This land is the traditional territory of the Wendat, the Anishnaabeg, the
Haudenosaunee, the Métis, and the Mississaugas of the Credit First Nation.

The Laurier Centre for the Study of Canada generously provided financial assistance for
the publication of this book.

University of Toronto Press acknowledges the financial support of the Government of
Canada, the Canada Council for the Arts, and the Ontario Arts Council, an agency of
the Government of Ontario, for its publishing activities.

**Canada Council
for the Arts**

**Conseil des Arts
du Canada**

ONTARIO ARTS COUNCIL
CONSEIL DES ARTS DE L'ONTARIO

an Ontario government agency
un organisme du gouvernement de l'Ontario

Funded by the   Financé par le
Government   gouvernement
of Canada   du Canada

Printed and bound by CPI Group (UK) Ltd, Croydon, CR0 4YY

There are no winners in war, whether soldier, civilian, animal, or nature. The family of Leslie Miller and Patricia Sinclair dedicate this diary to the memory of all who endured in the belief that it was the war to end all wars.

Contents

Leslie Howard Miller, 1889–1979. Credit: Miller family collection.

Foreword

The ridge was swarmed by Canadians. As on the day of the historic battle, one hundred years before, Canadians appeared in unanticipated numbers on 9 April 2017. Not the Department of Veterans Affairs, not the French government, not even the Parks Canada guides expected the more than 25,000 Canadians who travelled to Vimy that day to witness the ceremonies commemorating the anniversary. Among the hordes of visitors, 5,000 high school students thronged the Vimy Memorial grounds; they paraded their school banners and sang their national anthem repeatedly, astonishing event organizers with their numbers and fervour. The spectacle had an ironic resonance: exactly a century earlier, the German Army occupiers of Vimy Ridge were surprised, overwhelmed, and dislodged by members of the Canadian Expeditionary Force.

"April 9, 1917, will be in Canada's history one of the great days, a day of glory to furnish inspiration to her sons for generations," one war correspondent declared about the stunning victory. Such was the Battle of Vimy Ridge. Over four days following Easter weekend in 1917, nearly 100,000 Canadian soldiers – many just a few years older than the students observing the anniversary ceremony – climbed out of their trenches and seized the ground that British and French armies had failed to wrest from the Germans the previous two years. The cost was severe – 10,000 casualties, including more than 3,500 dead – but for the first time in that war to end all wars, a force of colonial soldiers had prevailed.

It was day four of the Vimy one hundredth anniversary commemoration trip I was taking part in. As historian and author of *Victory at Vimy: Canada Comes of Age, April 9–12, 1917*, I had been invited to offer context and tell the stories of individual Canadians who had taken this ridge to about fifty students from Uxbridge Secondary School, located northeast of Toronto. For these young people, the trip had become one of the best examples of experiential learning that they had ever known. After studying this iconic battle at home and in the classroom with the aid of books, video, and the internet, it was time for them to walk the ground, understand the distances and conditions, and view the graveyards of the fallen soldiers.

I could tell these teenagers had changed, even in the few days we'd been together on the road in France. One of them, Sam Futhy, a Grade 10 student, remarked on a visit to one of the Great War cemeteries: "When I saw the number of gravestones," he said, "I don't know. It just hit me."

Together, the students and I stopped and studied the restored Canadian trenches and the historic network of tunnels that Canadian miners, sodbusters, railroaders, and engineers had dug beneath the ridge in the months before the battle. I knelt down on one of the parapets and pointed to the ridge where the former German defensive lines had been situated in April 1917. I suggested any one of them could have thrown a baseball into the German lines; they were that close.

The farther up the ridge towards Hill 145 we trekked the larger loomed one of our country's most famous war monuments, the Vimy Memorial. Just beyond Walter Allward's two towering plinths commemorating the Great War, unveiled in July 1936, was where the students would attend the anniversary ceremony that day. There they stood solemnly through "The Last Post," a reciting of "For the Fallen" and "Reveille." They heard dignitaries – Prince Charles, President Gérard Hollande, and Prime Minister Justin Trudeau – speak in reverent terms of what had happened there a century ago. "As I see the faces gathered here – veterans, soldiers, caregivers, so many young people – I can't help but feel a torch is being passed," Trudeau said. "One hundred years later, we must say this, together. And we must believe it: Never again."

I couldn't help thinking that the prime minister's call to action had fallen on the most attentive ears possible. I learned that not only did these students look the part – with their Vimy commemorative jackets and sombre demeanour at a Great War memorial – but also that they were intellectually prepared. The day before, Sam Futhy had visited a Royal Newfoundland Regiment cemetery to honour a family relative, Ambrose Stride. Grade 11 student Scarlet Minshul had paid tribute to Uxbridge local Walter Gould, who had served at Vimy. And Grade 11 student Emma Runnalls brought her knowledge of Uxbridge-born Colonel Sam Sharpe, who saw his Ontario county battalion bloodied at Vimy – ten killed and thirty wounded simply repairing communication wire – on the first night of the battle. "I'm thankful to have had the chance to come here and do this," Emma told me.

One might sit at home in Canada and criticize these pilgrimages as just another field trip where young people of some means get a chance to zip off to exotic places, blow off some steam, and give the impression that they care. Well, I found evidence to the contrary. And I found it all around me. Following the observance that anniversary day, and as the crush of 25,000 spectators made its way to shuttle buses under the watchful eyes of gendarmerie security forces, a young man approached me. "Are you Ted Barris?" he asked. "You probably don't remember me, but we met here on the Vimy grounds ten years ago." Robb Phillips, then a twenty-something adult, reminded me of our first encounter at Vimy in 2007. Like the current group of student pilgrims, Phillips, a decade earlier a high school student from Pickering, Ontario, had saved and studied to get to Vimy to commemorate a relative, Corporal Joseph Kennedy of the 161st Huron Battalion. He still felt an attachment to Kennedy, wounded by shrapnel and gas, but still active during the Canadians' last hundred days of the Great War. He admitted the whole experience had changed him. "I'm here out of respect and love of history," he said. And on that hundredth anniversary day, Phillips wore the same green khaki army shirt he had worn in 2007, with the name "Joseph Kennedy" inscribed on a white patch sewn above his breast pocket. "I just had to come back!"

When the original Vimy veterans reached the top of the ridge, between 9 and 12 April 1917, the French press called their achievement "Canada's Easter gift to France." When the modern pilgrims swarmed over the historic site, a hundred years later, they heard average French citizens applaud them wildly. Among those citizens was a local electrical worker. When he was asked why he had given up his Sunday off for a pilgrimage to Vimy, he shrugged: "Back then, you came out for us," he said. "Today, we come out for you."

There is no indication that any of the Uxbridge high school teenagers, or even history-smitten Vimy returnee Robb Phillips, will ever have to live up to the prime minister's plea of "Never again!" But walking there among those battlefields and war memorials, they certainly realized a greater chance of success than those who dare to ignore the history of war altogether.

Of course, part of learning the lessons of history comes from the study of those who lived it. And that study delivers the greatest impact when history's witnesses write things down. Fortunately, the practice of composing letters and keeping a diary was common among women and men of Leslie Howard Miller's generation. His journal writing commences on 10 January 1915, after he purchases a diary and begins to reflect on his wartime journey from enlistment, in October 1914, while working as a school principal near Stoughton, Saskatchewan and continues until the day before spring in 1919 when he walks up the gangway of the SS *Cedric* for his transatlantic journey home to Canada. What lies between the lines of this diary is a truly Canadian story. Miller, unlike so many of his Great War comrades, was born in Canada (thousands in the CEF were native to the British Isles and thus patriotically drawn into the war to defend Mother England). Miller's ancestors had helped found Upper Canada. So, when he enlisted, it was as a Canadian fighting a Canadian fight. That he survived, when 60,000 of his compatriots did not, is miracle enough.

As appropriate bookends to the diary, writer and historian Graham Broad offers the reader a picture in words of Leslie Miller before the Great War and after. And it is in Broad's vivid biographical account where we learn about Miller's epiphany to share his sole souvenirs of the war in Europe with those who visited his farm in Ontario in the years that followed his safe return. Whether collected from the shattered woods atop Vimy Ridge or elsewhere, Miller brought dozens of acorns home from France and planted them on his property, actually lining the roadway to his farm house. His planting became the inspiration for the name of his farm – the Vimy Oaks. And his gift of commemoration would come full circle, one day returning descendant oak seedlings to former battlefields in France whence the original acorns came.

For me, and for students of history reading the diary entries that follow, Miller's drive to be an educator shines through. He offers the realities of life recorded in the trenches, while he keeps us grounded with his unique reflections on soldiers (on both sides) and civilians consumed by the war. Of Vimy he offers just statistics – "we took 12,000 prisoners and 150 guns" – and the realization that it was a "great attack" and a nearby village was "utterly destroyed by our shellfire."

There along the farm lane where he lived out his postwar life, Leslie Miller used his Vimy Oaks to teach those who stopped to look and listen that from united effort came restored freedom, from a threatened species of oak came rebirth, and from a war to end all wars came lessons for peaceful renewal a hundred years on and beyond.

The invitation to write this foreword has additional meaning for me. As a resident of Scarborough, where I was raised in the 1950s and 1960s, I rode my bicycle and walked by Miller's historic oaks hundreds of times without realizing their significance. Now, many years later, I share the honour of inviting you into the life of a homegrown son of Canada, a volunteer in its military service, and a teacher of its values.

Ted Barris

Miller Family Acknowledgments

Leslie Miller had a brother, Carman, who was a child during the First World War and with whom Leslie kept up a correspondence during and after the war. Carman married in 1938 and had two children, Brandt and Dan, who, after the death of Carman, inherited Leslie's diaries and photographs from the war. Brandt and Dan undertook to transcribe the diaries into digital form in a first step towards eventual publication.

Leslie and Carman had a great-nephew, Richard Breakey, who, with help from his wife, Kathy, worked with Brandt and Dan to proofread the digital copy of the diaries.

Patricia Sinclair of Toronto was politically active in the Scarborough area of northeast Toronto in which Leslie's farm, Vimy Oaks, had been located. When she learned of the diary, she offered her services in getting it published. Her offer was welcomed by Brandt, Dan, and Richard.

This led to a meeting in France at the Vimy Memorial in April 2017, during the Vimy commemorations, out of which a close and collaborative relationship was established between Patricia, Brandt, Dan, and Richard.

Patricia Sinclair introduced the diary project to the University of Toronto Press, who undertook to publish it, and to the historian Graham Broad of King's University College at Western University, who annotated it, and together we put it into publishable form.

Editor's Acknowledgments

Preparing this diary for publication required the assistance of several people, but my first order of thanks goes to Leslie Miller's nephews Brandt and Dan Miller for entrusting their uncle's diary to me. Patricia Sinclair, who represented the family and proposed this project to me, deserves thanks for her detailed knowledge of the diary, which saved me from several embarrassing errors. Miller's diary arrived at an exceedingly busy time in my professional career, and the difficulties of finishing the edits were compounded by the COVID-19 pandemic and the ensuing upheaval in the academic world. The Miller family waited altogether too long for the finished project and I thank them for their patience.

UTP's Len Husband had been a generous and forthright editor, while Anne Laughlin's expert copy-editing has made the final product much better than it would have been. Thanks also to the three anonymous peer reviewers, who provided counsel that was both useful and reassuring. An additional thanks is owed to friends and colleagues at King's University College at Western University. An internal research grant from King's helped to offset costs associated with publication. My research assistants Katie Bastedo, Laura Fyfe, and Katrina Pasierbek aided in ensuring the integrity of the transcription. No one knows more about First World War photography than Carla-Jean Stokes, whose assistance in photo research for this project was invaluable. Emily Amarelo assisted me with proofreading at the 11th hour. Obviously, any remaining errors are my fault alone. As always, thanks go to my wife, Amanda Green, whose own painstaking and careful historical research continues to inspire me.

As the reader will learn, Leslie Miller was for a time a teacher. No doubt his students benefited from his erudition and generous spirit. I hope he would not object if I dedicated my own contributions to this work to

three professors who guided me and indeed kept me from coming to a
bad end, academically speaking: Professors Jack Blocker, Peter Hyland,
and the late Douglas Leighton at Huron University College in London,
Ontario. Each imparted qualities in me that I hope are recognizable in
what follows.

Introduction

This is no ordinary wartime diary, but Leslie H. Miller (1889–1979) was no ordinary soldier. Miller was a teacher who had been an outstanding undergraduate at the University of Toronto's Victoria College, and in this diary he recounts his four years of service in the Canadian Expeditionary Force (CEF) in bracing and at times even eloquent prose. Admittedly, some of his entries are strictly matter-of-fact, written with no greater intent, it seems, than to jog his memory at some future date. But when the fighting starts Miller brings to bear the sharp eye of a writer who might have been a leading war correspondent had he so desired. The battles he describes in the greatest detail, the St. Eloi Craters, Mont Sorrel, Courcelette, and Thiepval Ridge, are nearly forgotten today, but they seared themselves into the memory of the generation that fought them. Miller served in the signals – the branch of the service responsible for communications. He fought the war with telephones, telegraphs, flags, and flares rather than rifles and grenades, but there should be no mistaking him for a "rear echelon" soldier, ensconced far from the action, as his account of the 5th Canadian Infantry Battalion's 26 September 1916 assault on Thiepval Ridge makes clear:

> About midnight trouble began on our right in front of Courcelette. After a little bombing and M.G. fire, Fritz sent up S.O.S. (a red flare bursting into two) and the artillery on both sides opened up. Shells fell thick all round us and we expected to go up any instant. A heavy British shell twice fell short at Bn. Hq. and killed one of our scouts (Bell) wounding another.[1]

---

1 Leslie Miller, *War Diary*, 26 September 1916. Hereafter: Diary, date.

In 1915, a Canadian infantry battalion had a nominal strength of about 35 officers and 1,000 other ranks, organized into a headquarters and four rifle companies.[2] Signallers were attached to the headquarters, but battalion headquarters typically were located in a dugout only a short distance from the front, well within the range of enemy artillery. One gains some appreciation of the peril faced by headquarters personnel in Miller's entry for 27 September 1916, which recounts the terrible fate of the 13th Battalion headquarters, whose officers and men were burned to death when a shell collapsed the exit of their dugout after having set fire to the interior.[3] Moreover, signallers faced many of the same dangers as did men armed with rifles and bayonets. They manned listening posts in saps that jutted precariously into No Man's Land, where they endured terrifying hours to provide warning of enemy attacks. In the thick of battle, often moving alongside or just behind advancing infantry, signallers replaced severed telephone and telegraph wires and ran new ones, passed messages with lights and flags or carried them personally, and helped direct artillery fire from forward positions. More than once, too, Miller was pressed into service as a stretcher bearer even while the fighting raged on, as he describes in the same entry on 27 September 1916:

> We heard that Mr. Wilson, intelligence officer, was up in Hessian trench seriously wounded, so Pongo, Jim Pedley, I and 2 others volunteered to bring him. We crossed to Zollern trench under machine gun fire, and could not get beyond, for Pongo and Jim, as soon as they emerged from the trench with white flag and stretcher, were met by a burst of M.G. fire and twice driven back. Just then an H.E. shrapnel shell burst above us and we thought we would end our careers right there. Our scout guide got the heavy driving band on his head and staggered groaning, "I'm hit". The band fell at my feet and kicked up the dust. But it had struck the chap's helmet a glancing blow and only dinted the metal; he was quite all right in a minute. More shells burst above us and the Hun M.G. raked the trench savagely.[4]

---

2 William Robert Lang, *Organization, Administration and Equipment of His Majesty's Forces in Peace and War* (Toronto: Copp Clark, 1916), 117–18.

3 Diary, 27 September 1916. See also Library and Archives of Canada (LAC) RG9-III-D3, Vol. 4922, File 383, 13th Canadian Infantry Battalion War Diary, 26 September 1916.

4 Diary, 27 September 1916.

Miller's account of these battles reminds us of the annihilating character of trench warfare. At Thiepval Ridge in 1916, nearly half of Miller's battalion was killed or wounded in two days.[5] Yet even amid the brutality, filth, and sheer terror of the Western Front, Miller invariably finds moments to reflect on all that is beautiful and delicate in what remains. Rare birds, flowers in bloom, unfamiliar varietals of trees and shrubs, the gently undulating terrain of Flanders and the Somme, all those things that pique his apparently bottomless curiosity about the natural world find their way into the pages of the diary he so meticulously kept. From his billet in French Flanders in December 1915 he writes:

> At the foot of our hill to the south a sluggish stream meanders across a flat water-soaked meadow and on the other side is gathered into a straight ditch and runs leisurely off down the valley to the south. A quarter of a mile away it rushes over a steep clay bank to a level lower by about eight feet, boils up out of its pool thus formed by the ever rushing and plunging water, and rambles on merrily babbling to itself through a little narrow ravine completely overarched with shrubbery and low trees, swings round a bend and under a low bridge to dash over another low fall then on through a deeper ravine overshadowed and shut in by shrubbery. It is a merry little brook, a brook with a personality that appeals to me very much. Some writer has surely woven it into a story long before this. It is such a romantic thing, the kind of companion a dreaming youth or a girl with imagination and a love for nature would cherish, almost as part of life itself.[6]

This rather wistful sentiment might seem jarring to modern readers, who are more accustomed to thinking that war is and only can be hell. The First World War in particular is often remembered as uniquely and senselessly horrific. By the 1960s, a nearly monolithic understanding of the conflict had emerged in most of the nations that had fought it: it was remembered as a remorselessly cruel and pointless war, in which cold-hearted and incompetent generals sent waves of brave young men to their deaths in one futile trench battle after another. For years the war ground on, consuming untold tens of thousands of lives, for no greater purpose, so the narrative went, than to satisfy national honour. The men

---

5 LAC, RG9-III-D3, Vol. 4916, File 363, 5th Canadian Infantry Battalion War Diary, 27 September 1916.

6 Diary, 1 December 1915.

who survived – the "lions" who had been led by "donkeys" – were left broken in body and mind. At war's end, those who were able poured out their bitterness in disillusioned and despondent poetry, novels, memoirs, and works of art.[7] Seen in this light, it might even be tempting to dismiss Miller's lilting reflections as the naivety of an idealistic young man who had not yet experienced real combat, but for the fact that he continues to make them even after he becomes a seasoned combat veteran, such as in late May 1916 when he writes,

> After supper I walked across the fields a mile or more north of camp – a warm evening with a uniform grey layer of "stratus" covering the sky. Visited a slough where I found many yellowish green frogs of medium size trilling incessantly; a meadow and choked ditch with a few inches of water under the dank growth of grasses, with Lady's Smock, Buttercups, Ribwort Plantain, Common Sorrel, and a wealth of grasses which I had no means of naming; a hedge and bank with Poppies, Common Feverfew and much White Dead Nettle and Red Campion; a brook and waste field with Avens, Yellow Rocket and Grass Leaved Stitchwort.[8]

The more seasoned Miller is at times unsparing in depicting the horrors he faces: he describes fields of unburied corpses, friends exploded by artillery, and having to clamber over the body of a comrade shot through the throat directly in front of him. Those events lay ahead of him in December 1915, but he had seen enough to make this New Year's Eve 1915 reflection seem surprising, perhaps even callous, to readers today: "Farewell old year, for you have been the most eventful 12 months of my life. From [Winnipeg] through Shorncliffe to Flanders, no one will ever know how much I have enjoyed it."[9]

As a generation of scholars have demonstrated, the popular perception of the First World War as pointless, futile, and an indictment of the politicians and generals who waged it is the result of a complex interplay

---

7 Dan Todman, *The Great War: Myth and Memory* (London: Bloomsbury, 2005), provides a very good overview of this widely held perception while contesting it. The most famous and influential studies of First World War literature and art from the perspective of the disillusioned soldier are Paul Fussell, *The Great War and Modern Memory* (New York: Oxford University Press, 1975), and Modris Eksteins, *Rites of Spring* (Boston: Houghton Mifflin, 1989).

8 Diary, 29 May 1916.

9 Diary, 31 December 1916.

between historical fact and myth-making over time.[10] In the past thirty years, historians have assailed this monolithic understanding with a series of sledgehammer blows, shattering the claim that the war was fought for no good reason, that the generals were all incompetent and unfeeling, that the battles were singularly futile and achieved nothing, and that soldiers invariably returned from war devastated and disillusioned – although recent centenary events might lead us to question the extent to which historians influence the popular understanding of the past.[11] Undeniably, many soldiers really did return home bitter and cynical, broken in body and mind. But diaries such as Miller's serve as an important reminder that such experiences were not universal. Many soldiers preferred, in the years to come, to remember not the anguish of loss but the good times: the bonds of camaraderie formed in the trenches, the exhilaration of life lived at a feverish pitch and with high purpose – as most soldiers, including Miller, believed in the cause for which they fought – and the reckless hijinks they got up to on leave. For many soldiers, especially those who came from remote regions of the Empire, the war truly was a great adventure.[12] Some historians have argued that Dominion troops were tourists of a kind. The war, after all, offered opportunities to see first-hand the famous regions of the Old World that most young men from places such as Canada could never have imagined visiting. So perhaps it is not surprising that Miller devotes the same kind of attention to his periods of leave in England, Scotland, and, after the war ends, Belgium, that he does to battles and his sojourns in the natural world. While on leave in the United Kingdom, he visits many of the same sites frequented by tourists today: the Tower of London, St. Paul's, Madame Tussauds, Edinburgh's Royal Mile, and Holyrood Palace. But he differs from ordinary tourists in that his every waking moment is suffused with his vast intellectual curiosity: he attends

---

10 Scholars who have studied the evolution of the "social memory" of the First World War include Jonathan Vance, *Death So Noble: Memory, Meaning, and the First World War* (Vancouver: University of British Columbia Press, 1997), and Jay Winter, *Sites of Memory, Sites of Mourning: The Great War in European Cultural History* (Cambridge: Cambridge University Press, 1995).

11 Among the many historians who have challenged the characterization of trench warfare as futile and British generals as entirely incompetent is Gary Sheffield in *Forgotten Victory: The First World War, Myths and Realities* (London: Review, 2002).

12 For a summary of the argument, see Bart Ziino, "A Kind of Round Trip: Australian Soldiers and the Tourist Analogy, 1914–1918," *War and Society* 24, no. 2 (October 2006): 39–52.

lectures on politics and history, goes to plays, films, concerts, and the opera. Yet the call to duty is omnipresent. Given the chance to extend his leave in December 1916, he declines, eager to get back to the front and his friends.[13]

If the modern reader is amazed that a soldier on leave would be eager to get back to the front, it is important to remember that the generation that fought the First World War was born in the late nineteenth century, when early and sudden deaths were commonplace and the material conditions of life were far harsher than those experienced by most people today. This is not to say that they valued life less, only that their upbringing may have better prepared them for the risks and hardships they faced in the trenches. Leslie Miller himself was born 5 October 1889 in Milliken, Ontario, a rural community now largely part of Scarborough, a district of Toronto, the son of William Miller and the former Emma Risebrough.[14] It was in this tiny cosmos of late-nineteenth-century rural life that Miller, along with his beloved sister Nellie, cultivated a lifelong fascination for the natural world. The keen observer's eye so often on display in his diary was honed in rural Ontario and already on full display when, in his late teens, he won the not inconsiderable prize of $3 for a series of birdwatching notes that were published in the Toronto *Globe*. "The day has been bright, but cool," he wrote in his April 1907 winning entry,

> The see-see-see of numberless kinglets enticed me to the woods. They were fairly overcome with the joy of the season, and the woods seemed literally teeming with those tiny birds. From the wooded hill overlooking my tanglewood I gazed down on the oaks which border the road. A solitary bird about the size of a robin met my eye. The shining bronze of its back, head, neck and throat, the paler breast and belly puzzled me. Nor did the bird deign to utter a sound. The long, sharp-pointed bill looked familiar, and that striking yellow eye. Finally he considered that he had posed enough. How long his tail seemed, and what a peculiar flight![15]

It is difficult for Canadians today to imagine that bygone world, a time when bright children were amused by such things as birdwatching and

---

13 Diary, 14 December 1916.
14 My thanks to Brandt Miller for providing the family history produced by his father Carman. Letter from Brandt Miller to the author, 13 August 2018.
15 "Nature Notes from my Notebooks, by L.H. Miller," *Globe*, 20 April 1907. Nellie's observations were also frequently published in the Toronto *Globe*.

when the majority of the country's population – about equal in number to the inhabitants of London, England – resided in small towns or on farms, without electricity and well before automobiles were an everyday sight. It was a world where no one had ever heard music on the radio, seen a colour photograph, or knew the word "airport." In those last decades before widespread vaccination, polio, measles, and even smallpox remained dreaded diseases, and few children grew to adulthood without the loss of a sibling or close relative. Deaths from farm, industrial, and shipping accidents were routine and mass deaths were common. In Canada, the first half of 1914 alone saw the sinking of the RMS *Empress of Ireland* in the mouth of the St. Lawrence, resulting in over 1,000 deaths, and the Hillcrest, Alberta, mine disaster, which killed 200. Moreover, for young men such as Miller, who endured years of frigid Canadian winters in drafty farmhouses (or for other young men who had worked in the mines in Cobalt or Cape Breton, or on fishing boats off the coast of the Maritimes), the material conditions of life along the Western Front were probably not so far removed from their everyday civilian life as we might imagine. It is notable that, in what is otherwise a remarkably forthright diary, Miller rarely grouses about living at or near the front. True, we can share his elation when, from time to time, he is able to take a bath and put on clean clothes, such as when he goes on leave for the first time in December 1916: "The beds at the Club are soft and warm, and oh, the comfort of clean sheets and pajamas once more."[16] But when writing from the front he does not complain much about the food, the rain, the mud, the cold, or even about the lice and rats that were constant tormenters in the trenches. Cold, sickness, vermin – these were routine parts of life for most people raised in the late nineteenth and early twentieth centuries.

When the war erupted in August 1914, Miller was employed as a teacher and school principal in tiny Stoughton, Saskatchewan. In October, he enlisted in the 20th Border Horse, a cavalry regiment of the Canadian Militia. Here he would have received a rudimentary but generally sound introduction to soldiering as it was understood and practised in Canada in 1914. But the militia stood apart from the striking arm of Canada's army, the Canadian Expeditionary Force, until late in the war. The unglamorous home-front duties militia regiments performed did not entail heroics that earned ambitious young men Victoria Crosses.

---

16 Diary, 4 December 1916.

So in mid-December, Miller and several of his chums from Stoughton enlisted in the CEF's 32nd Battalion at Winnipeg.[17] Just nine weeks later he embarked for England and the real war. Like most battalions raised for the CEF, the 32nd was designated a reserve unit and was broken up, its personnel fed into existing front-line battalions. In October 1915, Miller transferred to the 5th Battalion and embarked for France, where he spent most of the next two years.

Two things distinguished Miller as an outlier among early volunteers in the CEF. The first is that he was born in Canada. Indeed, with some pride the family traced its paternal line in Canada to the mid-eighteenth century.[18] While Canadians would later construct a nation-building myth around the First World War, it is too often forgotten that Canada in 1914 was a country whose demographics were heavily affected by immigration. Over one million immigrants, the majority male, young, and from the British Isles, had arrived in the three years preceding the war, often lured by generous land grants offered by the Canadian government.[19] When the war erupted in August 1914, they and their other compatriots enlisted to fight as much for Britain as for Canada. Some 70 per cent of the First Canadian Contingent, which embarked for England in October 1914, had been born in the United Kingdom.[20] Miller himself departed with the Second Contingent, of which 60 per cent was British-born, in 1915. It was facts such as these that prompted one contemporary observer to remark in mid-1915 that the CEF was, to date, "a British army recruited on Canadian soil."[21] By war's end, nearly 40 per cent of the CEF and probably half of those who served overseas had been born in the United Kingdom.[22] Canadians today might find

17 LAC, Personal Records of the First World War, Canadian Expeditionary Force (CEF), RG 150, Accession 1992–93/166, Box 6191-41, Leslie Howard Miller. Hereafter "Miller, Service File."

18 Miller's genealogy traces his paternal line to one Nicholas Miller, born 1760, himself the son of two German immigrants to the New World. Simon Miller (1889) "When Yonge Street was an Indian Trail," in W.L. Smith, *The Makers of Canada: The Pioneers of Old Ontario* (Toronto, 1923), 127–32.

19 Statistics Canada, "150 Years of Immigration to Canada" https://www150.statcan .gc.ca/n1/pub/11-630-x/11-630-x2016006-eng.htm Accessed 13 March 2018.

20 Desmond Morton, *When Your Number's Up: The Canadian Soldier in the First World War* (Toronto: Vintage, 1993), 9.

21 Herbert Ames, quoted in Terry Copp, *Montreal at War, 1914–1918* (montrealatwar .com/2017/07/12/mobilizing).

22 Chris Sharpe, "Enlistment in the Canadian Expeditionary Force, 1914–1918: A Re-Evaluation," *Canadian Military History* 24, no. 1 (Winter/Spring 2015): 53.

this fact wounding to national pride, but most British Canadians of that era saw little distinction between being Canadian and being a member of the larger British Empire. There was, as yet, no distinct category of Canadian citizenship and the country was not fully autonomous. Rather, it was a singular source of pride for many English-speaking Canadians that their country was the most populous and most senior of the British Dominions. Historians have debated the extent to which Canadian participation in the war resulted in an emergent sense of nationhood (with the Battle of Vimy Ridge in particular giving rise to a great deal of fanciful myth-making) but it is also true that the war, and especially the issue of conscription, was highly divisive at home, rending the national fabric almost beyond repair. But Leslie Miller makes no bones about any of that.

The second characteristic that marks Miller as unusual among rank-and-file CEF recruits was his level of education. For two years, beginning in September 1910, Miller pursued a degree in the faculty of arts at the University of Toronto's Victoria College, this at a time when perhaps one Canadian in a hundred attended university. The university offered a rigorous, language intensive degree, which included, as was customary in the liberal arts at the time, a healthy dose of mathematics. Miller earned outstanding grades, but chose not to complete his degree, perhaps because the lure of teaching opportunities in Canada's bourgeoning West was too great.[23] In 1913–14, he took the course of study at the Normal School in Regina, Saskatchewan, and then accepted a position as teacher and school principal in Stoughton.

With two years at university and a further year at the Normal School behind him, Miller could easily have taken a commission as an officer in the CEF. Instead, he enlisted as a private, perhaps in the hope of staying with his chums from Stoughton. Few members of the rank and file had Miller's level of education. A good many were illiterate. Miller had been raised on a farm but his diary reveals him to be intellectual and bookish. Without ever succumbing to pretension, he cites Byron and Shelley and paintings by Millet. He reads and reads, devouring history, politics, and biography, but also westerns and "lumberman" stories – books that transported him to a pristine natural world so unlike the shattered landscape of No Man's Land. "The scene is laid in upper Michigan," he writes on 27 March 1916 about the now-forgotten bestseller *The Blazed*

Trail, by Stewart Edward White. "The breathing fragrance and majesty of the pine woods is in every paragraph ... we must have a good edition of this book in our home library."[24] Bored during long, uneventful night shifts by the telephone, he finds time to transcribe poems, write in his diary, and discuss philosophy, poetry, and politics with a handful of officers and men of comparable education.

What did his comrades in the rank and file make of him, this eloquent and intellectual signaller? Certainly he thought all the world of them, never once writing a harsh word about a comrade, or even about his officers, although he does seethe that the 50th Battalion's assault on 3 June 1917 was "a bloody mix-up, and nothing but butchery."[25] Only once, at war's end, does he betray a hint of bitterness, and then only about a specific group – the chaplains! After a Canadian Corps victory service held in the liberated Belgian city of Mons, he writes,

> Padres have conspicuously failed in this war and only the few whose religion disappeared in their humanity have made good. But they'll go back and claim all the glory for themselves and *their* God in whom nobody believes. They never touched men, only thought they did. A soldier's religion is beyond their understanding.[26]

Yet the next day finds him arranging motor transport for a passing nun and a "flock of orphans." "I think the sister was praying," he writes, "for I saw her counting her beads all the time ... her prayer was certainly answered."[27]

From the outset, Miller served in the signals. Perhaps no other branch of the service so clearly demonstrates the extent to which the First World War was fought at a technological crossroads.[28] In some respects, signallers communicated using methods that would have been familiar to the generals of the ancient world: they delivered messages on foot and horseback, or with carrier pigeons or flags. But they also operated electric lights, telephones, telegraphs, and, with increasing frequency, the wireless. Wireless in the context of the First World War refers to

---

24 Diary, 27 March 1916.
25 Diary, 3 June 1917.
26 Diary, 17 November 1918.
27 Diary, 18 November 1918.
28 On the signals generally, see *The British Army and Signals Intelligence during the First World War*, ed. John Ferris (Wolfeboro Falls, NH: Army Records Society, 1992).

wireless *telegraphy* – that is, the radio transmission of Morse code – and not wireless *telephony*, in which speech was transmitted. The latter was still experimental and not deployed by the British Army until the final months of war, and it was never used in combat.[29] Nonetheless, wireless offered significant advantages over the telephone, whose hard wires were often cut by artillery fire.

But wireless was particularly vulnerable to eavesdropping. It was for this reason that Miller had to prove he could translate German prior to his transfer to the Canadian Corps Wireless Section in January 1917. The wireless section's war diary gives some indication of the experimental nature of the technology at that time. Some posts were immediately able to intercept enemy messages of "a fair amount of importance" while others were unable to overhear anything except other Canadian stations.[30] This was challenging and highly technical work, not suitable for just anyone – indeed the personnel of one of the section's six posts were disbanded when they proved unequal to the task.[31] By contrast, Miller seems to have demonstrated his value to his superiors, no doubt in part because of his excellent command of the German language. He spent the summer of 1917 attached to the British First Army's Wireless Company; then, having returned to the Canadian Corps through the intervention of one of his officers, he was promoted to corporal at the end of July and to sergeant in December. In the summer of 1918, after a ten-week course of instruction at the Canadian School of Military Engineering in Seaforth, England, Miller was commissioned lieutenant and posted to the 3rd Canadian Division's Wireless Company. This entailed a hefty pay raise: a lieutenant's base salary of two dollars per day and field allowance of sixty cents were two and a half times a private's pay.[32] Yet Miller seems uninterested in such matters as rank, mentioning a promotion only once in a laconic August

---

29 Unlike the Royal Navy, the British Army was highly conservative in its adoption of wireless until 1917, perhaps because of the immense technical challenges it still posed. On this, see Brian Hall, "The British Army and Wireless Communication," *War in History* 19, no. 3 (July 2012): 290–312, and the same author's *Communications and British Operations on the Western Front: 1914–1918* (Cambridge: Cambridge University Press, 2017).

30 LAC, RG9-III-D-3, Vol. 5006, File 696, War Diaries, Canadian Corps Wireless Section, 17 January 1917.

31 War Diary, Canadian Corps Wireless Section, 9/10 January 1917.

32 Canada, Department of Militia and Defence, *Canadian Expeditionary Force Units: Instructions Governing Organization and Administration* (Ottawa: Government Printing Bureau, 1916).

1917 entry: "Wheeled to Hersin-Coupigny to get my mail for past week. Found I had been made acting corporal during my absence."[33]

Regrettably, Miller's habitual diary writing drops off sharply around the same time. It could be that his new duties kept him from writing as often as he would have liked. It may also be that he fell into a routine that he did not feel worth recording. He spends nearly four months of 1918 training, with his final course of instruction ending on 10 November 1918 – the day before the armistice. The end of the war seems to invigorate him, and for the remainder of November and December 1918 he appears to be his old self again. For nearly two months he writes at length about liberated Belgium and the people he meets there. He recounts their stories of life under German occupation with empathy and in detail. But by 1919 he seems to have little more to say. He concludes the diary with a series of perfunctory entries which suggest that he had grown weary of it all. On 20 March 1919, he boarded the S.S. *Cedric*, bound for Canada. It was four years and a month since had he departed Halifax. Perhaps fittingly, he chose that moment to close.

This is the war recorded on an intimate scale. Miller has surprisingly little to say about the wider conflict and nothing at all about politics back home, in the United Kingdom, or even about the momentous events that overtook Russia in 1917. Could he still claim, in early 1919, that he had "enjoyed" his experience, as he had written on New Year's Eve, 1915? Did he still feel that way, three years later, after he had been through so much? The diary offers no answer to that question. Miller never explains what the war meant to him – although he allows a moment of nationalistic pride while in liberated Mons – nor does he say why he enlisted in the first place. Perhaps he considered it too obvious to state, or he might have believed that anyone who had not fought could not understand. Or it may be that, like many in the generation that fought in the First World War, he struggled to understand what had happened to him and to his country. There is a tendency in contemporary commemorations, from Remembrance Day ceremonies to occasions marking the anniversaries of significant battles, to impose a singular meaning, a kind of collective memory and understanding, upon the First World War. But this tendency should be resisted. The men who fought the war and their families at home did not share a uniform understanding of the war, and they debated what it meant

---

33 Diary, 6 August 1917.

to them for decades to come. It would be incredible if we could find consensus where they could not.

First World War diaries are rarer than might be expected. Most of the men and women who served did not keep one. The majority of diaries that were written, like the vast majority of letters and postcards that flowed ceaselessly across the Atlantic, were later lost, or thrown out when the writers or recipients died. Students and scholars of history are fortunate that Leslie Miller's heirs had the foresight to keep his diary so that others could benefit from his erudite and inquisitive mind. Any diary of a soldier who served in that terrible conflict of a century ago is of value. Diaries of the length, thoroughness, and eloquence of Miller's are treasures, and it gives me great pleasure to present it for publication on behalf of his descendants.

A Note on Provenance, Sources, and Method

Miller's diary covers three books and nearly 400 pages in all. He sent at least one of the diaries home while he was still posted overseas.[34] These remained in his possession until his death in December 1979, when they were inherited by his younger brother, Carman. Since Carman's death, they have been in the keeping of Carman's sons, Leslie Miller's nephews Brandt and Dan Miller. This annotated edition is based in large part on a transcription of the diary produced by Brandt and Dan, along with Leslie Miller's great-nephew Richard and his wife, Kathy Breakey. I have verified that transcription for accuracy against copies of the original. My transcription differs slightly from theirs in that I chose to retain Miller's original spelling and punctuation precisely, even where errors occur, as they inevitably do from time to time. In addition, I retained the acronyms and short forms that Miller employed throughout the diary even though he did not always abbreviate consistently. Generally speaking, however, "Div" stood for division, "Bde" for Brigade, "Battn" or "Bn" for Battalion, and "Coy" for Company. He used standard or easily understood short forms for military ranks. I have noted a few cases where it was not possible to determine what he was referring to.

In preparing the diary for publication, I added several hundred annotations. In addition, I included several explanatory notes concerning major events in the body of the text itself where more detail than a footnote

---

34 Diary, 24 October 1916.

could provide was necessary. Readers can, of course, skip the annotations altogether, consult them occasionally for reference, or read them as part of the larger narrative as they prefer. It is my hope, however, that the annotations will illuminate aspects of the diary and put Miller's entries into a broader context. I acknowledge that there is a danger of committing what David Hackett Fisher calls "the historian's fallacy" here – that is, the danger of hindsight bias – but this is always true for historians. It is one of the paradoxes of the study of history that we can never have an unmediated encounter with the past. In one crucial respect we always know more about the past than the people who actually lived through it: we know what happens next and they did not.

In annotating the diary, I struggled between my obligation to provide necessary context, especially for readers unfamiliar with the First World War, and the sinister temptation of pedantry. I felt it that was unnecessary, for example, to tell the reader what the famous Madame Tussauds wax museum is, but I deemed it necessary to identify some of the likenesses Miller encountered there, including those of Admiral Jellicoe and such forgotten heroes as Charles Fryatt and Jack Cornwell. At the behest of the Miller family, I inserted certain footnotes concerning aspects of the war not directly pertaining to the text. These notes might strike some readers as tangential but the family's intent is pedagogical, with the hope of engaging younger readers. Similarly, the accompanying photos in some cases refer directly to people, places, and events mentioned in the diary. The originals were in most cases Miller's own photos, several of which he subsequently pasted in the back of one of the diaries. In other cases I have included illustrative photos at the family's request, once again in the hopes that younger readers in particular might find them stimulating.

I struggled with how to cite my own annotations. Providing a full bibliographical reference for each of the 500-odd notations would have dramatically increased the length and cost of this work. Instead, I offer the following notes on sources, which I hope will suffice.

For the most part, I identified the many authors, actors, politicians, and poets mentioned by Miller using biographical sources, many of them now available online, including the *Oxford Dictionary of National Biography* and the *Dictionary of Canadian Biography*. I confess that the blessing and scourge of the modern information age, Wikipedia, was on occasion useful – although I always took the trouble to verify its claims where possible. Place names posed particular challenges, especially given the variable spellings (both Flemish and French) of certain places in Belgium. For nearly three years, Miller was punctilious about noting nearly every city, town, and village he passed through. I found it unduly cumbersome and, in this age of Google, unnecessary to annotate each one. Instead, I identified a representative few that are of importance to his service. While wishing to avoid condescension, I also did not wish to make assumptions about the reader's nationality and knowledge of geography. So while I did not think it necessary, for example, to tell the reader that Paris is the capital of France, I did not assume that every non-Canadian reader would know that Ottawa is the capital of Canada. *Historical Statistics of Canada* was my main source for facts, including population figures, for places in Canada.[35] Comparable figures for France I derived largely from data sheets available online through the École des hautes études en sciences sociales. Finally, Gerald Gliddon's *Somme 1916: A Battlefield Companion* proved particularly invaluable in identifying various places associated with the Battle of the Somme.

Identifying the soldiers with whom Miller served proved to be my single most laborious task. As their names were important enough to him to record, and some became his fast friends, I considered it of great importance to provide at least some detail of their service. I did so using six principal sources. Of the greatest value was the Personnel Records of the First World War database located online at the Library and Archives of Canada (LAC).[36] This long-delayed project to digitize over 600,000 service files was completed while this manuscript was in draft. In addition, the online database of the Commonwealth War Graves Commission was indispensable for locating the graves (or names on memorials) of those comrades of Miller's who were killed or died in service.[37] Several of the men Miller served with transferred to the Royal Flying Corps (RFC), whose personnel records are held at the National Archives (UK) but are availability digitally via the genealogy website Findmypast. A side note: details concerning the aerial combats that Miller refers to from time to time are derived from an extraordinary reference work, Trevor Henshaw's *The Sky Their Battlefield II*.[38] The 5th Battalion also published fascinating Christmas "trench papers" in 1915 and 1916, entitled *A Bouquet from the Front*, copies of which exist in the archives of the

---

35 *Historical Statistics of Canada*, 2nd ed., archived on line at https://www150.statcan.gc.ca/n1/en/catalogue/11-516-X.

36 LAC, Personnel Records of the First World War (http://www.bac-lac.gc.ca/eng/discover/military-heritage/first-world-war/personnel-records/Pages/search.aspx).

37 Commonwealth War Graves Commission (https://www.cwgc.org/find/find-war-dead/)

38 Trevor Henshaw, *The Sky Their Battlefield II* (Hertfordshire: Fetubi Books, 2014).

Canadian War Museum.[39] Apart from offering a generally fascinating, and often very funny, glimpse into the everyday lives of Canadian soldiers in France, the papers helped me to determine the identity of certain officers whom Miller only identifies by surname. The War Diaries of the various units with which Miller served, also digitized and online at LAC, were of value in identifying personnel Miller refers to, and also in providing additional details of the engagements he describes.[40] Miller's own accounts accord very well with those of the battalion diarists. Finally, Miller's own loose-leaf notes on personnel he served with proved useful in confirming what I found elsewhere or in pointing me in the right direction.

Nonetheless, even by cross-referencing the sources above, it was not always possible to determine conclusively the identity of every soldier Miller mentions. Searches for certain common surnames yielded hundreds, and in some cases thousands, of candidate files in the CEF database. In addition, Miller was sometimes uncertain or incorrect about the spelling of his comrades' names, further complicating attempts to determine who they were. In my annotations, I indicate four degrees of certainty about the identity of the men Miller served with: those who I positively identified (their basic biographical and service details are noted); personnel to whom my annotations *probably* refer; personnel to whom my annotations *might* refer; and personnel who could not be identified for one reason or another. It was often not possible to determine from the records the date of death of the men in question if they did not die during the war. Given the numerous names in question, I hope the reader will forgive me for forgoing the complex genealogical searches necessary to find out. I hope I have at least rescued them from oblivion.

Oblivion will not be the fate of Miller's memory. Not only is his name attached to the imaginative and touching Vimy Oaks project, which I discuss in the Afterword, but the publication of this diary will, I hope, extend his legacy and breathe new life into our understanding of the war in which he served.

Graham Broad
King's University College at Western University
London, Ontario, Canada

---

39 Canadian War Museum Archives, 5th Battalion Canadian Expeditionary Force, *A Bouquet from the Front,* 1915–1916.
40 LAC, War Diaries of the First World War (https://www.bac-lac.gc.ca/eng/discover /military-heritage/first-world-war/Pages/war-diaries.aspx).

First Diary

Owner

No. 81593

Pte. Leslie H. Miller

Signal Section

5th Canadian Battn.

1st Canadian Div.

British Expeditionary Force

France

Next of Kin

Mr. Wm. Miller (father)

Milliken

Ontario Canada

Owner

no. 81593
Pte. Leslie H. Miller
Signal Section
5th Canadian Battn
1st Canadian Div.
British Expeditionary Force
France

Next of Kin
Mr. Wm. Miller (father)
Milliken
Ontario.
Canada

War Diary

SUNDAY, JAN. 10, 1915.
Bought book yesterday at Russel
Lang's and decided to commence
a war diary. Enlisted in Stoughton
Sask. about Oct. 10, 1914 while I
was acting as Principal of the
School there. Capt. J. Mackay who
has since become d. Lieut. in the
32nd Battn. was recruiting officer
there. Passed physical exatn in
Weyburn Thurs. Nov. 5.
mobilization in Weyburn was
ordered Sat. Nov. 7, and I joined
the forces Mon. evening Nov. 9.
There were about 80 of us in
Weyburn, and we drilled for
just 3 weeks under Maj. Washington
Capts. Wheatley and Mackay,
and Sergt-Mj. Ames. Geo. Ledson
and I lived at the Waverley Hotel
a few days until George was sent
back to Stoughton temporarily
rejected. Then I met W. J. Jolly,
a Y. M. C. A. acquaintance from
Regina, and he had me live up
town with him in his very

The title and first page of Leslie Miller's first wartime diary.
Credit: Miller family collection.

1915

Sun., Jan. 10:

Bought book yesterday at Russel Langs and decided to commence a war diary. Enlisted in Stoughton, Sask. about Oct. 10, 1914 while I was acting as principal of the School there.[1] Capt. J. Mackay who has since become a Lieut. in the 32nd Battn. was recruiting officer there.[2] Passed physical exam in Weyburn Thurs., Nov. 5.[3] Mobilization in Weyburn was ordered Sat., Nov. 7, and I joined the forces Mon. evening, Nov. 9.

There were about 80 of us in Weyburn, and we drilled for just 3 weeks under Maj. Washington, Capts. Wheatley and Mackay, and Sergt.-Maj. Ames.[4] Geo. Leeson and I lived at the Waverley Hotel a few days until George was sent back to Stoughton temporarily rejected.[5] Then I met

---

1 Stoughton, Saskatchewan: A very small village 100 kilometres southeast of Regina, population in 1914 about 200. Miller enlisted in the 20th Border Horse, a militia regiment, before joining the CEF.

2 32nd Battn: An infantry battalion of the CEF authorized in November 1914. Mobilized out of Winnipeg, it embarked for Britain in February 1915.

3 Weyburn, town in south Saskatchewan. Population in 1914 about 2,500.

4 MacKay: Actually Captain John Alexander *McKay* (1883–1959). Served in the 20th Border Horse (militia) before joining the 32nd Battalion. Washington: Major Ferguson Coleman Washington (b. 1880) of Weyburn, Saskatchewan, 20th Border Rifles; later commanding officer of the 10th Canadian Mounted Rifles. Wheatley: Captain Frank Melville Wheatley (b. 1887), born London, England. Ames: Sergeant-Major Walter Thomas Ames (b. 1874), born London, England, a veteran of the Boer War.

5 Leeson: George Edward Leeson (1888–?), originally of Elmwood, Ontario; attested Winnipeg, December 1914. Twice wounded in action.

W.J. Jolly, a Y.M.C.A. acquaintance from Regina, and he had me live up town with him in his very comfortable room with a fine family who gave me a hearty welcome.[6] The other chaps who had to take quarters in the Post Office and in a vacant store at rear of McKinnon's were cold, dirty, and lousy, with neither comfort nor conveniences.[7]

We were paraded up to MacKinnon's store to get gloves one morning. As we were halted in line and many of the employees were at windows and doors looking us over, I spied Dick Beckett nearby. He took me to the Fletcher home where he lives and I met some lovely people. Mr. F. is Free Methodist Minister. I met Elias Wood on the street one morning and we had a brief chat.

Spent two Sundays with Dick Beckett and the Fletchers very happily. Spent one week-end back in Stoughton. Visited the Weyburn Collegiate Institute one afternoon and heard the Principal teach a class in literature. Went out one night with a picked party to a patriotic concert in South Weyburn School near Maj. W's home.

We were a mixed lot in point of clothing. A dozen wore khaki, another dozen including myself, had red coats, black riding breeches with white stripe, leggings, and blue cap with white band. We reported in front of P.O. 6 a.m., paraded to the fair grounds singing "Tipperary" for physical drill, breakfast at Tony's restaurant at 7, rifle drill 8:30 to 11:30, dinner, route march or drill 2 till 5, supper and free for evening.[8] We made a great many 6 mile route-marches in the neighbourhood of the town, as the fine weather favoured that form of "sport". Spent one day at the rifle range, the most strenuous day of drill, marching, and shooting I have put in. Left Weyburn with a great send-off 9 a.m. Nov. 30 and reached Winnipeg 9 p.m. Maj. W. with 14 cavalry men went to Yorkton, while all the remainder of us came on as infantry to Winnipeg.

We Weyburn men joined D Coy. of 32nd Battn. I became a coy. signaller training under Lieut. Hedley, a Moose Jaw school teacher.[9] A week ago the Battn. organization was altered, and now there are 4 coys and 16 staff signallers. We are stationed at the Exhibition grounds living, eating, and drilling in the various buildings. The 27th and 28th Battns.

6 Jolly: Probably William James Jolly (1879–1916), born Toronto; attested Edmonton,
   Alberta, June 1915, killed in action October 1916.
7 McKinnon's: A department store founded in Weyburn by Neil McKinnon in 1902.
8 Tipperary: "A Long Way to Tipperary," a popular song written by Jack Judge in 1912.
9 Hedley: Lieutenant (later Major) Harold Douglas Hedley, MC (1889–1961), of
   St. Mary's, Ontario; attested Winnipeg, December 1914.

Leslie H. Miller, in studio portrait taken in Regina in the spring
of 1914. Credit: Miller family collection.

are stationed in Wpg. also.[10] We all expect to be included in the 2nd
Canadian Contingent soon to leave for England.[11] Last Monday we all
received our first inoculation with anti-typhoid serum. Some 20 fellows
fainted during the operation; understand one officer was among the
victims. Some soldiers these Canadians! We are to get two more doses
of the same at ten-day intervals.

---

10 Wpg: With about 150,000 residents, Winnipeg was the capital of Manitoba and in
   1914 the most populous Canadian city west of Toronto.
11 Second Contingent: The First Canadian Contingent was the unofficial name for the
   first formations of the Canadian Expeditionary Force to go overseas. The contingent
   sailed for England in October 1914. The Second Contingent departed in a series of
   convoys between late January and May 1915. The First and Second Canadian Divisions, respectively, were formed from their ranks.

Regina Normal School spring term 1914, teachers of the first and second classes. Group at top left: N.B. Eadie, L.H. Miller, E.N. Wallwin, W. Mountford. Credit: Miller family collection.

Am going down to Selkirk Y.M.C.A. to spend evening with Stuart Thompson as I have done many times since I came to Wpg.[12] We usually chat a while, dine at Julius Café or C.V.C., attend service at Trinity Methodist Church, and by the time we get back it is roll-call at barracks. One evening at Trinity Church I met W. Mountford of my class at Regina

12 Thompson: Stuart Logan Thompson (1885–1961) was Miller's friend in Selkirk, where he resided in the YMCA. He subsequently attested at Winnipeg in February 1916 and served in the 44th Battalion (Manitoba) signals in France. In 1924, Thompson married Miller's sister, Nellie (see entry of 3 December 1915). He subsequently became a highly regarded naturalist, author of three books and many articles, and became president of the Toronto Field Naturalists Club.

1915

Folkstone, England,

Private Miller, 32nd Battalion, in a photo taken in Folkestone, England,
sometime in early 1915 when he was training at nearby
Shorncliffe. Credit: Miller family collection.

Normal.[13] Stuart is as full of Nature Lore as ever, retains all his former
interest in and zeal for collecting, is busy in Y.M.C.A. work, and teaches
S.S. class – certainly makes good use of his time.[14]

Wpg. provides many varied forms of recreation for the soldiers. To
me the Y.M.C.A. and Public Baths are most attractive. Old "D" Coy.
had a 4-hr. concert for themselves in their barrack room the night following New Year's. This week the Battn. gave one for selves and friends
in auditorium of King Edward School. We have some most amusing
entertainers among our number. Bugler Wheelhouse was formerly
an English comedian and is very funny, though ordinarily quiet and

---

13 Regina Normal: "Normal school" is an obsolescent term for schools that trained teachers.
14 S.S. Probably "Sunday School."

unassuming.[15] Different churches and societies have opened reading and recreation rooms for us through the city. Most popular are the large room in King Edward School fitted for reading, writing, music, and rest, and the St. John's Ambulance room at 320 Main, small but cozy, but free lunch is served as a special attraction. The theatres draw large numbers of soldiers into their audiences. Xmas day I saw "A Bird of Paradise" at Walker Theatre, and New Year's "Peg O' My Heart" at the Dominion.[16]

Fri., Feb. 19:

The 32nd Battn. left Wpg. at 9 p.m. last Tues., Feb. 16. We travelled in 2 trains via G.T.P. signal staff with right half Battn. on first train.[17] Reached Fort William next day at noon. Our half Battn. left the train and had a short march through the streets. We were taken thence by C.P.R. locomotives over C.P.R. line to North Bay.[18] Reached Chapleau next morning at day-break. Detrained at Cartier at 10 a.m. and again at Sudbury at noon, for marching and physical exercise. Reached North Bay at about 5 p.m. Thence we went by G.T.R. south to Scotia Jct. and east to Ottawa and Montreal.[19] Passed through Ottawa at 5 a.m., so saw nothing of the city. Kirkpatrick of the signallers was taken off sick here and sent to hospital.[20] Reached Montreal at 9 today and had a half-hour march there. Crossing the St. Lawrence south of the city we

---

15 Wheelhouse: Private Robert Clive Wheelhouse (1888–1915) of Yorkshire, England. Killed 21 May 1915 serving with the 10th Battalion at Battle of Festubert. Commemorated on the Vimy Memorial.

16 "A Bird of Paradise": 1912 play by Richard Walton Tully (1877–1945), American playwright. "Peg O' My Heart": Highly successful 1912 Broadway play by John Hartley Manners, later made into a silent film (1922). "The Dominion": Winnipeg's 1,100-seat Dominion Theatre opened in 1904 and featured such innovations as electric lights and steam heat.

17 G.T.P.: Grand Trunk Pacific railway, connecting Winnipeg to Prince Rupert, British Columbia.

18 C.P.R.: Canadian Pacific Railway.

19 G.T.R.: Grand Trunk Railway. Ottawa: Capital of Canada, population in 1915 about 125,000. Montreal: In 1915, Montreal was Canada's biggest city, with a population of approximately 500,000.

20 Kirkpatrick: Probably Clarence Victor Kirkpatrick (1896–1916), born Woodstock, New Brunswick; attested Winnipeg, December 1914. Killed in action 4 June 1916. Commemorated on the Menin Gate in Ypres.

proceeded by Intercolonial through southern Quebec.[21] Have just passed through St. Hyacinthe, a pretty little French town of several thousand inhabitants. A big soft-looking youth warmly clad in a coonskin coat asked me if I wasn't afraid to go to the war. My answer must have disappointed him, for he plainly felt afraid of it himself. All the inlets of Lake Superior and the Lake itself are frozen over. Lake Nipigon at North Bay is also entirely frozen. The St. Lawrence at Montreal is all frozen with the exception of one or two narrow open gaps where the dark water runs swiftly for a mile or so in the open air and then disappears under the ice.

It is difficult at Montreal to distinguish between the many rivers and lakes. We crossed and passed by several large rivers or branches of a river and I could not say whether I saw the Ottawa or not. From the centre of the railway bridge over the St. Lawrence one gets a fine view of the river above and below as well as both shores.

South of the St. Lawrence the land is perfectly flat, but away to the S.W. a few low, round-topped mountains rise from the level landscape.

Sat., Feb. 20:

Passed Chaudiere Jct. in south Quebec at sunset. All along the south of the St. Lawrence many rivers of 50 to 300 ft. across flow northward at a rapid rate, and at about 100 ft. below the level of the railway line. At a few points we thought we could see the St. Lawrence away below us and a mile or two to the northwest. During the late afternoon we saw the blue rounded hills on the north side of the river. At night we saw the lights of Quebec far away below us in the northwest. Passed Rimouski at 1 a.m. and thought of how the *Empress of Ireland* sank in the icy waters near there. Reached Campbellton at daybreak and put time on one hour.[22] Passed arm of Bay of Chaleur which was entirely frozen over. At Newcastle on Miramichi Bay met several enthusiastic people.

---

21 Intercolonial: Railway that connected the original Canadian provinces of Ontario, Quebec, Nova Scotia, and New Brunswick. It was absorbed by the Canadian National Railway after the First World War.

22 *Empress of Ireland:* Liner of the Canadian Pacific Steamship company that sank after a collision with the Norwegian collier *Storstad* in the St. Lawrence on 29 May 1914; 1,012 passengers and crew perished.

Exchanged addresses with Miss Eulah M. Stuart, Newcastle, Miramichi, N.B., a high school girl of that place.[23]

The line of the I.R.C. through N.B. is nearly all through hills and woods.[24] All the land is wooded with evergreens and hardwoods. Detrained at Moncton and marched through the streets, led by the local band. All the town turned out and gave us a most enthusiastic welcome. Exchanged addresses with Viola J. Lockhart, 13 Foundry Street, Moncton, N.B., and Lillian M. Smith, 101 Botsford Street, Moncton, N.B., and Dorothy M. Blakney, Sunny Brae, N.B.[25]

Noticed the tide flats and hay lands in the Isthmus of Chignecto, and saw the brown ocean water flowing among the wilderness of broken ice.[26] What look like rivers here are really long, winding inlets which receive the tidal flow. Crows were flying about at various points along this part of the line. Hardly any snow is left here, but there is more snow in northern N.B. than anywhere along the line from Winnipeg.

Reached Truro at 7 p.m. and Halifax at nine.[27] Pulled into the quay expecting to embark at once, but were disappointed and forced to spend the night on the train.

Sun., Feb. 21 (Noon):

There are two cruisers of war in the harbour, and the transport liners are lying at the docks. We cannot get any satisfaction as to when we change from train to boat, or what our destination is – some say Bermuda, while others are sure it is England.[28]

Took a march through the streets of the city from ten to eleven this morn. The weather is delightful, sunny, clear blue skies, with a fresh breeze blowing off the sea. There is no snow at all, and the harbour is

---

23 Stuart: See entry of 25 April 1915.

24 I.R.C.: Intercolonial Railway of Canada. See entry of 19 February 1915.

25 Lockhart: Miller keeps in touch with "Olie" Lockhart, noting correspondence with her in several future entries.

26 Isthmus: The Isthmus of Chignecto connects the Nova Scotian peninsula to the mainland.

27 Halifax: Capital of the province of Nova Scotia and one of the busiest ports in the British Empire during the First World War. Its population in 1915 was about 100,000.

28 Bermuda: Canadian battalions garrisoned Bermuda during the first two years of the war. Patricia Sinclair writes, "It wasn't until November 1915 that the British West Indies Regiment (BWIR) was formed after the personal intervention of King George V insisting that 'men of every class, creed and colour' be allowed to enlist. BWIR comprised 11 battalions; 15,600 volunteer soldiers, two-thirds came from Jamaica." See Heather Jones, *For King and Country: The British Monarchy and the First World War* (Cambridge University Press, 2021).

entirely free of ice. Flocks of gulls are skimming over the harbour and hovering about the ships. Pigeons in flocks are to be seen flying quickly here and there over the city.

The streets leading back from the water-front climb the steep slope that encircles the harbour. One wonders how anything but light traffic can be carried on in such a place. This city is decidedly English in character, especially when you consider the crooked streets, style of houses, and the ways of the people.

Had leave from 1 to 4 p.m. Geo. Leeson and I went to a restaurant and had a real dinner such as we had not been able to get since leaving Wpg. Roamed about the city for an hour but found little of interest because our time was so short. Spent the night on the train.

Mon., Feb. 22:

Embarked at nine this morning on the S.S. *Vaderland* of the White Star Line.[29] It took over two hours for our Battn. to come on board, and another half Battn. followed us on to the same boat. The 30th of B.C. and the 23rd of Quebec are going over with us as supplementary reserve Battns. for the 1st Division.[30] This boat carries 1,900 passengers. While we were at dinner onboard she left the wharf and moved off to anchorage in the harbour to make room for other ships to take on troops at the docks.

Was on duty three hours this afternoon on the ship's bridge with Cornish and Nicholls, sending messages by flag-wagging to the signal station on the fortified island in the harbour.[31] Found to our immense satisfaction that we can send and receive much better than the signallers stationed here. It was a novel experience being upon the captain's bridge in communication with the fort over a mile away across the harbour, this possible by mere flag-waving. I felt the value of the three previous months of training. Henceforth, we of the signalling staff are to be on duty on the bridge 4/24 hours per day throughout the voyage to keep

---

29 *Vaderland:* A 12,000-tonne, two-funnel liner launched in 1900. Pressed into service as a troopship, it was sunk by *U-70* in June 1917 off Ireland.

30 The 1st Canadian Division: Formed from the First Contingent and, at the time of Miller's entry, in the process of embarking for France.

31 Cornish: Charles George Cornish (1889–1953), born London, England; attested Winnipeg, December 1914; wounded at Vimy Ridge, 9 April 1917 and subsequently discharged on medical grounds. See entries for December 1916 when Miller, on leave, visits the Cornish family. Nicholls: William James Mayne Nicholls (b. 1892), born Chile; attested Winnipeg December 1914.

in touch with the other transports. It is a beautiful sight I have just been viewing from the deck this evening at seven after dark. The sky is clear and dotted with countless stars, centred by the moon nearing full. Only a light breeze ruffles the surface of the water in the harbour and the swell is imperceptible. From across the water the lights of the city twinkle and gleam in a crescent about the head of the inlet.

It is hardly possible for me to realize that I am looking at the last bit of Canadian soil I shall see for many months to come, and possibly forever. The low, round-topped hills that surround the bay will stamp themselves in picture upon our memory and make us long for an early return to the same scenes as a step nearer home. But at present we are thinking only of getting out upon the ocean and nearer the work to which we have set our hands.

We get no mail and very little news from the outside world. Have not read any war news since leaving Winnipeg. Life while travelling seems like a dream because we are entirely cut off from previous relationships and experiences. We are enjoying everything very much.

Tues., Feb. 23:

Sailed out from Halifax harbour at 7 a.m. The *Missanabie* led the way, followed by our *Vaderland* and the *Megantic* in the rear.[32] All are being escorted by H.M. light cruiser *Essex*.[33] Every man was on deck as the island and forts were passed, the city disappeared in its own smoke, and the harbour inlet opened out into the heaving ocean. Gradually the land sank from our view in the northwest behind us as we steamed southeast in line into the open sea. Tonight there is nothing in sight but the heaving waste of dark blue waters stretching away in every direction to the horizon.

Was on duty noon to 4 p.m. on the bridge signalling to the ships next ahead and astern. The sky was clear, and a fresh easterly breeze was blowing. Conditions for our work were good, and we put several messages through. Each boat was usually a half mile distant from its next companion. The sea is comparatively smooth, nothing but the long steady

---

32 *Missanabie*: New Canadian Pacific liner (launched June 1914) used as a troopship. Sunk September 1918 by a U-boat. *Megantic*: Single funnel 15,000-tonne White Star Line passenger liner launched 1908.

33 *Essex*: A *Monmouth*-class armoured cruiser launched in 1901. Used mainly for escort duties, the ship was scrapped in 1921.

swell running. Our boat however is not so large but that it sways and dips considerably. Several of the boys are already quite sick.

8:30 P.M. Have just been up on the bridge sending and receiving messages with lamps. Saw the Sable Island light gleaming in the darkness at the horizon on our port bow, i.e. in the N.E.

Fri., Feb. 26:

Had a steady run through very fine weather, quite warm and summer-like after the Canadian cold. Flocks of small terns, grey with black wing tips, and a few gulls follow the ship continuously. Have been on duty the last two days 4 to 8 p.m. Am going on 8 to 12 tonight.

Mon., Mar. 1:

On duty yesterday morning midnight to 4 a.m. A clear moonlight night. A light swell with a few foam-crested waves ("white horses") was running. The other ships were as plainly visible as during daylight. Signalling with lights was a pleasure. From the bridge the view was splendid: the four ships in line gliding steadily through the water; the light and shadow on the waves ever changing and moving; the "white horses" speeding along until they broke and disappeared while others formed as quickly and started swiftly away on their brief courses; our own ship, her wet decks, white rails, and tapering masts clearly outlined against the watery background, gently rising and falling, the prow now dipping deep into a wave as she plunged into a hollow, and again soaring upward like a bird as she rose on the next wave. It was a scene that inspired me with silent wonder and admiration. It was too beautiful to allow the mind to dwell upon the destructive power of the sea and the watery depths that lay below us. One rather thinks of the wonderful buoyant force of the water beneath, the ease and grace with which the ship rides over the uneven surface of the waters, and the skill of the mariner which enables him to hold to his course without any deviation, always knowing just where he is, the direction he is sailing, the course he is to follow and how to hold his craft to that course, the distance the ship has covered, and the rate of speed.

On duty this morning from 4 to 8 a.m. It rained all last evening and was foggy until sunrise. A strong lookout was kept all last night: crow's nest, one in bow, two on bridge. We lost sight of *Essex* and *Missanabie*, but kept in touch with the *Megantic* following us. Our Captain was quite

DISTANCES COVERED DAILY

Feb. 23....20 MI.	Feb. 28.... 280 MI.
" 24....311 "	Mar. 1....284 MI
" 25....284 "	Mar. 2....305 MI
" 26...256 "	Mar. 3....285 MI
" 27....259 "	

SPEED AVERAGE 11.72 MI. PER HOUR
FOR FEB. 23 NOON TO MAR. 2 NOON.
HALIFAX TO LIVERPOOL 2485 MI.

cool, and said he was sure the others were on our starboard bow ahead. None of us could see anything, but he claimed he saw a streak of smoke in that direction. *Megantic* kept signalling "Can you see the others?" but our Captain laughed at their anxiety. The previous afternoon the *Essex* had sent us orders to hold present course and speed until fog cleared. If we were then separated, a rendezvous was named by its lat. and long. where we were all to meet again. As the light increased the fog cleared slightly, and the crow's nest sang out "ships on starboard bow." We soon were able to make out the two leading ships of our line, running in a course parallel with ours but a mile to the starboard. Within an hour we were all in line again and proceeding as usual. At about five a.m. while we were all anxiously looking out for signs of our leading ships, a dull booming sound was heard. Some of us thought it was aboard our own ship, while others were sure it came from the distance on starboard bow. The Captain certainly wore an anxious look until the fog had cleared and we had sighted the *Essex*.

A merchant vessel with two masts and single funnel between, met us and passed on the horizon to port, evidently a steamer bound for an American port.

Tues., Mar. 2:

We are now (8 p.m.) within less than 200 miles from the coast of Ireland. Mail has been collected and is to be put off at Queenstown.[34] It is reported we are to reach that port before daybreak. We have travelled this far with no lights showing by night save stern lamp carefully shaded

---

34 Queenstown: Seaport town on the south coast of Ireland. Renamed Cobh in 1920.

and red port light. The bridge is kept in darkness. A shaded light may be used in the chart room and wheel house, but the helmsman works in the dark. A new order was issued this afternoon forbidding the use of flashing signals by ships and the lighting of the red port light tonight and tomorrow night. No smoking is allowed on deck. Today the crew uncovered the lifeboats and made them ready for instant launching.[35] As far as it is possible we are prepared against German submarine attack. We are now running at full speed and the ship is bobbing up and down in a most unusual manner. We have had several alarm calls to drill us in use of life belts. We are all assigned to lifeboats and know just where to go in case of accident. The sea is remarkably calm, and there is a thick fog and southeast wind.

Wed. Mar. 3:

We are nearing the coast of Ireland, and expect to reach Queenstown about 3 a.m. tomorrow. New birds began to appear about the ship this afternoon. All the voyage through we have had numbers of little white terns with black wing tips, about the same size as the black terns of Sask. They occasionally alight on the water, apparently to pick up morsels of food. Their little bodies float high in the water, and dance on the ripples and waves like bits of cork. Larger gulls of a grey colour are occasionally seen singly or in pairs. At 2:30 p.m. a large brown bird with long pointed wings, barred and flecked with cinnamon and white, appeared wheeling about the ship. Its spread of wing would certainly be at least 30 in. About the same time a greyish white bird with dark wing tips and of similar size and general appearance was seen wheeling about the ship low over the waves. The two birds resembled each other in so many points that I thought they might be male and female of the same species. The 2nd officer of the ship could not clear up my doubt, but merely said they were gulls such as one often sees off the Irish coast. Once at about 3 p.m. a number of porpoise crossed our course just under our bows, leaping out of the water as they passed. I was on the bridge reading a message, and could not give these interesting fish any attention, much to my regret. A dorsal fin showed prominently

---

35 Here Miller describes precautions against submarine attack. Three weeks earlier, the Germans had announced that a "war zone" existed in the waters surrounding the British Isles, marking the beginning of the first period of unrestricted submarine warfare.

and a yellow patch at the base of the fin. They only leaped partly out of the water but had sufficient speed to pass over twice their length before disappearing again. They are probably 3 or 4 ft. in length.

Last night and again this evening I noticed an interesting phenomenon in the wake of our vessel where the water was being churned up by the propellers. Now and again a luminous ball about the size of a baseball could be seen at a depth of a few feet, apparently drawn in by the propeller and then sent whirling away astern. It seemed as if phosphorescent sea creatures of some kind were disturbed by our propeller and made to show their light, then quickly caught in the suction and sent hurrying along in the temporary currents thus set up. Their appearance was so intermittent and irregular that I do not think the phenomenon was merely due to the action of the propeller blades on the water.

Thurs., Mar. 4:

(3 P.M.) Entered Queenstown Harbour this morning at six, and cast anchor to await orders. The entrance to the harbour is about five miles long running generally northward. The inner harbour is spacious, possibly two miles across at some points, but only a narrow passage can be used by ships of deep draught. Torpedo boats and cruisers were guarding the entrance and our ship had to observe several formalities to secure admission. This is evidently a small naval base as three or four cruisers or battleships are lying at the naval docks.

The surrounding country is quite hilly, and steep hillsides rise from the water's edge in some parts. Forts crown the principal hills along the entrance channel. The city is situated mainly on the steep north side of the inner harbour. The streets run parallel to the shore, one above and behind another. The houses are built accordingly, and as the ship passed up to the docks we could see the whole front part of the town. A splendid cathedral in the centre attracts the eye by its massive proportions and soaring spire.[36]

We cheered heartily as our boat passed along, and the natives responded by waving flags, handkerchiefs, and aprons from the streets and windows of the houses. The whole landscape is green of one shade or another. Evergreens are abundant (evidently fir trees). The deciduous

---

36 Cathedral: Reference to St. Colman's, a Gothic revival Cathedral whose construction began in 1867 but which was not completed and consecrated until a month after Miller laid eyes on it, March 1915.

trees show their swollen buds like a beginning of foliage. Evergreen vines, hedges, and shrubbery cover the hillsides and walls, hiding much of the brick and stone from view. Grey clouds hang low over the town, and there are frequent threats and beginnings of drizzling rain.

The streets seem to be paved with stone, and stone walls protect the precipitous side of every street that parallels the shore. Elaborately built stone flights of steps lead down from the higher streets to the quay. Everything looks fresh, clean, and neatly kept and cared for.

Jaunting cars are the commonest vehicles seen on the streets.[37] All vehicles are two-wheeled, and are drawn by one horse. The reason of this is evident in the steep streets and the sharp corners that must be turned. A few motor cars are to be seen. Among the civilians women and children are most in evidence. Nearly all men of young and middle age are wearing military or naval or merchant marine uniforms. The reception given us was most hearty, but we cannot get ashore to greet and be greeted at close quarters, much to the disappointment of all.

At present we are lying at the dock beside the *Megantic*, and the *Missanabie* is a short distance away at anchor. We are awaiting orders to proceed to our next destination, but there is a persistent rumour that we disembark here and proceed to Curragh Camp.[38]

Crows fly about in flocks across the harbour during the early morning, and singly or in small bands among the trees on shore during the day. They seem very bold and sure of their safety, for they often alight on the house roofs and in the open streets. A new species of gull has just joined the others (already mentioned) in the harbour – size of herring gull with same colours but back, wings and tail are black with narrow white margins. Hundreds of gulls hover about the ship or rest on the smooth water around us.

The tide has been running out since we entered. In the entrance channel it seemed as if we were in a strong river flowing seaward. The water on the quay retaining walls has fallen about 12 ft. Many shallow places about the harbour lie uncovered as mud flats or islands of mud. Groves of evergreens and hillsides covered with trees and shrubbery are much in evidence in the landscape as seen from the harbour. But some open cultivated areas divided up by hedges into little fields of many shapes and sizes lie back over the high ground to east and west of our anchorage.

---

37 Jaunting car: Two-wheeled light carriage drawn by a horse.
38 Curragh Camp: Historic army base and training camp, located on a plain in County Kildaire, Ireland.

Grass in the meadows is green, of a brownish hue. We see cows grazing
on the hillsides in a few places. The air is damp and cool with a fresh
breeze blowing in from the harbour mouth.

Fri., Mar. 5:

The *Megantic* moved out into the harbour at 7 a.m. and the *Vaderland* took
her place at the dock. Officers went on shore until noon. We spent the time
watching the ship being coaled up, buying post cards and fruit from vendors
who came on board or passed their wares from wharf to deck by means of
baskets on ropes. These vendors are several stout old Irish women about as
broad as long. They seem to be as strong as men, handling their boxes and
barrels of fruit with ease. They are always pleasant, have a happy faculty
for introducing their wares, and drawing one into conversation. For quick
repartee they beat any soldier on board, and several officers who passed
jokes about their wares were well paid back in kind amid roars of laughter
from the men. Had a route march of about 5 miles this afternoon 3:30 to
5. The battn. passed east by a main street that gradually ascended the hill
along the water front; then along shaded lanes and winding roads through
a large private estate, northward down the hill and out among the farms;
then westward and south we marched to re-enter the town. Passing by the
magnificent cathedral in the centre of the town we returned to our boat.

The streets are very narrow, about like our Winnipeg or Toronto streets
without the sidewalks. They don't know what a street like Main in Wpg.
or Spadina Ave. in Toronto is. There are no electric cars and very few
autos. The jaunting car is the most frequently used passenger vehicle.
There are a few two-wheeled cabs. All vehicles for carrying loads are
carts, many drawn by a single small donkey. A team of horses is a rare
sight on the street, as all vehicles are two-wheeled and for one horse.

Most of the fences are neatly-built stone walls, sometimes as high as
8 ft. Between fields, thick hedges are mostly used for the same purpose
but here and there one sees a lone modern wire fence. The hedges are
usually of hawthorn, but many other trees and shrubs grow among them
while vines climb about over walls and trees. The walls when old become
very pretty. Dirt has accumulated in the chinks and crevices among the
stones so that many species of small plants take root and grow luxuriantly.
Mosses of the richest green are much in evidence. Many species of little
wall ferns may be found, with leaves a few inches in length; these are
growing at this season and are quite green in colour. At one place we found
little daisies about two inches tall, white with yellow centre, growing on

the top of a wall. Ivy and other creeping and climbing plants cover such walls in places so that one sees more green vegetation than brown stone.

On two farms, plowing was going on in the fields. Two-horse teams and single furrow walking plows are used, same as in Ontario. In one field, there was grain six inches high. The meadows are all green, and some cattle and sheep are out grazing, but the grass is quite short. Hay and pasture fields are more numerous than cultivated grain fields. Saw first Robin while on this march. Two of them were hopping about in a hedge singing a cheery warbling song. Apparently the breast of the female is pale orange while that of the male is red. I am told that these birds are permanent residents here and in all the south parts of the British Isles.

Crows are very abundant and seemed to be quite fearless, alighting on roofs or on the ground within fifty yards of where people were standing. Heard other small birds singing among the branches of trees along by the road, but could not notice any distinguishing marks so as to identify them.

This has been a lovely day with clear sky and fresh cool westerly wind. Should judge the temperature was over 60° while we were marching. Early March seems to correspond to early May in Ontario and early June in Sask. with regard to the climatic conditions and the progress of plant growth. Of course the growing season is much longer here than in Canada and growth is correspondingly slower. They never get the weeks of continuous heat and showers that ripen our crops so quickly in July and August. And evergreens of many kinds are so much in evidence that the two landscapes cannot be compared by any casual observer. We saw beds of violet and yellow crocuses in bloom. They grow just like the prairie crocus, but are much more graceful and delicate in appearance. A bushy shrub about 4 or 5 ft. high which grows along the roadside is beginning to bloom. Its flowers are golden yellow and about 1½ in. across. The branches are very prickly, and these dangerous weapons are concealed by the leaves. One of our chaps, eager to get early flowers as souvenirs, grasped a branch to pluck it off, but let go so suddenly that everyone saw what a sharp disappointment he had received. (Later at Shorncliffe I identified this shrub as gorse).[39] A few other small plants and shrubs are in bloom. Many shrubs and small trees of a tropical

---

39 This parenthetical remark was added at the beginning of the next page of Miller's diary.

appearance are planted in the grounds of the estate though which we passed, and they appear to flourish here.

Sat., Mar. 6:

During the forenoon two torpedo-boat-destroyers steamed up the harbour and anchored beside us. At 2:30 p.m. we left the dock and passed to the outer harbour, anchoring there. The people cheered us and waved farewell from one end of the town to the other and from beach to hilltop. The *Megantic*, we are told has gone on to Liverpool. The *Missanabie* followed us later. Escorted by the two destroyers the two transports left the harbour for the open sea at sunset. Tonight we are running east along the south coast of Ireland. The sea is calm and wind light. Shore lights, buoy lights, and light-house beacons are flashing all along our northern horizon.

On duty on bridge with Cornish 6 to 10 p.m. The *Missanabie* followed us, while the destroyers ran ahead on either bow. Not a light is showing on any of the boats. We can hardly distinguish the destroyers on the darkening sea, although they are little more than 200 yds. distant. It seems incredible that those two shadowy patches moving silently along over the darkly heaving water are the only guarantee of safety we have tonight from the lurking German submarine with its deadly torpedoes. While the British fleet locks the German in his own harbours, daring him to come out and fight, and with another squadron batters the forts of the Dardanelles, making the Turk tremble in his home city on the Bosphorus, these two little dark coloured engines of destruction steal silently into Queenstown harbour and bid us proceed to our destination under their protection.[40]

Sun., Mar. 7:

Arrived in Avonmouth at the docks at 10:30 a.m.[41] Have seen land on both sides of the Bristol Channel since 3 a.m. The shore is high and composed of rolling land with many low hills. Trees cover the landscape in

---

40 Dardanelles: The Dardanelles or Gallipoli Campaign began three weeks before Miller wrote this entry. A strategically significant strait in Turkey, connecting the Aegean to the Sea of Marmara, the Dardanelles were the object of a major Allied naval operation in February and March, called off in mid-March after heavy losses. The land campaign continued until January 1916. Home city: A reference to Istanbul, located on the Bosphorus, which connects the Sea of Marmara to the Black Sea.
41 Avonmouth: Port of Bristol on the mouth of the Avon River in South West England.

groves, woods, and rows along roads and fence lines. The river is high and the water very muddy. Took the train on Great Western Ry. at 2:30 p.m. Passed through Reading, London at 7 p.m., and reached Shorncliffe at nine in evening.[42] It was very dark and drizzling rain and I was completely turned round, not knowing where I was. After a mile march we went into barracks and had soon made ourselves comfortable.

Mon., Mar. 8:

Cold and wet this morning, snowing at times. The ground is very muddy, but the macadamised roads make good clean walking in spite of the wet.[43] The artillery are out training on this parade ground this morning. But we Canadians are wandering around like a flock of lost sheep with no leader. At 9:30 no orders have been issued and we are doing nothing but explore the barrack area. Find conditions for training much better than anything we have had yet. Our barrack rooms are spacious, well ventilated and lighted, and with care we should be able to keep our quarters clean and respectable. We actually have iron bedsteads, mattresses and plenty of warm blankets, whereas in Winnipeg we just had mattresses on the floor and where the water ran down some of our beds froze fast. Two small stoves in each hut supply all the heat we need and we are issued with coal enough to keep the fires going.

Wed., Mar. 10:

Work is gradually settling down to a regular routine, and we are trying to make ourselves at home in our new surroundings. One of our first and most amusing difficulties is to get acquainted with English money. Paying a sixpence for a ha'penny paper, and getting back fivepence ha'penny seems like getting back ten times more than you gave. It is a problem to keep one's pocket clear of heavy coins, for the small paper money is the pound note and the 10 s. note. The sixpence coin is very handy. The paper money is much lighter and thinner than ours and requires half the carrying space. After introduction to the coinage however, you soon

---

42 Shorncliffe Army Camp, Kent, England. Situated adjacent to the town of Folkestone on a plateau overlooking the English Channel, the camp was a training and staging ground for troops heading to France. The Canadian Training Division was established there in April 1915 from the nucleus of the 23rd, 30th, and 32nd Battalions.

43 Macadamised: A road constructed of layers of crushed stone.

find it very convenient. So many small articles cost a penny or tuppence. A box of boot dubbin, a box of metal polish, a nail brush, a little pad of 150 detachable blank leaves, a packet of stationery, a photo card packet, and dozens of small useful articles can be had for a penny. Some of these same things cost from 5 to 15 cents in Canada. I have a new glass put in my wrist watch at Dingwalls in Wpg. for 25¢. Had it replaced yesterday in Cheriton for a sixpence. A Joseph Rogers jackknife with two blades cost me a shilling here, and I have bought the same type of knife in Canada for 75¢.[44] They are selling two oranges for a penny at the canteen (small Spanish oranges). They sold us large California oranges at 8 for 25¢ on the train in Canada. I can have a good time on a shilling a day and buy all the small articles I need. On two shillings a fellow can have all he needs, and buy a lot of extra food in addition. I should think that living here costs about one half what it does in Canada.

The spring birds appear to be returning, for the place is musical with bird songs all day long. I was watching some birds sitting on the roof of a hut and whistling when one of our fellows came along and said they were starlings. These birds are common about the barrack area. This is the bird they are introducing into the New England States with some success. But it is certainly neither a handsome bird in appearance, nor yet a singer of any merit. At the same time, we noticed a small grey sparrow-like bird fluttering in the air above us and chirruping a very sweet song somewhat like the spring song of the Prairie Horned Lark. I was told it was the Skylark. I at once had Shelley's famous poem running through my mind, and it seems a true description of the bird.[45] This morning the air is full of bird songs, and most of the lovely chorus comes from the throats of Skylarks. It is such delightful music to have poured forth in the upper air over our camp every morning. Whether cloudy or fine, the same cheering melodies are heard.

Fri., Mar. 12:

The 32nd, 30th and 23rd Battns. were reviewed at 3:30 p.m. by Gen. Barrington and several other British officers of high rank.[46] The General

---

44 Joseph Rogers: British cutlery maker, in business since the eighteenth century. Manufactured a line of multiplex knives, sometimes generically referred to today as "Swiss Army" knives.

45 Shelley: Miller is referring to Percy Bysshe Shelley's poem "To a Skylark" (1820).

46 Barrington: Might be Thomas Percy Barrington (1867–1951) of the Royal Irish Rifles.

Miller, standing at left in this photo from early 1915,
served in the signals, the branch of the service responsible
for communications. Credit: Miller family collection.

has a very pleasant manner, and chatted with several of the privates in
the ranks. He seemed well-pleased with our appearance. He told us we
should not have to use lamps in signalling; so there is a lot of hard work
removed from our course of training.

The parade ground was very muddy when we started last Monday,
but it is rapidly drying up, and today was in good condition for marching
with the exception of a few wet spots. We have had very little sunshine
since our arrival, and the air feels so damp that I wonder any moisture
will evaporate in such an atmosphere.

On Wednesday afternoon during parade a biplane passed over our
camp flying at a considerable height in a westerly direction. When near
us, the loud rattling of the engine exhaust attracted our attention, but
this sound rapidly grew fainter. Gradually the machine appeared smaller
and smaller and the noise died away, until like a bird it disappeared in
the clouds that hung low in the west. This is the first aeroplane I have
ever seen.

We have been greatly amused the last two evenings by the boys who come to the barracks in threes and fours to sing for pennies. Last night some boys sang us "Wee folk, good folk, trooping all together" and other songs which they said they had learned at school.[47] This evening four of the toughest looking specimens of boyhood I have yet seen came in to entertain us. Their clothes were old, dirty, and worn; their boots mud-covered wrecks of footwear; faces dirty with coal dust and filth, wearing an expression that showed a thorough knowledge of all the deviltry of the streets. Their songs were so comical that everybody burst into peals of laughter, but some of the language was the filthiest I have ever heard from small boys of 8 to 10 years. One cannot expect much however from the street urchins of a town where, apart from the soldiers, as many women as men are seen drinking at the public bars. All the bartenders are maids as is the custom in this country.

Fri., Apr. 3:

Good Friday; no drill today but church service at the garrison church in forenoon and half holiday afterward. In the afternoon, Geo. L. and I went to Folkestone and took in the show at the Victoria Pier Pavilion.[48] A most remarkable wrestling match was shown on one reel of pictures. It was just like reality and very fast; the contestants were certainly professional wrestlers of first class. Prairie life and scenery seems to provide the plot and colour for many of the picture plays shown here. At every show I attend some such are given. They seem to take a strong hold on the imagination of English people. A very bright picture of Western life is always painted.

Mon., Apr. 5:

Easter Monday and another half holiday, but as it has rained most of the day, many of us are remaining in the barracks. We started on a new daily routine this morning: rise at 6; drill 6:30 to 7:30; breakfast and clean-up 7:30 to 9:00; drill 9 to 12:45; dinner 12:45 to 2 p.m.; drill 2 to 5; supper 5:30; free till 9; lights out at 9:45.

---

47 Geo. L.: George Leeson. See entry of 10 January 1915. "Wee folk": Song derived from the poem "The Faeries" by Irish poet William Allingham (1824–1889).

48 Victoria Pier Pavilion: Featuring moving pictures, roller skating, dancing, and an 800-seat pavilion, the Victoria Pier, jutting from Folkestone's promenade onto the Channel, was a popular destination for troops stationed locally.

Had my first swim in sea water yesterday in the swimming bath on the beach at Folkestone. To a beginner the sea water is very disagreeable, for the least quantity entering one's mouth or nose irritates terribly, tasting like very strong brine. This tank is apparently the only one in Folkestone, a town of 34,000 people. It is not at all in the same class as those in the Winnipeg and Regina Y.M.C.A.'s, being small and possessing no diving facilities worth mentioning, too shallow anyway. We get hot sea or fresh water baths in tubs at nine pence each, and swims at 4 pence. I prefer the former.

Sun., Apr. 25:

Our Battn. was placed under quarantine for measles on Friday, and we do not yet know how long we will be so confined. We carry on drill as usual, but there was no church parade today. Yesterday afternoon most of the fellows played football or watched the games. Picked teams from A and B coys. played a match game. Others, like myself, remained in the barracks and read or wrote letters.

In the evening a concert was arranged in our room by the 28 occupants. A few from the other platoons came in to take part or enjoy it. Different fellows sang such songs as "Commissionaire", "The Strand at Night-Time", "Pass It Along to Father", "I See You've Got Your Old Brown Hat On", "If I Were King of England".[49] About a third of the fellows had had enough canteen beer to be happy and loose-tongued. So there was an abundance of wit and humour in evidence. A few boxing-bouts were arranged, and I had a turn with the gloves.

Finally we had coffee brought in from the cook-house; we fried onions and sliced mutton in our mess-tins over the coal fires in the heaters. I made cocoa, and with a few added delicacies purchased at the canteen, we made a banquet. "Lights Out" was blown before we had finished, but we left things in an indescribable confusion, and got into bed as fast as possible. The cleaning up this morning was a discouraging business, but everyone voted the affair a success.

This morning it was dull and raining continuously. We sat around the barrack room and read the weekly papers while a cheery coal fire burned in the grate. Everybody feels under the weather, some are playing cards,

---

49 "The Strand at Night Time": Lyric from "People You Meet in the Strand" by Reuben
    Hill. "Pass It Along to Father": Song by Harry Von Tilzer and Vincent Bryan,
    composed around 1908. "I See You've Got Your Old Brown Hat On": Song by Robert
    Gorman and Tom Lowan, composed in 1905.

smoking and chatting. A few of us have been practising bayonet fighting with dummy weapons and masks.

This seems such a long way from the life I have always loved in Canada. At times my present experience seems like a dream or illusion. When I consider the food we eat, the lack of comforts we endure, and the kind of work we spend our days at, I wonder how we can endure the change. And yet I cannot point definitely to one feature of our life and say, "This is a crime and ought not to be". I have never enjoyed perfect health for so long a period before. George Leeson, my chum from Stoughton, says I have grown very fat since enlisting. I sleep soundly every night, and blankets seem to give as much comfort and warmth as proper clean sheets and bed clothes. We can keep reasonably clean here as easily as in civilian life. We have all the warm, comfortable clothes we need. We don't get much pay, but we always know when pay-day will come, and a fellow can live quite as usual with no money in his pocket for a week. I carried a lonely halfpenny in my pocket 5 days, and then one of the fellows loaned me a sixpence which I promptly blew in on a tin of syrup. As long as I stay in barracks, all I need is morning papers and food extras from the canteen to supplement the regular issue from the cook-house. The Cheriton steam laundry does all our washing for which two shillings a month is kept out of our pay.[50] We can send all the laundry we like or none at all, but the charge remains the same for each soldier.

A course in signalling and field telephony has been going on for 2 weeks at the 17th Battn. barracks. Four signallers from each Canadian Battn. in the camp are taking it. Sergt. Jardine, Cpl. Pritchard, Pte. Alexander and I are the 32nd representatives.[51] We expect that the successful members of this class will be the first chosen to go to the front.

Another terrific battle between the British and German forces is in progress at Ypres and along the Yser Canal.[52] The Belgians have been

---

50 Cheriton: Another adjacent town, now a suburb of Folkestone.
51 Jardine: Percy Clayton Jardine (b. 1893), born Prince Edward Island; attested Winnipeg December 1914. Alexander: Probably Henry James (1878-), born England; attested Winnipeg December 1914; died of wounds 23 June 1916; buried Lijssenthoek Military Cemetery, Belgium.
52 Battle: Refers to the Second Battle of Ypres (22 April–25 May 1915), the first action fought by the 1st Canadian Division. Northeast of the town of Ypres, the Canadians bore the brunt of the first major German poison gas attack of the war and held the line for four days in the face of a heavy assault, suffering 6,000 casualties.

driven back over a mile, but south of Ypres the British have advanced taking Hill 60.[53] We hear the Canadians distinguished themselves by a brilliant charge which saved a situation. 1,700 Canadian casualties is the rumour. Drafts of reinforcements are being drawn from the Battns. here in camp. Our Battn. Medical Officer, Dr. Gardner, is leaving for France to-day.[54] We expect to go at any time now, but there is no certainty.

Received in mail letters from Mother, Viola Lockhart of Moncton, N.B., Dorothy Blakney of Sunny Brae, N.B., Eulah Stuart and her mother Mrs. H.H. Stuart, Box 68, Newcastle, Miramichi, N.B. The Moncton girls send cheery refreshing bits of news, offering to send me papers and other reading matter. Eulah Stuart is a school girl of 13 years. Mrs. Stuart writes a long, interesting, very kind-hearted letter. Mr. Stuart is a school teacher, Methodist local preacher and a socialist. They are all very much interested in us Canadian soldiers and wish me to send them news as they have no friend in the army. Mrs. Stuart also sent a lovely box of chocolates which I shared with the boys in this hut. The people of the maritime provinces are intensely loyal. Such gifts and letters are much appreciated by us. You can get nearer to a soldier's heart with a box of candy or a cake than with all the fine words or polished speeches of praise that could ever be written or spoken. We have grown weary of words from admirers.

Editor's Note: Miller's diary entry for 27 April appears prior to the 26 April entry.

Tues., Apr. 27:

Last night at seven o'clock "B" coy. and one platoon of "A" coy. left for France. They had about two hours notice of their departure, and as a result there was terrible confusion and haste. Fifteen minutes before they had to fall in the new Webb equipment was served out to them. No one knew how to put it together nor adjust it on his back. The fellows just shoved the separate pieces into their packs and haversacks and carried many things loose in their hands. Many did not get all the necessary parts, and some left pieces behind in disgust. The poor fellows went off in sad confusion, disgust, and discomfort. It was a disgrace to those in command and the men are quite angry that it should be possible for such things to occur.

---

53 Hill 60: A tactically significant promontory southeast of Ypres, contested until 1918.
54 Gardner: Probably Major (later Lt. Col.) Robert Lorne Gardner (b. 1878), graduate of McGill and a long-serving officer with the Canadian Army Medical Corps.

George Leeson, Miller's friend in Stoughton with whom he served in the
32nd Battalion. Leeson later served with the 10th Battalion and survived the
war despite being twice wounded. Credit: Miller family collection.

My Stoughton chum Geo. Leeson went with his company, and we have
been forced to part. George and I have kept together constantly since
joining, and we had hoped to stay together right through.

Three of us signallers slept together in this hut last night where 28 men
have been sleeping. It was so quiet; we seemed lost and were almost
afraid to speak in the vacant room. I wish we were all going now, for
this is not home with the other fellows gone. Other companies are going
in a few days, and we signallers expect to be away by Sunday.

It has been cloudy and very cool all day with a heavy gale blowing.
I do not think such a day could be so disagreeable in Sask. The spring
weather here has little apparent advantage over that in Canada, only
that there are few or no frosts.

Mon., Apr. 26:

"B" Coy left for France at 7 this evening. They took the boat at Folkestone for an unknown port in France. So all the Weyburn boys and Geo. Leeson, my chum, have passed off into the unknown. We parted like men; I have never had hand-shakes that were so full of feeling-just a firm clasp, a glance into the eyes, with a hurried "Goodbye and Good Luck", and they marched away into the darkness.

Sun., May 2:

For three days following "B" coy's departure, four of us lived alone in a barrack room where 28 men had previously lived. We found it very quiet and lonely. Then we moved over and lived with "A" coy a few days. "A", "C", and "D" coys. left for France this evening. They marched under orders to Folkestone one evening last week, but a thick fog came up on the Channel very suddenly and boat passages were cancelled for a time. So the boys had to return to camp very disappointed. However, their hopes are now realized and they too are "somewhere" in France.

About 100 officers, non-coms, and men are left behind. Some men have been sick, or absent on leave, while others like myself are on special courses or duties. This is now a Base Battn. training reinforcements for four battalions for the first Contingent. New men keep coming in from various sources, and our officers and N.C.O.'s train them and send them on to the front as they are needed.

Mon., May 3:

At about 11 a.m. while our class was working at buzzer practice out on the downs by the sea, we heard artillery firing in the direction of Dover.[55] A few minutes later a strange aeroplane appeared flying over Folkestone at an immense height. This was evidently the German "Taube" reported at many places along southeastern Kent today and fired on at Dover by anti-aircraft guns.[56]

---

55 Buzzer practice: The "buzzer" was a hybrid telephone-telegraph device. It had the advantage of being able to transmit Morse code over bad lines that could not carry a voice.

56 Taube: The Etrich Taube, a German monoplane notable for its birdlike appearance. Short-ranged and obsolete by 1914. The reported machine probably was not a Taube as the model had been removed from front-line service by early 1915.

Tues., May 4:

Our signalling class [Jardine, Pritchard, Stubbington, Norris, Mattingly, Lieuts. Underhill and McReady] worked on buzzer practice in the trenches on the downs by the sea from 8 to 10 p.m. for practice at night work.[57]

Wed., May 5:

For half an hour in mid-forenoon, heavy artillery fire was heard in an easterly direction on or across the Strait of Dover. The firing began slowly with shots at regular intervals of half a minute, then increased to a rapid bombardment for a few minutes, but quickly died away and ceased. Nearly every day we hear intermittent cannonading in the distance from south, east, or northeast. No explanation is ever offered by the newspapers, but we do not think all this ammunition is being used merely for practice.

Attended a lecture given in the Folkestone town hall by Wm. Le Queux, the eminent writer, novelist, and secret-service man.[58] Subject: "The Spy Peril in England". The speaker is a stout man of medium stature, much of the John Bull type; has a very good delivery for a lecturer; gives a strong impression because of the facts he discloses and not because of fluency or oratory. He has worked with and ahead of our War Office, has shown them the danger of the spy peril, and caused them to take measures to deal with it. He knows European politics and secret service work like a book, and has visited every part of Europe from Corfu to St. Petersburg in carrying on his work, either as a novelist hunting material for stories, or as a British secret service agent. I hear his books highly recommended, but have not yet had the pleasure of reading any.

---

57 Stubbington: William Henry Stubbington (b. 1875), born England; attested Valcartier, September 1914; a 14-year veteran of the Royal Navy and three-year veteran of the Canadian militia. Underhill: Ernest LeRoyal Underhill (1893–1968), born Woodstock, Ontario; attested Valcartier September 1914. McReady: Could not be identified. Norris: Could not be identified. Mattingly: Arthur William Mattingly (b.1893), born England, attested Valcartier September 1914.

58 Le Queux: William Le Queux (1864–1927), Anglo-French writer, pioneer pilot, and radio enthusiast. Best known for writing two sensationalist novels in the "invasion scare" genre, including *The Great War in England in 1897* (1894) and *Invasion of 1910* (1906). The latter, serialized by the *Daily Mail*, sold over a million copies and was made into an early film.

Mon., May 10:

For three days it has been quite cool and cloudy with high winds.

I walked up to Caesar's Camp Hill at sunset, and obtained a splendid view of the sea and the narrow plain on which lie Folkestone, Cheriton, and the camp.[59]

The trees are almost in full leaf. The gardens are gay with flowers – hyacinth, candytuft, forget-me-nots, wall flower, fleur-de-lis, and many kinds I do not know. The woods are fragrant with bluebells and many varieties of wild flowers. The hillsides on the downs are golden with gorse blooms. The Leas and the wooded cliffs below are a veritable paradise. The pleasure that thousands of people get out of those places is incalculable. On a Sunday afternoon one sees all kinds of people there – old people seated on the park seats in nooks among the trees overlooking the sea; whole families on the promenades; children down on the shingly beach, some paddling into the edge of the waves as they break and recede on the hard smooth sand or shingle; couples walking about arm in arm or spooning in some quiet corner among the shrubbery; soldiers by the hundreds wandering aimlessly about or sunning themselves as they lie in the gravel.

Editor's Note: Miller breaks with chronology to add the following parenthetic entry:

Fri., May 7:

Lusitania torpedoed and sunk off Kinsale Head, Ireland, at 2:30 p.m.[60] Over 1,400 lives lost.

Thurs., May 13:

It was clear and fine yesterday, a beautiful day in lovely Kent. You cannot imagine what that means unless you see for yourself the scenery that we enjoy day after day.

---

59 Caesar's Camp Hill: Not to be confused with Caesar's Camp Hillfort in Surrey. Caesar's Camp Hill is the local name for Folkestone Castle, medieval Norman earthworks overlooking the town and English Channel coast.

60 *Lusitania:* A reference to the famous Cunard liner, sunk by German submarine *U-20*. The heavy loss of civilian life (1,200 killed) resulted in an increase in anti-German sentiment in Allied countries and in the United States.

We had planned to go to Hythe for musketry on the ranges, but the trip had to be postponed, for it has rained heavily all day.

Wed., May 19:

Kitchener has just issued a call for 300,000 more men for his army.[61] On the streets of the local towns a youthful civilian is an uncommon sight and seems ashamed of himself. I met one on Cheriton Road this evening with a girl leaning on his arm. Some English soldiers standing at the edge of the pavement remarked, "Are you looking for the Recruiting Office?" The fellow got mad and made an angry reply as best he could. But all the soldiers laughed and the poor civilian looked mighty unhappy as he walked away.

Attended a lecture in Folkestone town hall by Hilaire Belloc on "Progress of the War up to the Present".[62] The speaker is a short, stout man, bare-faced, looks like the pictures we see of Winston Churchill of the Admiralty, or of Thackeray without the glasses; speaks with a rather thick voice with much exertion of the vocal organs; but is cool and thoughtful, understands his subject thoroughly; speaks fluently without hesitancy, commands the whole attention of his audience.[63] No one seemed to notice how the time was passing. Belloc has a great reputation here as a historian, and the hall was filled. Only about half the audience was civilian.

Speaker dwelt mainly on the Galician and Dardanelles operations.[64] The Germans have forced the whole southern Russian line from the Vistula to the Carpathians back upon Prjemysl, forcing them to abandon the Carpathian passes and leave behind all their wounded – over 100,000.[65] Unless the Russian line is broken and crumpled up in the next few days, the German case is hopeless, and this has not happened yet; the whole line has swung back intact for 95 miles, and Prjemysl is now likely to be retaken by the Germans. Russia has enormous reserves of men, but cannot arm and equip them yet, nor

---

61 Kitchener: Field Marshal Herbert Kitchener (1850–1916), British Secretary of State for War. The volunteer army raised on his orders was known as "Kitchener's Army."
62 Hilaire Belloc: Enormously prolific Anglo-French writer and politician (1870–1953).
63 Thackeray: British novelist William Makepeace Thackeray (1811–1863).
64 Dardanelles: Another reference to the ongoing Gallipoli campaign.
65 Prjemysl: Przemyśl, a fortified Austro-Hungarian town that fell to the Russians on 22 March 1915.

munition her heavy artillery. For this reason the Dardanelles operations are of vital importance so that the Allies may ship the required munitions to Russia.

There are three main difficulties to be overcome in the Dardanelles, – (1) Landing, (2) Capturing Achi Baba, (3) Capturing the great plateau that commands the Narrows.[66] The first seemed impossible but is now accomplished. The second is under way, but the first attempt has proved a costly failure. The third still lies untouched. Success depends on the munition train at the command of the Allies. The speaker does not inspire optimism unless there is sufficient cause for it. He says the Dardanelles operations may fail, yes, it is quite probable they will fail. At any rate a task of extreme difficulty lies before the Allied forces there. If these heights on the western tongue of the Gallipoli peninsula are taken, the forts at the Narrows must fall at once and Constantinople pass into the Allies' hands. Then munitions will be poured into the Russian ports on the Black Sea and the Russian advance will be made inevitable.

The Austro-German forces have been superior in numbers to those of the Allies until this month. Three great periods of reinforcement gave them an immense superiority in numbers in October, December and March. Their latest reinforcement has drained the country of all available men, and they must win decisive victory within the next six weeks, or fail utterly. Their strength must wane rapidly after June.

The Allies started out with much smaller armies than the Germans, and their numbers slowly decreased until on in the winter. Now they are reinforcing rapidly, and are already slightly superior in numbers. This inequality of numbers must grow very rapidly in the Allies' favour during the next few weeks. Already on the Western front the Allied armies exceed the German by from 30 to 50 percent in numbers.

Two kinds of peace are possible. If the Russians are seriously defeated now, Germany can hold back her Western enemies indefinitely, and an inconclusive peace will have to be made. Germany would retain most of Belgium, but would make concessions to France. But if we win at the Dardanelles and in the meantime the Russians hold their line intact, the German is doomed to be conquered and will have to submit to a humiliating peace.

---

66 Achi Baba: A height commanding the Gallipoli Peninsula and one of the focal points of Allied attacks during the campaign. It remained in Turkish hands.

The speaker made no mention of Italy, although the papers give us to understand that her decision for war is to be made to-morrow.[67]

Just before the meeting was called to order by the chairman, I was amazed to hear in rapid succession the yells of Toronto Varsity, Queen's, and Magill given from different parts of the hall.[68] I learn that a large number of Magill medical men are here for the Army Medical Corps. Who the Queens and Toronto men were I do not know. The 18th and 21st Battns. of infantry are both here from Ontario, and I believe the 21st is a Toronto Regt.[69] They are at West Sandling camp some four miles west of here near Hythe.

Mon., June 28:[70]

The Permanent School of Signalling for Canadian Battns. and units opened this morning in the Garrison Gymnasium with Acting Sergt. Pritchard in charge and I as assistant instructor. After having done nothing for the past fortnight (with the exception of a great deal of reading) I now have 22 men to instruct in reading and sending Morse code on the field telephone. I have 12 men of the 42nd Black Watch and 10 of the C.M.R.'s.[71] I live in the 32nd barracks, but have no Battn. parades to attend.

Sat., July 10:

Bought for 4 pence an apple that was grown in Tasmania, weighing a pound. Grown in Australia and eaten in England by a Canadian, it

---

67 Italy: A member of the Triple Alliance (with Germany and Austria-Hungary),
     Italy revoked its commitment to the Central Powers and joined the Allies
     in May 1915.
68 Toronto, Queen's, "Magill": Here Miller refers to three Canadian universities: the
     University of Toronto, Queen's University in Kingston, Ontario, and *McGill* Univer-
     sity in Montreal, Quebec.
69 18th Battalion, CEF: Recruited in and mobilized from London, Ontario. 21st Battal-
     ion, CEF: Miller was mistaken. The 21st Battalion recruited in eastern Ontario and
     was mobilized at Kingston, Ontario, which may account for the number of Queen's
     University men at the meeting. Both battalions were attached to the 4th Canadian
     Brigade, 2nd Infantry Division.
70 The gap of six weeks in Miller's diary cannot be explained, except perhaps by his
     apparent boredom (he notes a fortnight of nothing occurring in the 28 June entry).
     His service records indicate that he was admitted to hospital for five days (24–29
     May 1915) in Shorncliffe, however, for a minor ailment.
71 42nd Black Watch: Refers to the 42nd Battalion Royal Highlanders of Montreal, not
     its namesake the Royal Regiment of Scotland. C.M.R.'s: Canadian Mounted Rifles.

had travelled half way round the world. Such apples are on sale at all the fruit stores now. So our wonderful Empire brings the ends of the earth into touch with one another. When the fruit season in England is over, the orchards of the other side of the world still keep her markets supplied.

I have been buying tomatoes of late for from 6 to 8 pence per pound. I learn that practically all English-grown tomatoes are grown in hot-houses, as they will not ripen in the open. The growing season here covers almost nine months of the year as compared to our six months, and yet because Canada is a land of sunshine we have the advantage in rapid growth and early ripening. At present we seldom have an entire day clear of clouds, and often for 3 or 4 days together we scarce see the sun right in this midsummer month. And the excessive moisture in the atmosphere seems to weaken the power of the sunlight.

It is reported this afternoon that the entire hostile force in German S.W. Africa has surrendered to Gen. Botha.[72] So the Empire continues to grow. But in Europe the issue is as yet not so certain.

Fri., July 16:

The 32nd Battn. has been up to full strength for a fortnight now, owing to the recent arrival of new detachments of the 44th, 45th and 53rd Bns. from Canada. A draft of the 44th and 45th was to have left for France this evening, together with drafts from other reserve Bns., numbering several thousand in all. At 7:30 they marched off amid a dense fog and heavy downpour of rain. But no boats put across the Channel under such weather conditions, and the boys all returned to barracks 9 p.m.

I have been reading Gene S. Porter's books of late, and sending them home to Nellie.[73] First I read "Song of the Cardinal", then "Harvester" and "At the Foot of the Rainbow". Enjoyed them all because of the Nature Lore they contain and because the writer sets a high ideal for manhood and womanhood. But in truth the books are weak in their effeminacy

---

72 Surrender: Refers to the successful British 1914–15 campaign in the German colony of German South West Africa, now Namibia. Botha: South African prime minister and general Louis Botha (1862–1919).

73 Nellie: Elizabeth Eleanor Miller (1899–1967), Leslie Miller's sister. She married Stuart Logan Thompson in 1924. See entry of 10 January 1915. Porter: Gene Stratton-Porter (1863–1924), American naturalist and novelist. Many of her works became bestsellers and were made into silent films.

and excessive idealism. Everything is just as it ought to be, and only the evil-doer ever suffers harm. I also sent home "Freckles" which I had read two years ago at Meeks in Sask. Have still "Girl of the Limber-Lost" to buy and read before the set is complete.

Thurs., Aug. 12:

During past 18 days I have had a class of signallers at Dibgate Camp (Div'l Cyclists Coy., 2nd Can. Div.) instructing them in field telephone and line work.[74] They wrote their exam yesterday and I have returned to my Battn. to continue training here. While instructing this last class, I held acting sergeant's rank, but have handed in my stripes as I do not think they need me any longer at the School of Signalling. I am now ready for the front as a signaller. I have vowed a dozen times lately that if they don't soon let me go as a signaller, I will give up the signalling, revert to the ranks as a private, and try to go out on the next draft of reinforcements.

It is a dull grey day, warm and calm. I am spending the morning in the little room where Sergt. Pritchard and I live, Hut A1.[75] Have just finished reading Gilbert Murray's new book, "The Foreign Policy of Sir Edward Grey", a very brilliant and interesting treatise on the subject.[76] At present I am spending nearly all spare time at reading. But while instructing I was busy day and night lecturing and preparing lectures. Yesterday received letters from home, C.B. Wood at Victoria B.C., and Olie Lockhart at Moncton, N.B.[77]

Here is a poem I picked up in the barrack room one day, written on a scrap of note paper. It refers to the wanderings of the 32nd Bn. up to their arrival at Shorncliffe Camp.

---

74 2nd Canadian Division: Formed in England in May 1915; embarked for France in
    September, forming the Canadian Corps together with the 1st Canadian Division.
75 Pritchard: Frederick Pritchard (1882–1916), born England, resident of Lloydmin-
    ster, Saskatchewan; attested Winnipeg September 1914. A veteran of the Boer War,
    Pritchard was killed in action August 1916.
76 Gilbert Murray: George Gilbert Aimé Murray (1866–1957), author of *The Foreign Pol-
    icy of Sir Edward Grey, 1906–1915*, one of the earliest works on the origins of the Great
    War. Australian born, Murray was principally a classicist and was Regius Professor
    of Greek at Oxford.
77 Lockhart: Viola Lockhart, see entry of 20 February 1915.

Miller's sister Nellie (Eleanor), to whom he wrote often during the war, in a photograph from 1916. She later married Stuart Thompson. Credit: Miller family collection.

The 32nd

Arise, ye "Thirty-second"
The call goes out "To Arms"
The bugles, drums, and trumpets
Are sounding war's alarms.
And on the train, we mount so gay,
And all of us do feel,
There never was a finer bunch
Sent out by Colonel Steele.
And over the Grand Trunk Road we fly
To meet him face to face.
And when we do, God help you Bill,

I think we'll end your race.
We left the Canadian harbour
As happy as could be,
And soon we were all sailing
Across the deep blue sea.
After several days sailing
Against a heavy sea
The *Vaderland* is anchored
In auld Ireland by the quay.
We threw kisses to the colleens,
And pennies to the boys.
We sang the dear old "Maple Leaf",
And raised an awful noise.
Then out again away we go
Across the briny foam,
To that little spot the Englishman
Will always call his home.
So once again we're settled down
As cosy as can be,
But instead of packing snow
It's mud clean to the knee.
– Author unknown, but undoubtedly a 32nd Bn. private.

Wed., Oct. 6:

Have been at the C.A.V.C. Remount Depot with Fidgett, R.E. Mayes, and Lavin, under Sergt. Windward ("Windy") at Ross Bks. since Sept. 7 feeding, grooming and riding horses, and cleaning stables.[78] There are four of us from each of the reserve battns. in camp like the 9th, 11th, 12th, 17th, 23rd, 30th, 32nd, 36th, 49th, etc. Yesterday a detachment of C.A.V.C. men came in from near Southampton, and now we are expecting soon to be returned to our Bns., a move that will please most of us mightily. We never had such rotten treatment before, in spite of the fact that we are strangers to the C.A.V.C., and we merely came here to help them out of the hole they were in. But in the army all men are equals and good and bad are treated alike. The fellows who get drunk occasionally and gamble all their spare time find favour in the sight of the N.C.O.'s,

---

78 C.A.V.C.: Canadian Army Veterinary Corps. Remount depot: Supplied trained
   horses for units in the field.

and seem to have a better time than those who keep sober and attend strictly to business.

I was on piquet duty at stables 6 to 10 o'clock last night, and this morning the same hours. It rained incessantly, and has only just cleared up a bit this afternoon. Autumn has set in in dead earnest with clouds, cold nights, and soaking rains. But I have worried little about the weather, and have been thoroughly enjoying camp life. The old tent leaks at night so that I have to take all my clothes to bed with me and put my waterproof over the lot – a tent within a tent. I have my head stuck between the pages of a book most of the time, now a war history, again a novel, or a book of poetry. I spent nearly a fortnight on Marie Corelli's "Innocent" and enjoyed every page of it, because it is a mirror of normal human life and character in a time of peace.[79] It takes one away from hard and cruel thoughts and makes you think quietly on the gentle things of life – love, ambition, art, etc. Am digging into Tennyson's and Matthew Arnold's poems just now, and also have a Nelson's History of the war as well.[80]

Tues., Oct. 12:

Left camp 7 a.m. entrained 9 a.m. passed through Ashford, Tonbridge, Guildford, Farnham. Prettiest rural scenery ever seen. Arrived Southampton 1:30 p.m. Embarked at 5 and boat left quay at 6:30. Passed Isle of Wight in darkness and could only see the lights. Reached open sea at 8:30.

Wed., Oct. 13:

Reached Le Havre 2:30 a.m.[81] France at last! Everything quiet in the harbour. Men keen to get ashore but no moving yet at 7:00 a.m.

Disembarked about 8 a.m. Lined up on quay – detachments of Canadians and Imperial Infantry. Marched inland about 7 miles to base camp and went under canvas for a time. This is indeed a fair land to a visitor from England, just like Southern Ont. or England. We are in a wooded

---

79 Corelli: Marie Corelli (1855–1924), immensely popular English novelist. *Innocent: Her Fancy and His Fact* was a bestseller at the time Miller read it.
80 Nelson's: Refers to the serialized *Nelson's History of the War* by John Buchan (1875–1940), Scottish author and politician, later (as the First Baron Tweedsmuir) the 15th Governor General of Canada.
81 Le Havre: French port city in Normandy, one of the principal disembarkation ports of the Allied expeditionary forces during the war.

and arable district where the land undulates gently in many low ridges and hollows. Sluggish streams abound. The roads are lined with poplars, continuous rows rising to near 60 ft. in height and spreading their crowns to meet inward and form an arch. We were marching through an avenue arched over with foliage far overhead and carpeted below with the first few leaves of autumn's gathering.

Thurs., Oct. 14:

Physical exercise for an hour in the morning on the parade ground followed by a mile run on the road. We passed through a quiet little French village in our valley where the children came out to see us and the women gazed from their windows greeting us with friendly smiles and gestures when near the street. It is a peculiar situation when you first realize that you are a foreigner in a strange land and an object of curiosity to the inhabitants. We rested all afternoon. Last night there was a lecture in the Y.M.C.A. hut on "Aircraft and Their Development" illustrated by lantern slides. This evening we had humorous entertainment given by some Tommies from the next camp.[82] Seldom have I seen better funny sketches given on the stage of a theatre, and the songs were all new, original, and referring to our present situation. The singer was the composer of 3 of these. There was "Down at the Base", "Tickler's Jam", "Camp Fare", "Old Blighty".

Fri., Oct. 15:

Spent day at training camp S.W. of here 2 mi. Had musketry tests, lectures on respirators and bombs. Saw first Indian troops in camp here.[83] Our march led up the side of a valley, the slope heavily wooded with grand old elms, beeches, chestnuts and others, undergrowth in places. The trees were all in rows skirting the road, or in groves, evidently planted there many years ago. To see the beauty of these splendid groves both from

---

82 Tommies: Affectionate slang for British soldiers, especially the rank and file, dating from at least the nineteenth century.

83 Indian troops: Here Miller refers to a unit of the Indian Expeditionary Force A. Consisting of one infantry and one cavalry corps, it served on the Western Front in 1914 and 1915. In all, over one million troops from India served overseas during the war and approximately 75,000 lost their lives. See George Morton-Jack, *The Indian Army on the Western Front: India's Epeditionary Force to France and Belgium in the First World War* (Cambridge: Cambridge Univeristy Press, 2014.)

Canadian-born photographer Charles Hilton DeWitt Girdwood took this
photo of Indian signallers in the summer of 1915. Over a million troops from
India, representing diverse linguistic and cultural identities, served overseas
in the First World War. Credit: Girdwood Collection,
British Library. Reproduced with the permission of the Controller
of HMSO and the King's Printer for Scotland.

the inside and as a part of the general landscape was sufficient evidence
to convince anyone of the wisdom of planting trees. The houses seem
to be built among the woods, they hide there and are scarcely seen in a
general view of this landscape. With us in Canada we build our homes
and perhaps have a few trees as decorations. I cannot but think what a
lovely land Sask. may yet become if the great mass of the people only
are brought to an understanding of the possible results of tree planting.

Sat., Oct. 16:

Spent morning on miniature rifle range, 25 yds. I had good results and
few had better scores to show than I. The great difficulty is to combine
speed with accuracy of fire. Many cannot work the bolt mechanism

rapidly and smoothly and being behind the others fail to take aim. I had my 10 rounds rapid fire all on my target while some had only 1 or 2 on their targets.[84] The French light vehicles seen on the roads are nearly all two-wheeled. I have only seen one wagon yet. When more than one horse is used they are hitched tandem, never side by side. The only plough I have seen at work was being drawn by 2 horses hitched thus. All light vehicles on the roads carry bells as we do in winter. It is odd to hear the bells jingling along the road in the distance; it makes one think it is winter and memory brings back many happy scenes. But we are having delightful weather, very warm and usually with the sky overcast with stratus clouds that break occasionally and give us a few rays of sunshine. It is usually clear all night long and starlight.

We expect to go east to-night and many of the boys are getting their hair clipped short in readiness. We get good encouraging news from the front now and everyone is keen to be there.

Sun., Oct. 17:

Left camp yesterday at 6 p.m., reached Havre at 8, entrained, left Havre at 11 p.m., travelled slowly and with many stops, and found ourselves in Rouen at 6 this morning.[85] Spent the entire day in Rouen. We are confined by sentries to the railway depot, a large shed with concrete floor where we deposited our equipment, and a large Y.M.C.A. reading and refreshment room. This latter is run by ladies who serve tea, coffee, and cocoa at a penny a bowl and bread and butter, buns and cake, tobacco and a few other soldier's needs. A number of Indians provided us with an interesting and amusing scene at the depot this afternoon loading onto cars a flock of sheep and goats. An English corporal was in charge and he could speak their language fluently – a senseless jabber to us. They are very friendly fellows, but beyond smiles of greeting and a little friendly assistance to them, we could not go. They are fine, tall, bronzed fellows. From the top of a freight car in the yards, I could only see a steel trestle bridge over the Seine, a splendid cathedral in the centre of the city, and a line of hills east of us some 4 or 500 ft. high.

---

84 Rifle: In 1915, the Canadians were still equipped with the domestically produced Ross Rifle, an accurate sporting weapon that proved unsuitable for the muddy conditions of the Western Front.

85 Rouen: City on the River Seine in Normandy. Cathedral: Notre-Dame de L'Assomption de Rouen, a medieval Gothic cathedral.

Mon., Oct. 18:

Left Rouen at 10:30 last night. Today passed Fontaine, Vichy, Abbeville, Conchil-le-temple Verton, Buvette, Etaples, Boulogne, Calais, St. Omer (1:30 p.m.), Hazebrouck, Bailleul (6:10 p.m.). Detrained at Steenwerck, marched to Bn. Q.M. Stores and were issued with rations, gas helmets, and tobacco.[86] Marched to dressing station and had medical inspection just behind trenches. All this time star shells were going up all along the eastern horizon and the guns were booming and rifles crackling just ahead behind the woods.[87] We entered a communication trench well under cover behind a little rise in the ground, passed through a maze of trenches for half a mile or so and landed in the second line reserve trench, were assigned to our dugouts and told to go to bed.[88] By this time the guns had become silent and there was only a little desultory sniping and machine gun fire, a few bombs being occasionally thrown across both ways.[89]

Tues., Oct. 19:

At 5:30 a.m. "stand to" to await attack and inspection by officer, but a few minutes later stand down and get breakfast. Was on a working party in front line trench 8:30 a.m. to noon, filling sandbags and building a traverse. The Germans threw over some shrapnel at 9 and later but everybody ducked behind parapets and no damage was done, although one shell exploded right above us.[90] Slept in dugout all afternoon and moved out at dark, being relieved by 8th Bn.[91] Just before moving out, our artillery threw a lot of high explosive into

---

86 Steenwerck: Small village (commune) in northern France, 20 kilometres southeast of Ypres. Gas helmet: Gas mask.

87 Star shells: Star shells contained magnesium flares in order to illuminate the battlefield at night or to pass signals.

88 Communication trench: Trenches connecting front-line, support, and reserve trenches used for moving men and materiel between them.

89 Bombs: Term for hand grenades, although sometimes generically used to refer to artillery shells.

90 Shrapnel: General name for anti-personnel artillery shells that scattered individual fragments. After Henry Shrapnel (1671–1842), British officer who conducted early experiments with shells of that kind.

91 8th Battalion: 8th Battalion CEF, organized from the 90th Winnipeg Rifles and 96th Lake Superior Regiment. Attached to the 2nd Infantry Brigade, First Canadian Army.

Messines in the German line and we got a few back which did no
damage save to cut off a tree in front of our first line parapet to the
left of my dugout. Our fellows gave the enemy about ten shells to
their one and had the last word too. Our shells made an awful row
over in Messines and the boys say they blew up a house where some
Germans were known to be.[92]

We came about 5 mi. behind the lines to our billets and after getting
some hot tea, slept soundly.

Wed., Oct. 20:

We have a little physical exercise 6:30–7 a.m. and an hour of platoon
drill in the p.m. Apart from that we are left to ourselves to keep ourselves and kits clean, read papers and write letters. We have good
drinking water but for washing a dirty stinking mudhole in a field
with no wash basin or drainage. For breakfast we get a slice of fried
bacon, bread, jam and tea. Dinner potatoes and hot meat from the field
kitchens. Supper – tea, bread, jam, cheese. It's the same every day. Met
Clements, one of the old 32nd Bn. signallers who has been here since
May 1, went thru Ypres and Festubert actions and is fed up with the
life.[93] I have met about fifteen fellows I knew at Shorncliffe – Ewson,
Brandie, Squair, and others.[94]

Thurs., Oct. 21:

Physical drill 6:30–7 a.m. In pm by way of a drill a Battn. attack and
charge on some trenches near the billets.

---

92 Messines: A Belgian town occupied by the Germans.
93 Clements: William Lee Clements (1893–1916), born Detroit, Michigan, a resident of
    Winnipeg; attested Winnipeg, December 1914. Killed in action 14 June 1916. Com-
    memorated on the Menin Gate.
94 Ewson: Harold Ewson (1892–1916), born England; attested Winnipeg, February 1915.
    Killed in action 27 September 1916. Commemorated on the Vimy Memorial. Brandie:
    Henry Brandie (b. 1891), born Scotland; attested Winnipeg, December 1914. Killed
    in action 21 August 1917. Buried in CWGC plot in Carvin Communal Cemetery,
    France. Squair: Private (later Lieutenant William Alexander Squair (b. 1892), born
    Manitoba; attested Winnipeg, December 1914.

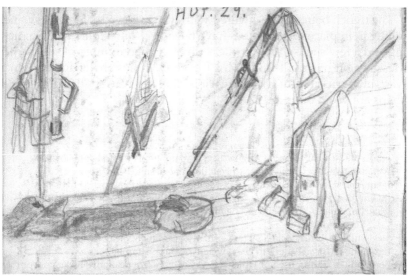

Sun., Oct. 24:

I was transferred from No. 15 section 8 platoon, B Coy. 5th Battn. to signal section of the 5th Battn. yesterday morning.[95] They put me on duty at the phone in orderly room during this forenoon and I had some experience learning their way of doing things here. I had my own ideas of how to manage the phone learned at Shorncliffe of course. But I had to forget all the rules I had learned and acquire the methods of this Battn. I received a good bawling out from Bde. office as a result of my ignorance, but am learning fast and will be proficient in a few more days. We came into the trenches at about 5 pm, relieving the 8th Battn. Met several of the old 32nd Boys as I passed up the communication trenches.

Mon., Oct. 25:

I and two others are in charge of C.A. front line trench phone station.[96] Was on duty 12–6 a.m. and 6–12 p.m. We are in a dugout some six or eight feet below ground with covered passage leading in. It is so dark that we have to burn candles both day and night. As there are corrugated iron, several thicknesses, sandbags and bricks above us, we are practically bomb proof. The old hands say even a Jack Johnson would hardly injure our retreat.[97] It has rained lightly all day.

The trench bottoms are covered with water, the sides are greasy and falling in in places. The Boches have been very quiet, only a little sniping and a few shells.[98] Our artillery threw a good number of shells into Messines on our right front. This trench (131) lies about due east and west, but turns at right L's where it joins 130 and runs south. Kitchener's chaps are south of us in 127.[99]

---

95 5th Battalion: Authorized in August 1914 as a mounted unit and dubbed 5th
    Battalion, Western Cavalry, the 5th kept its name despite being reorganized as an
    infantry unit before proceeding overseas in February 1915. Attached to the 2nd
    Infantry Brigade, 1st Canadian Division, the battalion was known as "Tuxford's
    Dandys," after its first commanding officer, Lt. Col. George Tuxford (1870–1943).
96 C.A.: Corps artillery.
97 Jack Johnson: British nickname for German 15-centimetre heavy artillery shell, after
    the famous African American heavyweight boxing champion.
98 Boches: Like "Fritz," used in Miller's 26 October entry, a pejorative nickname for the
    Germans.
99 Kitchener's chaps: A reference to one of the new battalions of the British Army.

It is very difficult to obtain firewood to boil our tea with. I was out rustling wood this morning, went away south to 127 and brought home an armful of wet muddy sticks. At supper we had a terrible time to get a fire. We split the driest wood we had very fine, and two of us on our hands and knees took turns at blowing under the fire. We had to keep blowing until the water came right to boiling. We do things here I would not have dreamed of in civilian life. This is a great experience to make a fellow resourceful.

We can send our mail out to be posted and receive our incoming mail every day. Parties go out to Hyde Park Corner in Ploegsteert Wood every day to meet the transport wagons and get rations and supplies.[100]

Tues., Oct. 26:

On duty 12 to 6 this p.m. Our artillery put a lot of shrapnel and high explosive shells over on Fritz' trenches today. We hear that Warneton and Messines are being bombarded with 12 in. howitzers, so doubtless we are strafing Fritz pretty hard.[101]

Out to Hqrs. at Ash house at 6:30 p.m. for water and rations. Snipers very busy tonight, as it is calm and bright moonlight. Bullets were singing over the trenches everywhere, and so many whistled around the well where I filled my water bottles that I thought I was being sniped at and I began to wonder if the bottles would ever get all filled. The trenches are very muddy and water lies along the bottom in many places. I came home plastered to the knees and with splashes and daubs all over me.

A German aeroplane was brought down behind our lines near here this morning.[102] Aircraft have been very busy all day and ours were continually passing overhead followed by tiny shrapnel clouds from German guns. One of our machine gunners was shot through a loophole as he lay facing the enemy. The bullet entered at his hip, passed right down a leg and came out on the calf of the leg. He was carried

---

100 Hyde Park Corner: Here, as in many other entries, Miller refers to the practice of giving trenches and rear-area locations familiar British names. Ploegsteert Wood: A rear-area camp, south of Ypres, near the Belgian village of Ploegsteert, referred to by British and Imperial troops as "Plugstreet."

101 Warneton: Occupied Belgian town, about 12 kilometres south of Ypres.

102 This machine was brought down by Captain Robert Lorraine (well-known English stage actor) and his observer, Lt. E.F.P. Lubbock of 5 Squadron, Royal Flying Corps. The German plane was flown by Uffz Otto Gerold (killed) and Ltn. Paul Bucholz (POW).

out in a bad condition. A German shell killed a red cross stretcher bearer and wounded another behind trench 128 on our right.[103] We are in trench 131.

Fri., Oct. 29:

The days pass by quietly with little to vary one's interest though there is a little shelling each day which rouses some excitement. There was a rather lively artillery duel to-day. Our fellows put a lot of small stuff from field guns over into their trenches and a few heavy H.E. into their front line.[104] They replied in the same way mostly at trench 132 on our left, but later a few regular busters landed quite near our dugout, shook things up uncomfortably and nearly stunk us out with the sulphur fumes. Then our fellows cut loose with the heavy stuff on their front trenches. By Jove but Lloyd George must put some awful explosive into his new shells, for the crashes fairly split the air and set the earth even in our lines rocking.[105] The Germans gave in and let our fellows have the last word. While this bombardment was going on, one of the signallers came into the dugout with the mail and handed me a letter from Nellie. It was written on Oct. 4, reached Shorncliffe Oct. 22, and here the 29th. At that rate they don't yet know I have left Shorncliffe; how far apart we are!

We were relieved by the 8th Battn. this afternoon and marched about two miles through the mud to Monk Farm where we took up quarters in huts newly-constructed.[106] The night sky is flashing with artillery fire and star shells. We are right among our own guns and they make a terrible row when they are in action. We can hear the rifle and machine gun fire very clearly here.

But most of the country houses are occupied by the natives who sell all kinds of needs to the soldiers and work their farms as best they can. Of course all this district is right within range of any of the German guns. The difficulty is that isolated buildings are very difficult to hit, and we

---

103   Red Cross stretcher bearer: Might be Christopher Watts (1873–1915) of the 2nd Division Supply Column, buried in CWGC Bailleul Communal Cemetery, France.
104   H.E.: High explosive.
105   Lloyd George: David Lloyd George (1863–1945), later UK prime minister (1916–1922), was at the time of Miller's remark minister of munitions.
106   Monk Farm: La Grande Munque Farm, a camp located northwest of Ploegsteert.

have such a mastery of the air that the enemy cannot observe the effect of their fire back here behind the hill and the woods.[107]

Fri., Nov. 5:

We returned to the trenches afternoon of Wed, Nov. 3. Came up Mud Lane to trench 127 and thence to trench 130, CB station. All communication trenches were caved in or half full of water and impassable and the way we came was bad enough. Besides my full kit with 120 rounds I had a blanket, waterproof coat, and a sack of rations and firewood. I am sure had I slipped and fallen, I could not have got on my feet again without dumping most of the load.

I had to go out to Hyde Park Corner the same night for rations and coal. It was very dark and I had no light. I tried Seaforth Ave. trench but found it blocked by water and cave-ins. A sentry told me to cut across on top and take a chance. I did so and made for the line of trees on Messines Road. Waded knee deep through a section of stretcher trench, made the road and the ration rendezvous. Returned by Mud Lane and trench 127 (Cheshires) as in the afternoon.[108] The most strenuous marching I have ever done; for the mud was so bad my feet slipped every time I put one ahead of the other. We had to jump across trenches, avoid wires, and mudholes too deep for anything but swimming. Every now and again a German flare would go up, light up the whole place and then go out leaving worse darkness than before.

The trenches were in a bad condition when we took them over from 8th Bn. Even front line trenches were barely passable in places owing to water and sides caved in. Nearly all dugouts were wet and many caved in. All available men are working night and day making the necessary repairs. They have built for each coy O.C. a battle dugout with walls of concrete and roof of heavy sheet iron, concrete, bricks and turf.[109] The top is level with the ground and presents no mark for the enemy.

---

107 Miller's subjective assessment overestimates Allied airpower: in fact, this period was referred to as the "Fokker Scourge," when German monoplanes, equipped with machine guns synchronized to fire through the propeller arc, attained air supremacy on the Western Front.

108 Cheshires: Cheshire Regiment, a British infantry regiment whose 1st battalion was serving on the Ypres salient.

109 Coy o.c.: Company "Officer Commanding," term used for the officer units smaller than a battalion in the British and Imperial armies. Commanding officer is the term used for larger units.

Front line scouts last night reported heavy enemy transport moving into Messines from north by Ypres-St. Eloi road and from east by Gapaard road. Word was sent over wires to an artillery battery and in a few minutes the German transports entering Messines from the east had a warm experience.

2 fifth C.M.R. signallers spent last night in our dugout.[110] A party of them are in the trenches for 24 hours getting acquainted with the work. One of their men was killed by shell-fire this morning. A stretcher bearer was shot through the leg yesterday morning. He was on top getting wood or water when a sniper got him.

Rum is issued to us every evening at the rate of a tablespoonful to each man.[111]

Our scouts go out to within a few yards of the German front line nearly every night. They locate their listening posts and sentries, map out the wire entanglements and saps which are thrown out in front, even hear work going on in their trenches at times.[112] Last night our scouts bombed one of their listening posts and a sentry at another position. Our fellows pull off all kinds of tricks on the Germans, but they very seldom retaliate. The initiative is certainly ours in this part of the line. Our artillery gives them twenty shells for every one they put back.

Mon., Nov. 8:

Relieved by 8th Bn.; came out to Bulford Camp huts via trench 127, Mud Lane and Hyde Park Corner.[113] Met the 10th Bn. going in and exchanged greetings with Geo. Leeson as they marched past.

The Germans shelled trench 128 as we were passing out through the subsidiary lines. One shell passed between Burdon and me (he was some 50 yards behind me) and exploded in a bank 100 ft on our right showering

---

110 Fifth C.M.R.: 5th Canadian Mounted Rifles, a mounted infantry unit raised in Quebec.

111 Rum: The rum ration was a tradition in the British Army. During the First World War, the standard "tot" was about 2 ounces. Regulations required it to be consumed in the presence of officers or senior NCOs to prevent hoarding.

112 Saps: Short trenches, typically dug to a distance of about thirty yards in the direction of the enemy trench. Sap heads were often used as listening posts to monitor and give advance warning of enemy activity, and were sometimes linked to one another at right angles to form a new trench line.

113 Bulford: This Western Front camp, located about five kilometres west of Messines, was named after the much better-known Bulford Camp on the Salisbury Plain.

us with dust and scattering splinters all about.[114] Others followed but we got out as fast as possible and no more came close.

Tues., Nov. 9:

The leaves are fast falling from the trees after turning yellow and fading out. There are no bright autumn colours on the foliage here, perhaps because there are no frosts before the summer season is past and the cool wet weather has stripped the trees. Rain has set in again this evening. It has been cloudy almost continuously of late, seldom are there even a few hours of clear sky when the airmen can carry on their observation work. As yet we have only had one light frost, and the weather keeps comparatively warm. Saw a 12 in. howitzer in action this morning about 80 rods from our billets.[115] At each discharge our hut shook and the metal roof rang. The gun was concealed in a canvas house painted on its exterior to look exactly like an ordinary Belgian dwelling of brick with doors, windows and tiled roof. The muzzle pointed through one end which could be temporarily removed clear to the gable. When the shot was fired the muzzle pointed up at about 70° elevation. The flame shot out all around the breech and muzzle and no one stood within 50 ft of it when being fired. 50 yds. to the right and left of the muzzle you could feel the wave of hot air hit you and the roar was deafening unless you put your fingers in your ears. The shells were of an enormous size, nearly 3 ft. long, and were handled by rolling them on a skidway or lifting them with a crane. The gunners said the shells went to a height of over three miles in their flight and dropped almost perpendicularly on their mark. This bombardment was directed at a church in the direction of Wytschaete. After about six shots the order came to cease fire. Evidently the object had been achieved.

Wed., Nov. 10:

Cool strong west wind, showery but clearing in the afternoon. Walked up the road to the limits of Neuve Eglise. It has been a village the size of

---

114 Burdon: Bert Allen Burdon (1894–?), born Cambridge, Massachusetts; a resident of Fredericton; attested Valcartier September 1914. See entry of 24 October 1916.

115 Howitzer: The standard British 12-inch heavy howitzer had not yet entered service. Miller might be referring to a somewhat lighter weapon or an experimental "one-off" gun.

Markham, but now is deserted.[116] Only a few houses are occupied by the natives and the others that are intact are in some cases used as billets for soldiers. I was not able to get into the village as it is out of bounds except to those on duty. The church tower is slightly damaged. Most windows in the buildings are gone and here and there a house has been partly demolished by shellfire from the German lines. The only life is the army transport moving through the streets and a few soldiers wandering here and there. I noticed the emplacement for another heavy howitzer being prepared – a spur railway line with a canvas painted house at the end built astride the rails to conceal the gun.

Paid 15 francs to-day. My 2nd pay since coming to [entry ends]

Tues., Nov. 16:

Came into the trenches Sat. afternoon the 13th. There has been a heavy bombardment all day, chiefly by our side. We have had every kind of shell going over in a continuous stream, heavy howitzers into Petit Douve farm and from field guns shrapnel and H.E. upon Fritz's front line and wire entanglements.[117] The Germans came back with a little shrapnel, but did no damage. Our fellows have brought a number of batteries of field guns right up to our support trenches where they are cleverly hid and have been in action for two days. The roar of guns and bursting shells has been incessant and deafening. We kept to our dugouts all day. No one knows just what the Germans mean by this silence in the face of our bombardment. Up to a month ago they replied to everything promptly and vigorously.

Lt. Pyman of B Coy. was shot through the calf of the leg yesterday morning and three of his men were wounded by snipers' bullets this morning. They were out walking about on top when they got it.[118]

It has been quite frosty the last two nights. This morning there was 1/4 inch ice on the pools and the crust of the mud was hard.

---

116 Markham: Then a town of about 5,000 in Ontario, now a city that is part of the Great Toronto Area.

117 Petit Douve: Le Petite Douve, name of a farm a kilometre southwest of Messines.

118 Pyman: Lieutenant (later Major) Colin Keith Lee Pyman, DSO (1884–1918). Survived wound to left leg described above; died from wounds received 10 August 1918.

Wed., Nov. 17:

This morning at 2:30 B coy. of our Bn. made a bombing attack from trench 130 upon the German lines opposite about 300 yds. away. Yesterday's bombardment had cut the German wire in places and badly mauled Petit Douve farm, the German fortress opposite 131. The scouts led the party up to the German parapet, the bombers following each carrying all the bombs possible. Lieut. Campbell led the party and scout Birch was there.[119] Signaller Burdon and Capt. Nash ran out a telephone line from the Colonel's position. But just in front of the German parapet, a moat 12 ft. wide with wire entanglements and several feet of water was encountered. Several of the boys got in this trap and had to be pulled out by their mates. So they threw all their bombs into the German trenches and ran back, getting off without a casualty. Only a few rifles and a machine gun was fired at them. Then our artillery opened up and the German trenches were rained with shrapnel and high explosive for over an hour. Petit Douve was again given a dose from the heavy howitzers.

Simultaneous with our attack, the 7th Bn. trenches 132–135 made a similar attack upon the Germans opposite them. The moon, nearing full, had just gone down, it was cloudy and had just commenced to rain lightly. They carried foot-bridges for crossing the moat which they knew quite well protected the enemy trenches. They got right into the trenches before the Germans knew what happened. They went 80 yds. up the trench, captured 12 Germans, bombed several dugouts in which men were sleeping (threw a hairbrush bomb into one and said they got six men there), and were back in their own trench by the time the Germans were about.[120] Then the fools, thinking our men still among them, threw bombs in their own trenches. But instantly our field guns opened on them and gave them a terrific bombardment. There would be men up and moving about exposed all through their lines and they must have suffered heavily in casualties. The German artillery made scarcely any reply, only two whizz-bangs came into our trenches.[121] We expected a retaliation to-day, but the enemy did not make a single show of activity.

---

119 Campbell: Could not be identified.
120 Grenade consisting of an explosive affixed to a paddle.
121 Whizz-bangs: Term generally applied to high-velocity German artillery whose shells were heard to "whizz" before the "bang" of the gun itself, because the shell travelled faster than the speed of sound.

The prisoners taken were closely questioned by our officers. They are Prussian Landwehr who have served in Galicia against the Russians and more recently were at the Loos battle of six weeks ago.[122] They were sent up here for a rest as this is considered a quiet part of the line. They were glad to be taken and treated so well. They get plenty of food and clothing but say their folks at home don't get the food they require. They hate their officers and wish we had captured or killed them. Three officers had just left the place when our men entered and so just missed becoming involved. The men say the officers avoid the front line as much as possible.

The 7th Bn. lost one man killed and one wounded.

Thurs., Nov. 18:

Much aeroplane activity all day. We have a pom-pom anti-aircraft gun on the hill behind us – a new type that fires automatically a stream of tiny shrapnel shells.[123] A German aeroplane with engine shut off came circling down out of the clouds right above us. The observer was leaning far out as if they had lost their bearings. Instantly the pom-pom on the hill, all our machine guns, and scores of rifles opened fire. But by some miracle of good luck the machine got off safe, making straight for the German lines. A few minutes later a biplane of ours passed overhead, went away back over the German lines as if to offer a challenge. The Germans had three planes over us at one time, an unusual sight, for our men have kept the lines too well patrolled of late to allow a German machine within sight.

Everyone is talking about the way the Germans have received our activity. Never before have they refused to retaliate to our offensive movements. They do not seem to have enough guns on this front to reply to ours, and for the few they have there is surely little ammunition. Their shells are few and far between.

Yesterday afternoon, we saw Messines bombarded by one of our 12 in. howitzers. The village is in full view from trench 128, being on a hill top across the Douve from our position and a mile and a half distant.

---

122 Loos: The Battle of Loos (25 September–8 October 1915) was the British Army's biggest offensive of the war to date, fought about 25 kilometres south of Miller's position of the Ypres Salient. The attacks failed, incurring heavy losses.

123 Pom-Pom: Several weapons went by this nickname. Miller might be referring to the QF 2 pounder Mark II, an early anti-aircraft gun often used by the Royal Navy, or he might be referring to anti-aircraft artillery in general.

We would hear a whirring roar far overhead and gradually approaching Messines. Suddenly a brown column of dust was seen to spring into the air gradually spreading as it rose, overtopping the ruined tower in the middle of the town. Then the sound reached us in a terrific roar which shook the ground even in our lines. Some of the old 5th boys said they had never seen shells explode like it with such an uproar. When the dust cloud settled, the whole of Messines was enveloped and lost to sight for several minutes. The destruction must have been enormous.

Relieved by the 8th Bn. this p.m. and came out to Grande Muncke Farm through a drizzling rain.

Mon., Nov. 22:

Our brigade is moving back into Army Corps reserve for a fortnight. We left Grande Muncke Farm at 10 a.m. and marched via Bailleul and St. Jans Cappel to Berthen and into billets on a hilltop in a lovely bit of country.[124] We arrived just at dark, 4 p.m., and were sent to a loft on a farm. We had made ourselves comfortable for the night, had enjoyed some hot coffee in the farm kitchen, and I was already in bed and nearly asleep, when another better billet was reported and we all moved half a mile through the dark to another farm. We soon had straw and were comfortable in a closed box stall in a brick hop-barn. Enjoyed coffee in the kitchen with the farm people and then retired.

Tues., Nov. 23:

Was assistant cook for the signallers today. We have a fine big kitchen in the house with chairs, a table and a stove, real luxuries to us. The people are very kind and courteous; seem anxious to help us in every way possible. They have put up 7,000 soldiers here at different times but still give us a hearty welcome. We notice such a difference between the French and Belgians in this respect. Just across the boundary in Belgium a few miles away they are so mean and suspicious with us. But here it is like being among friends.

---

124 St. Jans Cappel: A very small town in northeastern France, near the border with Belgium. Berthen, about two kilometres northwest of there, had a population of about 600 prior to the war.

Wed., Nov. 24:

Cool and drizzling rain now and again. Our Battn. is all split up and scattered over a wide area of country. Hdqrs. is here on Mt. Kokereele with D Company.[125] Transport is at St. Jans Cappel and it is from 2 to 3 miles from any one company to any other. Other Battns of the Brigade are in the same situation.

We are in a lovely bit of hill country on a hilltop ourselves and with other hills of the same size around us, picturesque valleys lying between. Down west of us lies the village of Berthen, a group of red-roofed cottages gathered about a large brick "Ecole des Enfants" and an old church with lofty spire.[126] West and northwest other hills rise and limit the outlook, but the valley and village is a gem to hold one's attention. Southward the level plain reaches away to the horizon where SSE we see the spire and roofs of Bailleul. Eastward we have a valley and another hill higher and more extensive than this, crowned with groves of trees and a number of windmills of the local type. The road from Berthen eastward describes a wide arc to the north up over this hill and away to the Belgian frontier and Westoutre. Just north of us is Boescheppe.

I went down to Berthen this morning; bought a granite mug at a little store for 1 fr. 25 centimes, – an exorbitant price as the lady here at the farm says, for we are Canadians and prices go up when they see our maple leaf badges. At this store the lady spoke and understood a little English. But I bought a towel in another store where I had to speak French to make myself understood. I could say all I required, but I had difficulty understanding what was said to me. However, I had quite a conversation with the lady in French. These ordinary people as a rule know far more English than we do of French, a state of affairs that we ought to be ashamed of. We have been too selfish and think too much of our own language. When a call came a few days ago from Army Corps Hdqrs. for a man able to write shorthand and knowing German well so as to tap their telephone lines and steal information, there was not a man qualified for the position.

I had a chat with the proprietor of this farm this morning. He has soixante hectares (about 150 acres) in the farm. His brother was a French soldier

---

125 Mt. Kokereele: Somewhat overblown name for a hill in French Flanders.
126 Old church: St. Blaise, dating from the sixteenth century, destroyed by German bombing in 1940.

killed in the Champagne in July this year. The Germans were here ten days in October 1914. Many units of troops passed along the roads and soldiers were billeted in Berthen and all the neighbouring farms, but strange to say they never came to this farm. They took horses, hay, oats, etc. from the farmers and paid nothing in return. Many people from the district fled before the invasion as refugees. The young men who remained were taken away and have never been heard of since, but it is believed they are in Germany working under compulsion. Neither the men nor the women left this farm and they were never molested. When German troops were passing in the road by fields where these men were hoeing, the men kept their eyes on their work and never looked up until the troops were gone by.

Then the English came and 18 pdr. field guns were in action on the hills around Berthen, and shells fell in the paddock by the barn here. Machine guns were used and after a little stiff fighting, the Germans retired eastward and over into Belgium. The proprietor of the farm says he lay in a sunken driveway by the house as the bullets whistled overhead, terrified because he had never heard anything like it before. (He crouched in the very spot and showed me how he had watched the battle.) He hates the Germans intensely and hopes they are beaten before the end of another year.

Wed., Dec. 1:

Still at the same billets on Mt. Kokereel. We have a telephone station at A Company a mile and a half south of here on the St. Jans Cappel-Locre Road. I was down there on duty two days lately. I had a very pretty view as I returned from duty there one morning just after sunrise. The red light of the sun gave an unusual tinge of colour to the landscape. It had frozen during the night, the ground was stiff and the pools glassed over, a touch of hoar frost silvered all the meadow grass and the branches of the hedges and trees. Below in the valley lay Berthen, a cluster of red-roofed houses, still wrapped in the silence of night time. The church bell was pealing soft and clear, and as it drew one's attention to itself there was the lofty spire pointing heavenward to direct one's thoughts to the source of all this peaceful beauty. In the background on the lofty Mt. des Chats, the old grey-walled monastery stood clearly defined in the morning light.[127] On the hill tops and rising ground dotted here and there over

---

127 Mt. des Cats Monastery: Trappist abbey located on Mont Des Cats, a hill adjacent the town of Godewaersvelde in French Flanders.

the landscape were numbers of these Flemish windmills, some standing idle as if wrapped in thought, while others revolved merrily, the canvas on their long arms glinting with frost and flashing back the sunbeams in intermittent reflection. It was such a complete picture of tranquillity yet pulsating with life and movement. It seemed to reflect the soul of this land and its people. I recalled Millet's "The Angelus" and, yes, I have seen all its elements right here in Flanders.[128] On nearly every farm we see women working in the fields all day long taking up the root crops.

At the foot of our hill to the south a sluggish stream meanders across a flat water-soaked meadow and on the other side is gathered into a straight ditch and runs leisurely off down the valley to the south. A quarter of a mile away it rushes over a steep clay bank to a level lower by about eight feet, boils up out of its pool thus formed by the ever rushing and plunging water, and rambles on merrily babbling to itself through a little narrow ravine completely overarched with shrubbery and low trees, swings round a bend and under a low bridge to dash over another low fall then on through a deeper ravine overshadowed and shut in by shrubbery. It is a merry little brook, a brook with a personality that appeals to me very much. Some writer has surely woven it into a story long before this. It is such a romantic thing, the kind of companion a dreaming youth or a girl with imagination and a love for nature would cherish, almost as part of life itself.

Yesterday Phillips and I spent the afternoon on a stroll over the hills southeast of here in the direction of Kemmel and Locre, especially Mt. Noir just on the French side of the frontier of Belgium.[129] The western side of Mt. Noir is crowned by a fine chateau that stands in a grove of pines and commands splendid views over the plain south and west towards Bailleul and far away beyond that town. East of the chateau a windmill stands on the highest point. Here you can see an immense stretch of level plain both to the north and to the south. Poperinghe seems to lie almost at the foot of the hill and due north. But what was on the horizon I could not say. It must have been forty miles away. The air was clear but the horizon was so far away as to appear a line of blue mist.

Mt. Noir is one of a ridge of six hills extending from Mt. des Chats eastward into Belgium. Mt. Kokereele is the second and Mt. Noir the

---

128 "The Angelus": Reference to *L'Angelus*, a 1857–8 painting by Jean-François Millet (1814–1875) depicting peasant farmers praying in a potato field. The painting was in the Louvre at the time of Miller's entry.

129 Probably William Maxwell Phillips (1895–?) of the 32nd Battalion. Born England, attested Winnipeg, December 1914.

third counting from the west. Both north and south of this ridge the land is absolutely flat and stretches away on the one side to the North Sea and the Scheldt and on the other side into France. The hills appear to consist of red sand underlaid by sandstone to an unknown depth. There is a covering of soil so that the gentle slopes are carefully cultivated right to the summits. There is a large quarry on the east side of Mt. Noir and the summit is being gradually removed. The other hills have been dug into so as to learn their nature for future purposes. The British R. Engineers work the quarry now and use the material for road making.[130]

We visited the next hill to the east and had a good view of the country around Ypres. Most of it was indistinct with blue haze, but we could see the flashes of the guns all along the battle front there.

Paid 65 francs this evening.

Thurs., Dec. 2:

Phillips and I walked into Bailleul at 11 a.m. and spent the day there, returning 8–9 p.m. I bought a 6 franc Ingersoll watch and spent 30 francs in all.[131] Met a number of the old 32 boys including Holmes, Russel, Macdonnel and others.[132] The band of the 27th Wpg. Regt. played on the town square in front of the town hall. Tried at six places to get a bath but failed and am still dirty.

Fri., Dec. 3:

Letters from Nellie and Stuart Thompson last night. Wrote Nellie and Olie Lockhart to-day.

On duty 1:30–5:30 a.m. and 11 p.m. to 2 a.m. (4th) at orderly room Mt. Kokereel.

---

130 R. Engineers: The Royal Engineers, responsible for constructing military installations, lines of transportation and communication, and other forms of technical support.

131 Ingersoll watch: Ingersoll was an American watchmaker, famous for producing a one-dollar pocket watch in 1896.

132 Holmes: Could not be identified. Russel: Could not be identified. Macdonnel: Private (later Captain) Victor MacDonnell (1892–1961), born Grenfell, Saskatchewan; attested Winnipeg, December 1914. The officer recording MacDonnell's medical file saw fit to note that MacDonnell "does not indulge in tobacco or alcohol" – a rare combination at the time.

PROGRESS
Let there be many windows to your soul,
That all the glory of the universe
May beautify it. Not the narrow pane
Of one poor creed can catch the radiant rays
That shine from countless sources. Tear away
The blinds of superstition; let the light
Pour through fair windows broad as Truth itself
And high as God.

Why should the spirit peer through some priest-curtained orifice,
     and grope
Along dim corridors of doubt, when all
The splendour from unfathomed seas of space
Might bathe it with the golden waves of love?
Sweep up the debris of decaying faiths;
Sweep down the cobwebs of worn-out beliefs
And throw your soul wide open to the light
Of Reason and of Knowledge.

Tune your ear
To all the wordless music of the stars
And to the voice of Nature and your heart
Shall turn to truth and goodness, as the plant
Turns to the sun
A thousand unseen hands
Reach down to help you to their peace-crowned heights,
And all the forces of the firmament
Shall fortify your strength.
Be not afraid
To thrust aside half-truths and grasp the whole.
POEMS OF LIFE
ELLA WHEELER WILCOX[133]

(copied from J. Pels' book Dec. 3, 1915 in orderly room, Mt. Kokereel
at 11–11:30 p.m.)[134]

---

133 Wilcox: Ella Wheeler Wilcox (1850–1919), American poet. *Poems of Life* (1902) was
      the collection in which the poem in question, "Progress," appeared.
134 Pels: John Street Pells (1891–?), born England, resident of Prince Albert, Saskatch-
      ewan; attested Valcartier, September 1916.

Thurs., Dec. 9:

Left billets at Berthen at 7 a.m. for Bulford camp and the firing line. We were assigned these billets until Dec. 14, but the C.M.R. brigade who occupy our position have done badly, have lost control of "no-man's land" and allowed the Germans to build a barrier on Messines Road, 170 yds from our parapet. So the 2nd Brigade has been suddenly called back to restore the original strength and conditions to that section of the front.

Sopp and Cpl. Lingford left CYA division for English Farm – the forward transport station.[135] Two others proceeded to Bulford early to take over that camp station. We others reeled up the line from Mt. Kokereele to CA and St. Jans Cappel CYA; had dinner in a French house in the village and in the afternoon marched via Bailleul to Bulford Camp. Met some Messines refugees in Bailleul and bought them some fruit. Reached Bulford at dark and found it enisled in a sea of oozy mud, the worst we had yet encountered.

Fri., Dec. 10:

Proceeded to the trenches in p.m. Jack Pells and I held the Bulford telephone until the 1st C.M.R.'s relieved us at 4 p.m. We are posted to C.F. company reserve station on the hill.[136]

We called at a Belgian house and had supper of hot coffee, fried eggs, and bread and butter. Jack forgot his waterproof and when we got up to Court Drêve 2 kilomètres away he thought of it and went back, giving me his rifle to carry on.

I found our dugout, the entrance caved in leaving only a manhole through at the top of the door, the floor covered with mud, without furniture or equipment as the vandal C.M.R.'s had torn everything down for fuel: beds, cupboard, shelves, desk, and stool. Rex and Phillips were scraping the floor in a mighty unpleasant humour and any C.M.R. who had happened to come that way would have surely encountered trouble

---

135 CYA: Probably a reference to the Morse code call sign of a wireless station. Sopp: Earnest John Sopp (1890–?), born England; attested Valcartier, Quebec, September 1914. Had served in the Royal Canadian Regiment prewar. Lingford: Corporal (later Sergeant) George Kenneth "Rex" Lingford (1885–1918), born England; attested Valcartier, September 1914. Killed in action 1 April 1 1918. Commemorated on the Vimy Memorial.

136 C.F.: Company field.

just then.[137] We spread a piece of revetting screen and some sandbags and made a bed on the floor. Pells was sent back to English Farm to spend the night and get a box for a new desk. Rex took the bunk and Phillips and I occupied the shake down on the floor. So we passed the night with alternate shifts to mind phone.

Sat., Dec. 11:

I had phone from midnight to 5 a.m. We cleaned up a bit and made plans for repairing the dugout. In the p.m. Pells returned with boards for a desk, and I went down to English Farm for the night. Sopp and Red Morris are there with four 10th Battn. signallers.[138]

Sun., Dec. 12:

A German plane flew over us this morning at a tremendous height, but two English planes came up and the Hun retreated. I returned to C.F. station in the evening, calling on Madeline for some hot coffee. I dried a lot of my things by her hot stove, for my pack was rolled into a ditch full of water when the transport wagons were unloaded at Hyde Park Corner the other night. I found the dugout a bit more shipshape with two bunks now instead of one. We four are staying here tonight as Capt. Nash had ordered it.

I went round by the Messines and Ash roads to Ash House Hdqrs. after dark for mail. I got a letter from Mother and one from Charlie Cornish. There was very little rifle fire on the front and not a single bullet came to sing its hissing note in my ears.

Mon., Dec. 13:

Fixed up a third bed with corrugated iron siding, a piece of revetting screen, and some sandbags on the floor. We are quite comfortable in our little home in the hillside. We get our meals cooked and provided ready for us at the company field kitchen across the road below the hill.

Our artillery bombarded the Messines road barrier yesterday afternoon and again at 11 p.m., but with little result as only one direct hit

---

137   Rex: Corporal Lingford. See entry of 9 December 1915.
138   Morris: Could not be identified.

was made. This shell which pierced the barrier in the afternoon sent the little company of Germans flying back to their own lines. But our fellows opened rapid fire and dropped six of them, the others returning to the barrier.

Tues., Dec. 14:

I met Nicholls yesterday p.m. He was trained as a signaller with the 32nd, came out here in July to the 8th Battn. and was working here on the hill with a fatigue party.[139] Met also another old signaller in the 8th who came out here in June and he is in the company ranks too. They have not all been so fortunate as I in getting on to their special work.

Artillery bombarded the barrier yesterday at 3 and 10 p.m. but with no better result than on the previous night.

From the crest of the hill above our dugout, I had a fine view of this portion of the battlefront yesterday morning. Across the valley of the Douve was the round hill which bears the ruins of Messines on its top. Only a thin mutilated portion of the church tower remains standing. There was not a sign of life to be seen; the fields looked scarred and disfigured, neglected and grown over with grass and weeds. Our 18 pdrs. behind me were barking intermittently and the shells went screaming overhead to burst with a puff of white smoke among the trees a mile away to the east.[140] Rifles frequently cracked angrily in the still air, and once or twice a machine gun spoke with its metallic and regular crackling. Charlie Cornish tells me in his letter that Ted Ward of the old 32nd Machine Gun Section was killed out here on Oct. 12, the day I left Shorncliffe.[141] Charlie is now in billet at Lyminge, Kent, as are most of the 32nd.

Casualties have been numerous in the 5th for two days past, as the Germans have shelled our front line heavily at times. The Sergt. Major of B Coy. got a Blighty,[142] while Lt. Cockrill M.G.O.[143] was marked on

---

139 Nicholls: See entry of 22 February 1915.

140 18 pounders: Ordnance QF 18 Pounder, a mainstay of British field artillery.

141 Ward: Edgar Ward (1891–1915), born England, attested Winnipeg, December 1914. Killed in action 12 October 1915. Buried at CWGC R.E. Farm Cemetery, Belgium.

142 "Blighty": This slang term for Britain also referred to a nonfatal wound, sufficiently serious to warrant being medically evacuated to the UK.

143 M.G.O.: Machine gun officer.

the face with shrapnel.[144] A Pte. in C Coy. got a dangerous bullet wound this morning.

Wed., Dec. 15:

Last night at eleven, our artillery again bombarded the German barrier on Messines Rd. They had previously bombarded with howitzers and field guns at 3–3:30 p.m. On Monday night a work party dug a sap out from our front line to within 50 yds. of the barrier. Plans for an assault were very carefully laid. The afternoon and night bombardment battered the barricade very badly, and the German reply was weak, with a few Jack Johnsons and heavy shrapnel.

Between midnight and 4 a.m. a working party lengthened the sap to within bombing distance of the barrier. A field gun was taken up Messines Road to our second barricade and trained on the enemy position. A trench mortar was put in position to use on the barrier.[145] Bombers were prepared, a telephone line was run up the sap from Hqrs., stretcher bearers and prisoners' escort were all then ready for business.

Promptly at 4 a.m., with a cold wind blowing lightly, a sky obscured with grey clouds, and quiet prevailing all along the front, our gun on Messines Rd. opened fire. Nearly 50 shots were fired at point blank range into the barrier as fast as the gun could be worked. Trench mortar and rifles opened on the barrier and the bombers prepared to charge from the sap head as soon as their support ceased fire. But just then Petit Douve Farm became a hive of clattering Maxims and the sap was swept by a hurricane of German bullets.[146] It seemed as if the bombers were foiled, for it was madness to attempt to leave the trenches in face of that storm of lead.

Capt. Jackson rushed to the phone and asked the artillery to open on Petit Douve.[147] Nine howitzers crashed in quick succession behind us,

---

144 Cockrill: Lieutenant Ashton Denis Cockrill (1887–1931), born England, attested Val-cartier, September 1914. Severely wounded 22 April 1916. See entry 24 April 1916.
145 Trench mortar: Lightweight artillery piece that launched a shell on a curved trajectory. See entry for 12 May 1916.
146 Maxims: Model of machine gun used by the Germans. Hiram Maxim (1840–1916), the Anglo-American inventor, developed the first fully automatic machine gun in 1883.
147 Jackson: Probably Ernest Charles Jackson, DSO (1886–1953), born Ontario; attested September 1914 (no location given).

and soon buried Petit Douve and the German machine guns in high explosive ruin, and the place was silent. Then our bombers made their rush and carried the barrier in a few seconds. Two Germans, the only survivors of a party of eight, surrendered promptly with hands up and "Mercy Kamerad" trembling on their lips. A hasty survey was made to be sure the place was clear, dead bodies were observed, but in view of a possible German bombardment, the prisoners were hurried off to the sap and back to our front line, while the bombers dived into the ditches at each side of the road.

But only a casual bombardment of trench 131 and the artillery area behind the hill followed. So after a while the work was completed. Wire entanglements were fixed on the enemies' side of the ruined barrier. Three Germans were found blown to bits by the shells and three riddled with rifle bullets. It was evident that no one escaped to tell the tale.

Our field gun was rushed by motor to the rear the instant they ceased fire. It was only just clear of its position when a H.E. shell hit the barrier and wrecked it. A minute later and the gun would have been lost and likely some of the hands. But our parties got off with only one man wounded in the arm. By daylight the sap had been extended to the barrier, barbed wire strung in front, preparation for counter attack made and everything restored to normal.

But no counter attack has come, and tonight the barrier is to be mined and blown sky high as a lesson to the Huns on what happens to such mad ventures.

There has been a violent bombardment of the enemy lines beyond the Lys River south and west of Armentieres from eleven am, still continuing at 2:30 p.m.[148] From our hilltop we can see the silver ribbon of the Lys among the trees and beyond it in the blue haze, the frequent flashes of bursting shells and the grey smoke clouds slowly dispersing. The roll of our artillery is like continuous thunder, varied now and again by our field guns barking angrily below the hill, and the German shells bursting in the neighbourhood.

Last night's two prisoners were questioned before the company O.C. then passed on to Ash House and questioned separately by the Colonel (Tuxford). By dawn they were back at Brigade for further questioning and then on to the rear and the prisoners' camps. They are of the 11th

---

148   Armentières: French town, population about 14,000 in 1914, 20 kilometres due south of Ypres. "Mademoiselle from Armentières" was a trench song about an aging prostitute, often sung with improvised and bawdy lyrics.

Prussian Guard. This is the same unit the 7th Bn. took prisoners from on Nov. 17th, last. They say some severe punishments were meted out for allowing that incident to occur. They testified that some of the Strathcona Horse, supposed to have been killed in their attack on the barrier, are really wounded and prisoners of war, a Lieut. (Galt?) among the number.[149]

Sun., Dec. 19:

From midnight until nine this morning, there was an incessant booming of guns on our left towards Ypres. At times our hut shook and the metal roof rattled. When we got up our eyes were all sore and smarting, full of tears, and everybody was rubbing and blinking. The Germans were making a gas attack and a N by E wind brought the dispersing and rarified poison down upon us. The effect lasted about two hours. The morning was clear and bright and the breeze gradually freshened. We hear the wind proved unfavourable and the Germans were repulsed. But we have no certain news yet. The bombardment continued intermittently during the day, which was marked by much aircraft activity. Tonight the cannonade has increased again to a steady rumble.

"Letters"[150]

What is the call
The bugle call
The call that has no betters
The silver call
That beats them all?

---

149   Strathcona's Horse: Lord Strathcona's Horse (Royal Canadians), a cavalry regiment privately raised during the Boer War. Lt. Galt: The confusion generated by the fog of war is evident here: John Galt of the Strathcona's Horse was reported missing 9 December 1915. He was subsequently listed as a wounded prisoner of war and then was declared to have died "on or since" that date. He is commemorated on the Menin Gate.

150   "Letters" appeared in a 1915 collection of thirteen poems entitled *Contingent Ditties*, written by Sergeant Frank Smith Brown (1893–1915) of the Princess Patricia's Canadian Light Infantry. Brown was born in Waterford, Ontario, and attested in August 1914. His poems proved enormously popular and were reprinted in Canada's major newspapers. As Miller's inclusion of "Letters" indicates, they apparently made the rounds in the trenches, too. Known as the "Poet of the Pats," Brown was killed in action 3 February 1915 at St. Eloi and is commemorated on the Menin Gate.

The music call for "Letters".

You can take a silver trumpet
And sound the dread "Alarm"
T.A. will spring to action
With his rifle 'neath his arm;
But if you want to see him jump
Or run like a streak of hail
Just take the same old bugle
And sound the call for "Mail".

No one who ain't been there himself
Can tell just what it means
To have a live epistle
From your home tucked in your jeans.
A dripping sweet John Collins
To a thirst you wouldn't sell
Ain't in it with the starving heart
That gets a word from Nell.

Or if the maiden's name is Kate,
or Jean, or Marguerite,
A scented word of love-kin makes
A week's dull drudgery sweet.
Why any mother's soldier son
Who hears that bugle cry
Just stops his heart and holds his breath
For fear he'll be passed by.

His hand is all a-tremble,
His eyes stick out like pegs,
He goes all of a quiver
From the ague in his legs.
And if his name's not on the list
He welts like a frozen bud
Until another mail call drags
Him plousing through the mud.

He ain't no correspondent
And his answers may be few;

His opportunities are slim
To write his billy doo.
But when he does, it is beneath
A spluttering pine-knot taper
With the broken nib of an ink-starved pen
On a scrap of cartridge paper.

Now the moral is for folks at home
Don't wait for him to write,
And don't just say, "Dear Tom – must close;
I hope this finds you right"
A good long newsy letter
Is the best that you can yield
In the way of downright service
To your Tommy in the field.

What is the call
The cheering call
That every other betters?
A silver call
A longed-for call –
The music call for "Letters".

Tues., Dec. 21:

Signallers and Pioneers of the 5th Battn. gave a Xmas dinner and concert
to a few friends in the Y.M.C.A. tent at Bulford Camp. Corpl. Rex Lingford
managed the preparations. Each man put in five francs and some of us ten.
We got three geese, sausages, cakes, Xmas puddings, and fruit in Bailleul.
We rented plates, knives and forks from the Belgian farmhouse across the
road, where we had coffee made for us. We had the geese roasted, vegetables
cooked, and sausage heated in one of the company field kitchens. The whole
event was a splendid success and everyone was satisfied and pleased. Capt.
Nash took the chair at the head of the long table at 7:30 and things began
to hum.[151] I was a waiter and had to slice and butter the bread to start with.

---

151 Nash: Captain John Foster Paton Nash (1866–1916), DSO. A veteran of the Boer
War. Born England; attested Valcartier, September 1914. Killed in action 23 April
1916; buried at CWGC Railway Dugouts Burial Ground, Belgium. Nash received
the DSO for bravery under fire at Festubert in May 1915. See also entry of 24 April
1916, describing Nash's death.

After the dinner, a two hour program of songs, toasts, and recitations was given. Sergt.-Major Mackie was chairman and toastmaster.[152] Charlie Haydon gave some of his popular French Canadian selections from Drummond.[153] L/Cpl. Sopp sang twice, and gave his imitation of a bee in a grocery store alighting on sugar, Gorgonzola, and then in a fit. That brought the house down. I recited twice, "The Revenge" and "Kentucky Philosophy".[154] We had a silent toast to our absent friends and loved ones, a very impressive part of the program. After "God Save the King" we joined hands in the magic circle and sang "Auld Lang Syne". Then we let our guests go, cleaned up a bit and soon turned in.

Wed., Dec. 22:

Returned to the trenches to relieve the 8th Bn., I going to CF Battn. reserve station on the hill by Hyde Park Corner with Rex L., Phillips and Red Morris.

Thurs., Dec. 23:

On duty 2–8 a.m. Then walked back to English Farm and Q.M. stores to get a new gas helmet and arrange for our rations. Had a cup of coffee with Madeline. On return met George Leeson up in the bush near our position. He is well and cheery and reports having had some good things from Stoughton ladies. Don Maclean is back in Stoughton. Geo. met Kirkpatrick in Bailleul recently – he is a battalion bomb thrower.[155]

I have contracted a bad cold, and on reaching the dugout, I felt all in, my whole system ached and I felt a dose of Grippe coming on.[156] Rex made me a hot drink with rum, sugar, water, and orange peel, and

---

152 Mackie: William Gowan Mackie (1886–1967), born Kincardineshire, Scotland, attested Valcartier, September 1914.

153 Haydon: Charles Willoughley Haydon (1892–1932), born Ontario, attested Valcartier, September 1914. Drummond: Probably refers to William Henry Drummond (1854–1807), Irish-Canadian poet whose work was widely read in the two decades before the First World War.

154 "The Revenge": Probably "The Revenge: A Ballad of the Fleet" by Tennyson. "Kentucky Philosophy": Poem by Harrison Robertson (1856–1939).

155 Kirk Patrick: Probably refers to Clarence Kirkpatrick. See entry of 19 February 1915.

156 French and obsolete English word for influenza.

I went to bed till night and my next shift of duty. Felt much better then and knew the cold broken.

Sat., Dec. 25:

3 a.m. On phone 2–6 a.m. It is rather quiet along the front. The guns up towards Ypres have been booming intermittently throughout the night. Exactly at midnight there was quite a burst of rifle and machine gun fire and six bomb explosions up towards the 7th Bn. position on our left.

The boys have been exchanging Xmas greetings over the wire. No mail last night as the posts are reported closed for some unknown reason. So we get no Xmas parcels for tomorrow.

Our dugout entrance has been caving in with the rains. I was digging it out yesterday pm but didn't get it all clear. We have been shelled severely here on the hill lately with some very heavy percussion stuff. Some of the 7th reserve company were wounded in their dugouts down behind the hill. A lot of H.E. shrapnel has been thrown into trenches 131 to 135. Our Bde Hqrs. has been shelled out twice since October. Their last move was from Court Drêve to Petit Pont Farm. A few of our batteries have been located and had to move to other positions.

Opened By the Censor
The First.
Miss Mary Angelina Craven-Hall,
Park Avenue, The Annex, Montreal

My Darling,
'Neath a fickle tallow light
A message of our love would I indite,
The message of a starved and aching heart,
Sick of the conflict, sick of slaughter's mart
It is to thee I turn. In spirit haste
To help me bear this desolated waste.
Thou art my constant comrade, and I feel
Thy presence o'er my wearied senses steal
I lit my comfort-pipe, and in the smoke
Behold! I saw thy face. To me it spoke
Of Love and Home, and all that goes to make
Life's even way the rose's colour take.
Oh! Would that I might hold thee to my breast,

Or, safe beneath thy care, sink into rest,
Or feel thy crushing lips in love's caress
Waft out the soldier's care to nothingness.
Oh! But again to see the gloried sun
Caught in thy tresses of the gold beam spun;
Oh! Once again to take thy trusting hand
And lead you through a fairy castled land.
Forget not in the city's monotone
The chant of faith to thee I sing alone
And ne'er forget the sacred word that binds
Our pulsing hearts, our intellects and minds.
May God in Heaven guard our treasure trove
Remember I am always thine.
With Love

The Second.
To Mrs. Hiram Billican,
Near Beulah
Minnedosa, Man.

Dear Jane,
I feel I cannot sleep;
In slush and mud four miles deep,
I'll snatch a little time to write
A line or so to you tonight.
I hope the kids aren't fallen sick,
And if they're bad just use the stick
I showed you how to make them mind.
But then you never were my kind
In handling kids you take the cake
I'm glad you're teaching May to bake
I'm sending you a pound or two,
And with it here's what you must do
Lay in a stock of coal and wood,
And kindlery and a pile of food.
Don't spend the rest, but take good care
To get the kids warm underwear.
About that darned old brindle cow
If she is milking up to now,
Don't sell her until by-and-by;

Get rid of her when she goes dry.
Tell John he's got to be a man
And feed the pigs on swill and bran;
And see he cleans the dirty pens,
Collects the eggs, and feeds the hens.
Be sure he doesn't start to smoke,
Or he'll be sick enough to croak.
If Harry's acting up the fool,
You'd better send him back to school.
Just keep an eye on Susie's lung,
And mind that Casey woman's tongue.
Don't fret or worry over me,
I am as right as I could be.
Now mind, I like to hear from home
And say, please send a fine toothed comb!
I guess I'll have to say ta-ta,
Kiss precious baby for his pa,
I hope he grows up good and strong
To be a soldier boy ... So long.
P.S. You ought to see the grub
They hand to us ... Your loving Hub.

The Grouch
"This world's made up of critters",
Said a Private from the ranks
Of cantaloupes and quitters
And most unlordly swanks.
Just take our Colour-Sergeant,
He's a bird when on the shout,
I wish I was the Colonel,
I'd hang the blighter out.
"There ain't no use in talking",
He continued, warming up,
That half-cut Corporal Smithers is
A dirty-dealing "pup."
He took me up before the beak;
You bet your life he did,
With evidence to hang me, sure
For bluff he takes the lid.
The Captain hands me out a snort

With his oogley-boozley nose;
And when he'd looked me up & down
And stared clean thro' my clo'es,
He up and says, "What makes you think
You're living in a cup?
What have you got to say? But wait,
Before you start, shut up!"
Now, say, that is some justice
For a Briton born to get,
The Captain and the Corporal
And the Sergeant have me set
They get me seven days C.B.[157]
And seven more if I
Refuse to get my hair cut.
When I'm told to by-and-by.
Great Caesar's white untarnished ghost
What's this they serve for beer?
Hey! Canteen Steward, what 'ye' mean?
We want no water here.
For water hasn't any use
Except to swab your face,
Put under bridges, or float ships,
Or sprinkle 'round the place.
There goes the call for dinner.
Gee! Ain't that bugler punk!
His tongue is simply rotten,
Or else the bugle's drunk.
I wish I was a bugler,
I'd show them how to blow,
What? Time up, Canteen Steward?
Well, suppose we'll have to go.
Gee whiz! Call that a dinner?
You could drive a mule train thro'
Between the vegetables in
That dope you call a stew.
If I was cook, you bet your shirt
I'd fix you up a treat;

---

157 C.B.: Confined to barracks.

But what's the use of grouching –
Great Scot! I've speared some meat!
Well, anyhow, I'm finished;
I guess I'll make the grade,
And dust my buttons off before
The bugle sounds parade.
Ain't it the limit? Same old street,
Parade the same old way.
Most every other afternoon
Should be a holiday.
"This world has awful tulips"
Finished Private from the ranks
"And ostriches, and canards,
And overbearing cranks.
You wait until I get a stripe,
I'll make myself a name.
But then, on second thoughts,
I guess I'll be about the same."

From "CONTINGENT DITTIES"
By SERGT FRANK S. BROWN[158]
P.P.C.L.I.[159]
(Killed at St. Eloi on his first day in the trenches.)

Sat., Dec. 25:

6 p.m. The day has passed off quietly. There has been heavy intermittent gunfire towards Ypres, but it was quiet on our front. There was a little sniping, and one of our men was wounded early this morning.

There was no exchange of compliments or singing across no-man's land as was forbidden by orders.[160] The spirit of the boys was "Give them hell, Xmas or no Xmas, for we want to be home in Canada a year

---

158 *Contingent Ditties:* See entry of 19 December.
159 PPCLI: Princess Patricia's Canadian Light Infantry. Privately raised, the PPCLI was the first Canadian battalion to serve and fight overseas.
160 A reference to the so-called Christmas Truce of December 1914, a subsequently mythologized event which saw some fraternization between soldiers on opposing sides in certain sectors of the front.

from now. We received a message of season's compliments and best wishes from "Arthur", Gov-Gen. of Canada.[161] I read this off the wire for our company.

We had a good Xmas dinner here in reserve, but they didn't fare so well in the front line, as they had no cooking facilities while we had the field kitchen. We had roast beef with thick brown gravy, mashed potato and carrot, haricot beans, steamed Xmas pudding with sauce, and we are getting beer this evening.

Tues., Dec. 28:

Came out to Grand Munque Farm billets. Red Morris and I took over the phone here at 3 p.m. and remained on duty till 8, while the 10th Battn. were moving out and our fellows coming in.

While I have been on C.F. station, I found B coy., 10th Bn. living in huts on the same hillside; so I met Geo. Leeson and some of the old 32nd boys frequently. I had a parcel from Olie Lockhart which brought cakes, candy, gum, wristlets and good wishes.[162]

Wed., Dec. 29:

A group of 17 aeroplanes (British) came up from the West this morning headed straight for the German lines.[163] When the first German anti-aircraft shell burst near them, they spread rapidly and continued their course. Hundreds of shells were fired amongst them, but not one took effect. A few turned back but quite a number scouted up and down over the German lines for half an hour before returning. They must have done some valuable work, for the air was very clear.

Last night about ten the comparative silence was broken by the dull explosion of a bomb somewhere in the British lines in front of Ploegsteert. Instantly several rifles and machine guns began to rattle. Another bomb went off, and a perfect roar of rapid fire ensued, continuing for perhaps

---

161 "Arthur": H.R.H. Prince Arthur, Duke of Connaught and Strathearn (1850–1942), Governor General of Canada (1911–16).

162 Wristlets: Term for a wrist watch, a relatively new invention that came into common use during the war.

163 17 aeroplanes: This would have been an extraordinarily large formation for the time.

15 minutes. But by this time the guns began to speak and battery after battery of howitzers and field guns took up the chorus until the roar and crash was deafening. From the window of our hut, the night sky appeared to be on fire, flash after flash and flare following flare all the way from here to Armentières. We understand the scrap was about the possession of some mine craters between the lines, and the result is we still hold them.

Fri., Dec. 31:

Farewell old year, for you have been the most eventful 12 months of my life. From Wpg. through Shorncliffe to Flanders, no one will ever know how I have enjoyed it, but perhaps this book will bear witness to some extent.

Had a letter from Harry Smith of Pheasant Plains School and answered it this morning. One of my Blackwood pupils, George Armstrong, has gone to Regina to enlist.[164] Had a parcel from Dick Becket of Weyburn yesterday – soap, candy, nuts, wristlets, handkerchiefs and good wishes. Had a box of cakes from mother yesterday. The Canadian mail has been much delayed and the Xmas parcels are coming in large numbers these days. I read that 84,000 Canadian parcels came to London P.O. in one day recently.

Runners are quartered with the signallers in our hut now, and they are putting in chicken-roost bunks for us so the hut will hold twice as many men as before.[165]

Weather is still very mild usually clear in mornings and cloudy after noon. Rains are frequent, winds light and variable. The grass keeps fresh and green and the buds on a few shrubs are big and seem ready to burst into foliage.

164　Armstrong: George Francis Armstrong (1887–?) of Saskatchewan; attested December 1915. Determined medically unfit and returned to Canada in April 1917.

165　Runner: Military courier who physically carried messages. As a signaller, Miller sometimes served in this capacity. One runner who gained fame during the war was Thomas Charles Longboat (Gagwe:gih) (1886–1949), of the Onodaga Nation, one of more than 4,000 Indigenous people who served in the CEF.

1916

Sun., Jan. 2:

The usual business proceeds and we do not distinguish Sundays from other days. Only the natives cease their daily toll and are to be seen dressed in their best going to church service in groups. We had bathing parade to the Div. baths at Bulford Camp this morning. In the afternoon, Col. Tuxford gave a farewell address to the Battn. as he is leaving to take command of a Brigade in England.[1]

Mon., Jan. 3:

Came into trenches at 3 p.m., a beautiful clear bright day with a warm S.W. wind blowing quite strong. It is odd to think of them frozen up in Canada and with snow everywhere. It is quite summer-like here.

As we were coming round Hyde Park Corner, the enemy were shelling the chateau on our left with a light field gun. Three direct hits were made as we passed up Mud Lane. Then they lifted and shelled the Corner and the dressing station, doing some damage as a Sergt. of the 8th was killed at the station.[2]

Sniping was pretty hot on 129, and an 8th Bn. boy had just been shot through the neck by a bullet coming through the parapet. He lay dying,

---

1 Tuxford's replacement was Major Hugh Dyer.
2 According to the 8th Battalion War Diary, dead at the dressing station was *Private* Phillip McDonald (1886–1916), born Quebec; attested Valcartier, September 1914, buried CWGC Berks Cemetery Extension, Belgium, killed in action 3 January 1916. McDonald was noted in the 8th Battalion war diary as a sniper who "had accounted for 42 Germans."

stretched out on a bath mat in the bottom of the front line trench.[3] Sopp, Hayden and I had to crawl over the dead body to get along to 130 where we were coming. This is the first case of "killed in action" that I have seen.

It looks like a rough time here this evening. An enemy trench mortar is throwing heavy bombs into Seaforth Farm and every time an explosion occurs, we are showered with fragments at our dugout. An enemy machine gun keeps sweeping this part of the line every few minutes, plastering the trees and the earth full of metal, almost playing a tune as the pitch varies with the movement to and fro.

Received letters from Olie Lockhart and Stuart Thompson and a card from Mother, dated December 14, 13 and 19.

Tues., Jan. 4:

Parcel with belt, gum, and fudge from Dorothy B. Wrote mother and Stuart Thompson. On duty 1–9 a.m. Very heavy artillery duel on this front, but trench 130 escaped well.

Wed., Jan. 5:

Aeroplanes active; Lively cannonade; much sniping, and M.G. fire. Man killed in C Coy. yesterday and another today.[4] Trenches in bad condition, parapets falling down, and drainage bad.

Sun., Jan. 9:

Came out to Bulford Camp, being relieved at 4:30 p.m. They have just put slat walks all about the camp and it is in splendid condition in spite of the mud. We have had a pretty hot time in the trenches, heavily shelled at Seaforth Farm and Ash House, one dugout was blown up, and two men were killed with bullets through the head. This has been a lovely day and numbers of our planes have been over the lines all the time, some going away back over Messines and Warneton. The artillery on our side was very active and in the pm we could hear

---

3 8th Battalion Boy: Probably Private Sydney Jameson (1890–1916), born in England; attested Valcartier, September 1914, buried CWGC Berks Cemetery Extension.

4 Men killed could be Private John Henry Baugh (1877–1916) on 4 January or Private F.W. Boyer (1885–1916) on 5 January. Boyer was an American serving with the CEF. Both are buried in CWGC Berks Cemetery.

Winston Churchill with French General Émile Fayolle on the
Western Front in France, 15 December 1915. A month later, Lt. Col. Churchill,
commanding the 6th Royal Scots Fusiliers, addressed Leslie Miller's
5th Battalion. Credit: Imperial War Museum Q49305.

the big howitzer shells going high overhead, their express train roar
dying away in the east and the explosion of the shells being too far
away for us to hear.

Mon., Jan. 10:

About 4 a.m. there was a terrific outburst of artillery fire just north of
us on 2nd Div. front, lasting half an hour or so. We all woke up, but do
not know why it occurred.

Moved to Petit Pont Farm this p.m. to assist Biggs and McGuire at
our EF station.[5] Austin has gone to Bailleul to Hospital. Our aeroplanes

---

5 Biggs: Ralph Percy Biggs (1894–?). Attested Valcartier, September 1914. Returned to
   action after being wounded in the right arm (see entry of 24 April 1916). At Vimy
   Ridge was wounded again and subsequently transferred to the Canadian Army
   Medical Corps. McGuire: Could not be identified.

very active and no enemy planes in sight. Our big guns at the rear are firing steadily these days.

Mon., Jan. 10:[6]

Reported at Petit Pont Farm to Grenade Coy. to work on phones with Biggs and McGuire.

Fri., Jan. 14:

5th and 7th Bns. with Bde. Grenade Coy. made attack on G.H.Q. lines, witnessed by Lt. Col. Winston Churchill, who afterwards addressed the men.[7]

Sat., Jan. 15:

Bde. men relieved us at Petit Pont Stn. at 2 p.m. Came into trenches at dusk to trench 129 with "C" Coy. It is nearly full moon now and bright all night long. Motor Mch. Gun Bde. have guns back on Messines Road and keep up an intermittent fire over our heads all night long.[8] This seems to be doing much to check enemy fire at night which was rather severe ten days ago.

Rec'd lovely box of chocolates from Mrs. Stuart of Newcastle, N.B. We cleaned them all up this evening.

Wed., Jan. 19:

British Tommies a mile or two on our right attacked German narrow salient under cover of gas, took a few prisoners (8?) and straightened out the line.

At night flashes of 3 German machine guns were observed, positions determined, artillery warned, and result – enemy shelled and silenced.

---

6 Date: Miller's second entry under that date, or an error in dating.

7 Attack: This was a practice attack, according to the 5th Battalion War Diary. Lt. Col. Winston Churchill: Refers, of course, to Winston Spencer Churchill (1874–1965), later prime minister of the UK. In November 1915, Churchill resigned from the government, in part because of his role in the planning of the disastrous Gallipoli campaign. He commanded the 6th Battalion, Royal Scots Fusiliers, on the Ypres Salient near Ploegsteert from January to March 1916 before returning to England.

8 Motor Machine Gun Brigade: The Canadian Expeditionary Force's first fully motorized unit, equipped with armoured cars mounting machine guns.

Artillery on this front destroyed a German battery yesterday. Our airmen are doing excellent work these fine days; some of our machines are whirring overhead all the time, but rarely do we ever see a German, and then only behind their own lines.

Fri., Jan. 21:

Relieved by the 8th and went to Bde. Reserve at Grande Munque.

Thurs., Jan. 27:

Came up to trenches, I to 129 with Biggs and McGuire. Sick with trench fever while out at Grande Munque, but only confined to bed four days. Fifth day visited Div'l baths and Romarin canteen, coming back thru Ploegsteert at dark.

Tues., Feb. 1:

Clear in afternoon. Three German Fokker planes circled overhead a while this afternoon.[9] They are the new machine that has created such a flutter of anxiety in England as they are supposed to be much faster than our best planes. They appear perfectly white against the blue sky. Our anti-aircraft guns were shooting very wildly far behind the German planes.

Wed., Feb. 2:

About noon, one of our howitzer btys. bombarded the German's Ash Rd. barrier just ahead of their front line. Some direct hits were made. It was great to see great sections of barbed wire with stakes and supports blown into the air. At each explosion of a shell, a great black mass of smoke, earth and debris sprang into the air and shell fragments fell even back in our trenches. The Germans have put a lot of work on this barricade lately, strengthening it against an attack from us. But our scouts have watched them and reported everything done.

---

9 Fokker: Dutch-German aircraft manufacturer, named for its founder, Anthony Fokker (1890–1939). In 1915 and early 1916 Fokker's monoplane, the Eindecker, dominated Allied opposition.

Sat., Feb. 5:

Tenth Bn. made night bombing attack this morning. Party went out early to cut wire. At 4 a.m. bombing party advanced through wire and encountered a covering patrol with a working party behind them on the German parapet. Our boys killed all the covering patrol, but the German working party opened rapid fire, and our fellows ran back "sauve qui peut."[10] On reaching our trench they were ten men short. Returning cautiously they brought in six wounded men, leaving four behind missing and probably killed.[11]

About ten days ago, Pongo Warr, our lineman, picked up on the Warneton Road a German message flag dropped by an aeroplane.[12] It contained a message addressed to the British Royal Flying Corps, giving names of airmen brought down within the German lines within a certain period, whether killed or taken prisoner, where buried or imprisoned. This shows the existence of an unwritten code of honour between the two air services. The message was sent to its destination, but the flag was sent back from Bde. to the finder.

Sun., Feb. 6:

The new Div. Baths across the road from Bulford Camp have been in operation since the New Year opened. Each time we are out from trenches we get a hot shower bath, change of sox, shirts, and underwear and sometime towels, and have the remainder of our clothing disinfected by steam.

Yesterday p.m. as we were out doing some Helio and flag work, Alexander of the old 32nd Signal Section, now in 2nd Bn., came across from their Div. reserve position at Dranoutre and we had quite a chat.[13] I went half way back with him, through Neuve Eglise and out on the

---

10 "Sauve qui peut": Colloquially, "every man for himself."

11 According to the 10th Battalion war diary, four men were killed in this "minor operation" that saw sharp, close-range fighting and perhaps 40–50 German casualties. In addition, several Germans were taken prisoner but "in getting through the out belt of wire under a very hot fire it became impossible to bring them out and they were killed." LAC, 10th Battalion War Diary, *Report on Minor Operation Carried Out on Night of 4th-5th February 1916*, RG9-III-D-3, Vol. 4919, File 372.

12 Warr: Horace Murchie Warr, born 1882 in St. Stephen, New Brunswick; attested Valcartier, September 1914. A "lineman" was responsible for the laying and maintenance of telephone and telegraph lines.

13 Alexander: See entry of 25 April 1915.

Dranoutre Rd. Saw Kemmel Hill, Mt. Noir, and Mt. des Chats. They occupy trench position in front of Wulverghem, which village Alex says is completely shot to pieces.

Bde. Band gives concerts every night in the Y.M.C.A. tent and render some very fine music. Last night they assisted the 5th Bn. give a concert. I told some jokes and recited "Kentucky Philosophy".

Tues., Feb. 8:

Back to trenches, "129" station.

Mon., Feb. 14:

Billets at Court Drêve; Sigs. in loft over house.

Wed., Feb. 16:

Shell lit in courtyard in p.m. killing team of mules, wounding five men (one fatally) including Sig. Jock Shaw, and blowing in all the windows facing the yard. Cherry trees in bloom.[14]

Sun., Feb. 20:

Trenches, "129" as usual for me.

Sat., Feb. 26:

Relieved & came to Bulford Camp.

Wed., Mar. 1:

Phillips & I visited Bailleul and Berthen. Welcomed home by all the Demol family. I gave Lucie my 32nd cap badge. Jim left on Jan. 7 to train in Southern France and will train until July before going on active service.

---

14 Shaw: Could not be identified, but no one of that name was killed in this incident, as Miller's slightly ambiguous wording might suggest. Dead was Ernest Harrison (1890–1916), born Michigan; attested Valcartier, September 1914, buried CWGC Bailleul Communal Cemetery. His death is not noted in the 5th Battalion War Diary.

Remarkably, Miller kept the day pass he and Private Phillips received 1 March
1916 to go to Bailleul and Berthen. Credit: Miller family collection.

They want us to come whenever we can and Mme. Demol says we are
all her boys and she is our "mère". It was like a trip home to make such
a visit. I have no better friends on this side of the ocean.

Last night E.F. Smith who has been Battn. Pigeoniero[15] took three fits
in succession and nearly died.[16] He has gone to hospital and is being sent
on down to the base still unconscious. Jack Pells gets his job at Bn. Hqrs.

---

15 Pigeoniero: Pigeon handler.
16 E.F. Smith: Edwin or Edward Francis Smith (1880–1918), born Montreal; attested
    Valcartier, September 1914. Smith had long suffered from mental illness and was
    given the light duty of caring for the battalion's pigeons. A medical officer noted at
    the time, "It was always a matter of wonder to us how he ever came to be passed for
    Active Service." Smith was subsequently diagnosed with syphilis and determined
    mentally unfit for service. He died in Montreal in October 1918 and is buried in a
    CWGC grave in Montreal's Mont Royal Cemetery. On the medical services, and
    specifically about Canadian Nursing Sisters, see Cynthia Toman, *Sister Soldiers of the
    Great War* (Vancouver: UBC Press, 2016).

Another of the chaps wounded at Court Drêve billet has died. Mackenzie who came on the Section a week ago has just gone to hospital sick. The Battle for Verdun is raging and the Germans are slowly approaching the inner forts.[17]

Thurs., Mar. 9:

Relieved by 8th, proceeded to Grande Munque billet.

Wed., Mar. 15:

Back to trenches.

There has been heavy artillery work lately, and aeroplanes are very active. New rapid fire pom-poms are doing good work in this sector. Verdun Battle has raged since Feb 26 and Germans have lost about 200,000 men to gain Douamont Ridge and Fort, no other result. We have had no Canadian mail for a fortnight and do not know the reason. I get my Weekly Times regularly, and daily papers are sold here every morning lately by Belgian boys. (Sergt) Tom Bennett of Weyburn and 32nd Bn., recently for 3 wks of "A" Coy 5th, was wounded last time in trenches, and is now in England.[18] Three men (Whitelaw, Christenson & Ruthven) were killed in one dugout by a whizz-bang penetrating the roof in trench 131.[19]

Sat., Mar. 18:

Our heavies are pounding Petit Douve position this morning. The upper air is roaring with passing shells and the crashes are terrific. It is the heaviest bombardment I have heard yet. Petit Douve has always

---

17 Verdun: The Battle of Verdun (21 February to 18 December 1916). A protracted battle fought between the French and German armies in and around the city of Verdun, resulting in a million casualties but no decisive victory for either side.

18 Bennett: Sergeant Thomas Bennett (1891–?), born London, England; a resident of Weyburn; attested Winnipeg, December 1914. Twice wounded; declared medically unfit for further service in 1918 and returned to Canada. W.L. Smith, *The Makers of Canada: The Pioneers of Old Ontario* (Toronto, 1923), 127.

19 The three killed died 6 March 1916. Christenson: Private James Christenson (1876–1916), born Iowa, a resident of Humboldt, Saskatchewan, attested December 1914. CWGC incorrectly lists last name as Christensen. Ruthven: Private Donald Ruthven (1892–1916), born England, attested Saskatoon, January 1915. Whitelaw, Alexander Francis (1893–1916), born Scotland, attested Minnedosa, Manitoba, December 1914. All three buried CWGC Berks Cemetery Extension, Belgium.

been a danger point for us and we bombard it periodically, but this is the heaviest yet.

Lovely weather now, warm days usually bright with sunshine, mild nights moonlit from sunset to almost dawn. The land is rapidly drying up; the farmers are plowing, planting and sowing every day; plant growth has quickened, and the spring birds are returning. Heard first skylark singing one bright morning a week ago over field south of moat at Grande Munque; now we hear them every day. Starlings and blackbirds have been common for weeks. There are five robins where one was two weeks ago, and oh how they sing! Saw two magpies recently, also many birds I can't identify. Some birds sing in the neighbourhood of the trenches all through these warm nights. During the day flocks of small birds hover above or cross over no-man's land frequently. Last night Joe De Pevre was wearing a lovely big yellow daffodil found in the deserted area behind the trenches. The willows are covered with catkins. Saw a water-hen of some kind swimming among the growing flags (already six inches above the water) in the moat by Grande Munque house.[20]

The Germans are retaliating with whizz-bangs at 11:05 a.m. and have wounded two men at the junction of 128 and 129 trenches.

Tues., Mar. 21:

Canadian mail held up since Mar. began to come through 2 days ago. I got 4 parcels of food, 4 of magazines, and 7 letters in this short time.

Thurs., Mar. 23:

Inoculated with anti-typhoid serum and given 48 hours complete rest (entire Battn. took this). Germans have fought to a standstill at Verdun, losing 250,000 men.[21] Russians are becoming active in the East. Trebizond is almost surrounded.[22]

---

20 Flags: Refers in this case to a species of the iris plant.
21 As violent as the Battle of Verdun was, the figure of 250,000 casualties, no doubt circulating in Allied propaganda at the time, is an exaggeration.
22 A reference to the Battle of Trebizond, February–April 1916, in which the Turkish Black Sea port of Trabzon (known historically as Trebizond) fell to a Russian attack. See also entry of 22 April 1916.

Sat., Mar. 25:

Jock Shaw and "Compris" returned from Le Havre base camp last night. Say they led a dog's life as soon as they left hospital and are glad to get back.

Quite a heavy fall of snow during last two nights and a day, melted almost as fast as it fell.

Mon., Mar. 27:

Battn. returned to trenches. Ralph Biggs, Goodwin, and I took over the transport station in hut by our Bn. Q.M. stores.[23] As the front line was short of phones, they took ours out. We are left here with nothing to do but take stock of the signal section stores prior to moving.

I have just received Stewart Edward White's book "The Blazed Trail" from F.M.W. and am reading it.[24] It is the best lumberman's story I have ever read, even beats Ralph Connor's best in places.[25] The scene is laid in upper Michigan, and deals with the career of a successful young lumberman, Harry Thorpe. The breathing fragrance and majesty of the pine woods is in every paragraph. The descriptions are clear and powerful. The excitement is intense in places, and, when well-launched, the plot moves swiftly, gathering momentum and becoming more absorbing after each new incident. We must have a good edition of this book in our home library.

Have just received home-knit sox from Mrs. H.H. Stuart, Florence Wood, and Mrs. Clarke (by Mother), also from Goodwin my mate here.

Weather keeps cool with strong west winds and heavy cumulus clouds. It rained two days but is drying up fast again.

---

23 Goodwin: Albert Ernest (1889–?), born England, attested Edmonton, February 1915. Goodwin, a telegrapher by trade, will be mentioned often in the entries that follow. He later transferred to the Royal Flying Corps.

24 "The Blazed Trail": 1902 novel by the American author Stewart Edward White (1873–1946). F.M.W.: Could not be identified.

25 Connor: Ralph Connor, pen name of Dr. Charles William Gordon (1860–1937), Canadian novelist who was among the British Empire's most widely read writers in the years preceding the First World War. Connor served as a chaplain during the war.

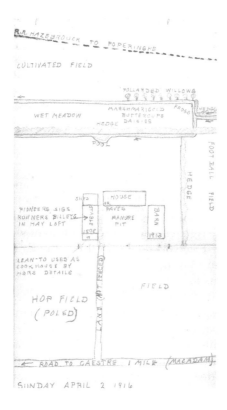

R.R. HAZEBROUCK TO POPERINGHE

CULTIVATED FIELD

POLLARDED WILLOWS

MARSHMARIGOLD ROAD
WET MEADOW   BUTTERCUPS
HEDGE   DAISIES   HEDGE

POOL

FOOT BALL FIELD

HEDGE

SHED   HOUSE
PIONEERS SIGN   PAVED
BONNERS BILLETS   MANURE   BARN
IN HAY LOFT   PIT   1913

LEAN-TO USED AS
COOKHOUSE BY
H & R S DETAILS   FIELD

HOP FIELD
(POLED)

LANE (NOT FENCED)

← ROAD TO CAESTRE 1 MILE (MACADAM)

SUNDAY APRIL 2 1916

Fri., Mar. 31:

Battn. relieved by Royal Fusiliers, left trenches last night, spent night at Grande Munque Farm.[26] Assembled at Grenade school field Petit Pont Corner at 2 p.m. today, and marched via Bailleul, Meteren, Flêtre, Caestre to new billets. Halted at sunset in a lovely green meadow just west of Bailleul where the field kitchens served hot cocoa. We rustled bread and cheese from farm houses. Reached Caestre and billets one mile north away on in the night, most of us done up with sore feet and general weariness. Shown into the loft above a substantial brick stable, the floor liberally strewn with soft hay, we turned in and were soon sound asleep.

---

26 Royal Fusiliers: Also known as the City of London Regiment, the Fusiliers were a storied British Army regiment tracing their history back to 1685.

Sat., Apr. 1:

A glorious day, as fine as spring could bring. Spent time exploring the place and here is a rough sketch.

Sun., Apr. 2:

Advanced party of 12 men, 1 L/cpl. and Lieut. McDonald (myself to represent Sig. Section) left Caestre billet 8 a.m., machine gun limber carrying our packs and equipment; marched by Berthen, Westoutre to Canada Huts half mile north of DICKEBUSCH.[27] Halted by Demols farm at Berthen and I called to see them. Mme. Demol, Marie Lucie and George gave me a warm welcome and regretted I could only stay 10 minutes. Again they proved their friendship in a way there was no mistaking. We halted 45 minutes in Westoutre at noon and lunched at the Estaminets.[28] It was a hot fine day and marching with just rifle to carry was a real pleasure.

Mon., Apr. 3:

We have a hut to ourselves and are doing nothing as yet up to noon. The cannon boomed incessantly last night and have only just now become a bit quiet at noon, this in the direction of St. Eloi.[29] A batch of 61 German prisoners has just been marched through camp, captured this morning over there. They were mostly young looking fellows in their early twenties, a very good-looking crowd. None of our fellows sneered or passed a single remark as they passed, although both sides of the road were thronged with Tommies and Canadians as they passed.

Editor's Note: The Battle of the St. Eloi Craters
On 3 April 1916 the 2nd Canadian Division relieved the British in heavily cratered and waterlogged terrain southeast of Ypres. In the subsequent confused and hard-fought brawl that became known as the Battle of St. Eloi Craters, the Canadians were defeated, suffering nearly 1,500 casualties. Miller and the 5th Battalion entered the line on 16

---

27 Dickebusch: Also Dikkebus, Belgian village approximately five kilometres southwest of Ypres towards Bailleul.
28 Estaminet(s): French café that also serves alcoholic beverages.
29 St. Eloi: Small town 5 kilometres south of Ypres.

April, just as the battle reached its final stages. The 5th was relieved late on 25 April,
having lost a tenth of its strength, but was subjected to an intense bombardment while
in support trenches the following day.

Wed., Apr. 5:

The Battn. marched in from Caestre to the Canada Huts, arriving at
nightfall.

Thurs., Apr. 6:

Heavy fighting at St. Eloi, about six miles S.E. of here. Germans shelled
camps in this area 5 p.m. till after dark. Killed 6 men, wounded a dozen
more, killed and wounded 8 of our horses; blew in the corner of a D coy
hut killing Runner Joe Galant and "Bung" Lever, the comic singer.[30] We
took shelter in ditches and behind trees, but at dark left camp, slept in
a trench until midnight when it came on rain, then got in an old shed,
taking straw from a stack for our beds.

Fri., Apr. 7:

Returned to camp and carried on as usual. But special instructions were
issued telling all units what to do in case Canada huts were shelled again.

Sat., Apr. 8:

Moved to another camp half a mile north of Canada Huts this afternoon.
Set to work at once to dig shell trenches in case of bombardment, although
we have very snug little huts.
    I am working with Virgin cooking for the Signal Section during the
absence of Donald Hay, the regular cook who is on leave to England.[31]

---

30 Gallant: Private Joseph Gallant (1891–1916) of Prince Edward Island; attested
    Dauphin, Manitoba. Lever: In fact, Private Victor Stanley *Laver* (1889–1916), born
    England; attested Saskatoon, January 1915. Both are commemorated in Aeroplane
    Cemetery, Belgium.
31 Virgin: Probably William Harold Virgin (1893–?), born USA; attested Toronto,
    November 1915. Hay: Donald Alex Hay (1888–1959), born Manitoba; attested Por-
    tage La Prairie, Manitoba, February 1915.

Sun., Apr. 9:

Very fine warm day. Spent day quietly in camp. In evening Highton and I walked to Dickebusch & back.[32]

Mon., Apr. 10:

Heavy bombardments night and day now with intervals of quiet or intermittent fire.

Went on sick parade to army dentists at Vlamertinghe, an hour's walk across the fields.[33] Left camp at nine and returned at one. The town is pretty much shot to pieces and few civilians live there. It is far more deserted and desolate than Dickebusch. The latter town is partially wrecked but there are many fine little stores and eating shops still doing business. Both cathedrals in these towns are unroofed and only a few sections of walls and the badly shattered towers are still standing. The interiors are buried in bricks and debris ten or fifteen feet deep.

A British plane was blown to pieces by a direct hit from a German anti-aircraft shell and the occupants killed.[34] Atmosphere very clear all day. We could see 5 German observation balloons around this Ypres salient, besides our own two, one at Kemmel Hill, and one at Poperinghe.[35]

A number of our officers and N.C.O.'s have been up at the front looking over our new position. Sergt. Jenkins was making the trip yesterday when he had his head blown off by a whizz-bang.[36] He is greatly missed.

---

32 Highton: Private (later Lieutenant) Harold Victor Highton (1892–1918), born England, attested Regina, May 1915. Transferred to the RFC May 1917. He was killed in action 25 March 1918 and is commemorated on the Arras Flying Services Memorial to the missing.

33 Vlamertinghe: Now a borough of Ypres, in 1916 Vlamertinge (correct spelling) was a village in West Flanders.

34 The machine in question was a Morane "Parasol," piloted by Lt. Col. Donald Swain Lewis, DSO (1886–1916), commanding officer of 2nd Wing, Royal Flying Corps, the highest-ranking officer of the British air services killed during the war. The other occupant of the aircraft was Captain Arthur Witherby Gale, officer commanding the Trench Mortar Batteries of the 3rd Division.

35 Observation balloons became a common sight along the front. Typically they were tethered a short distance behind the lines.

36 Jenkins: David Jones Capenhurst Jenkins (1892–1916), born Wales; attested Valcartier, September 1914. Buried in CWGC Railway Dugouts Burial Ground, Belgium.

Thurs., Apr. 13:

Reported to transport telephone station by the windmill S. of Ouderdom to do duty with L/Cpl. Ralph Biggs and Goodwin. We 3 live in a tent, without a floor, and we are very comfortable. The weather is cool with westerly and northerly gales, heavy cumulus clouds developing mostly into nimbus, with intervals of bright warm sunshine between. Hedges are at half-leaf, grass is growing luxuriantly, tree tops at a distance have a greenish brown tinge of bursting buds.

Sat., Apr. 15:

Visited dentist at Vlamertinghe. Saw a magpie in a field, and another leaving a nest in the topmost branches of a tall elm. Magpies are usually seen singly strutting over the ground in cultivated fields or perched in trees. A magpie is black and white while a jackdaw is pure black. I have only seen the former species.

Sun., Apr. 16:

Our Battn. went to trenches in this new position for first time. L/Cpl. Burdon came to transport station and took Ralph Biggs' place as he is gone up with the section.

Tues., Apr. 18:

Stuart Thompson has just arrived in England by S.S. *Olympic* from Halifax to Liverpool.[37]

Went to dentist at Vlamertinghe and had tooth filled. Passed through Reninghelst and Poperinghe on way, picking up rides on motor lorries half the distance.[38]

Moved our tent across the road yesterday to a spot among some reserve trenches and near the dugout we have chosen as phone station in

---

37 SS *Olympic*: Sister ship of the *Titanic, Olympic* was converted to a troopship during the war. Nearly one-fifth of Canadians who served overseas crossed the Atlantic aboard her.

38 Poperinghe: Town in West Flanders, with Ypres one of the only significant towns in Belgium not under German occupation and an important British army hub on the Western Front.

Miller's future brother-in-law, Stuart Thompson of the 44th
Battalion, CEF, photographed in 1916 at Hythe Ranges, a military facility near
Hythe on the English Channel coast. Credit: Miller family collection.

case of shelling. The Germans shell the main roads near here every fine
day, mostly about sunset.

Sat., Apr. 22:

Very wet cool weather; this is the 5th day of rain and heavy clouds.

Heavy cannonade east of Ypres at 3:30 a.m., dying away by 4 a.m.
This is anniversary of 2nd Battle of Ypres, and only the rain seems to be
preventing action in this sector.

L./Cpl. Sopp has been on leave to England since Apr. 10, and Donald
Hay returned from his last Sunday.

The hedges are in full leaf. Many trees and shrubs are unfolding their
buds rapidly and showing green.

It was reported in the papers of Thurs. that Trebizond has fallen into the hands of the Russians.[39]

Mon., Apr. 24:

Battn. leaves trenches tonight. Transport and Q.M. Stores broke camp at 11 a.m. and reached Poperinghe via Ouderdom by one o'clock. Located billets, Goodwin and I strolled about town looking at people and shop windows. This is a larger town than Bailleul, but has been shelled and bombed so much that many citizen homes are deserted and used as billets for troops. The 7th Bn. are occupying a hop factory, while we will have three coys. and Q.M. Stores in Sacred Heart Convent. Bn. Hqrs. is in a fine house in a block across the street.

Capt. J. Nash, D.S.O., our signalling ofr. was killed and Lieut. Cockerill wounded yesterday by a shell penetrating the dugout they were occupying.[40] Ralph Biggs was wounded in the arm, a nice "Blighty" for him.

Tues., Apr. 25:

Goodwin tended phone to midnight, then I till 4 a.m. German aeroplanes bombed Poperinghe at 3:30 to 4 a.m., dropping many bombs, but none near our house. One incendiary bomb fell in the square 100 yds. away. Motor machine guns and our aeroplanes finally drove them off at daylight. One coy ("B") reached billets at 5 a.m. The others and sigs missed the train at Ypres. They were relieved so late that they could not get out to the train in time, as it had to be away by daybreak. At 6 a.m. they are still stranded on the Ypres-Vlamertinghe Road, and motor busses are being sent for them. They were very heavily shelled yesterday in their position.

Battn. suffered about 80 casualties during 8 days in front line, and most of these occurred on last day.

---

39 Trebizond: See entry of 27 March 1916.
40 Nash: See entry of 21 December 1916. Cockerill: Lieutenant A.D. Cockrill. See entry 14 December 1915. Cockrill was partially buried by the collapse of the trench. His left arm was severely crushed: "like a bag of bones" was how it was described in his medical file. He returned to Canada in November 1916.

Wed., Apr. 26:

Brig. Gen. Lipsett addressed 5th Battn. in bandstand yard behind Y.M.C.A.[41] Said Battn. had just gone through heaviest bombardment yet experienced by any British troops, and we would not likely ever experience any worse. Our fellows stood it all splendidly and stuck to their positions; only disappointed because the German infantry did not attack as was expected. The 2nd Bde. had never lost a trench in the war.

Heavy bombardment all evening, like continuous thunder, rattling our windows at times. All troops in the salient are standing to. Germans are attacking position held by 2nd Canadians who relieved the 5th. Some German mines exploded; some of our trenches taken by Germans, then retaken by our bombers.[42] Enemy completely driven off. Our artillery develops terrific concentration of fire in these attacks. Our boys say it was splendid last Monday and the Germans suffered far more than us. Rumour says we have 1,600 guns in this salient alone.

Fri., Apr. 28:

The British Commander-in-Chief, Sir Douglas Haig, reviewed and inspected the Battn. at 4 p.m. in a meadow on the west side of Poperinghe.[43] Gen. Alderson (Corps), Gen. Currie (Div.), and Brig. Gen. Lipsett were

---

41 Lipsett: Major General Louis Lipsett (1874–1918), then brigadier general, commanding officer of 2nd Brigade. A British officer, Lipsett had close relations with the Canadians and had served as a training officer in Canada before the war. He later commanded the 3rd Canadian Division at Vimy Ridge. Killed in action 14 October 1918 while commanding the British 4th Division. Buried in Quéant Communal Cemetery British Extension, France.

42 Mine: Miller refers several times to mines and mining. Mining was the practice of digging tunnels under (or near to) the enemy's trenches and packing them with explosives, usually to be detonated moments before an attack.

43 Haig: General (later Field Marshal) Sir Douglas Haig (1861–1928), commanding officer of the British Expeditionary Force (BEF). Currie: Major General (later General) Sir Arthur Currie (1875–1933), then commanding officer of the 1st Canadian Division. Commanded the Canadian Corps from June 1917 onwards. Alderson: Lt. General Sir Edwin Alderson (1859–1927), British officer, then commanding the Canadian Corps.

present. Col. Dyer is on leave to Eng., so Maj. Page is in command.[44] The C.-in-C. walked down between the coys., and spoke to the Ofr. or N.C.O. i/c each detail. He is a very keen eyed man who seems to see everything, yet kind-heartedness is stamped on his features.

We next marched to the court yard behind the Y.M.C.A. where Gens. Currie and Alderson spoke to us. Both said they saw in the 5th a Bn. to be relied upon in any emergency. The C.-in-C. had said we looked like fighting men through and through.

Editor's Note: Miller recorded the names of several friends and correspondents on the following page of the diary.

No. 404860 Pte. E. Hooper[45]
No. 3 Platoon, "A" Coy, 35th Battn.
Bramshott Camp
Liphook, Hants, England
20th Bn., France after April 1st
Belle[46]
R.R. No. 1 Todmorden
#105624 Pte. G.F. Armstrong
D Coy, 68th Battn. Barracks
Regina, Sask.
Pte. Bryce Lockhart[47]

---

44 Dyer: Lt. Col. Hugh Marshall Dyer, KCB, CMG, DSO (1861–1938). The 5th Battalion's commanding officer since January, Dyer was born in Ireland but immigrated to Canada in 1881. He was a 12-year veteran of the 12th Manitoba Dragoons when he attested at Valcartier in September 1914. In July 1917 Dyer was promoted to brigadier general and placed in command of the 7th Canadian Infantry Brigade. Page: Major Lionel Frank Page, CB, DSO and Two Bars (1884–1944), born England, resident of Red Deer, Alberta, attested Valcartier, September 1914. Promoted to Lt. Col. In March 1917, Page took command of the 50th Battalion. He was wounded in a gas attack on 2 November 1918. Page served again in the Second World War, commanding the newly formed 4th Canadian Armoured Division in 1941 and subsequently acting as general officer commander in chief, Atlantic Command. He died of natural causes in 1944.

45 Hooper: Ernest Hooper (1896–1916). Born Barrie, Ontario; attested Toronto, April 1915, killed in action 2 June 1916. Buried CWGC Bedford House Cemetery. It is not clear what Hooper's relation to Miller is. See entry of 14 November 1917.

46 Belle: Miller's sister, Isabella Muriel Miller (1896–1983). She later married Frederick Clifford (Cliff) Penson, also a veteran of the war.

47 Lockhart: Private (later Lieutenant) Bruce Melvin Lockhart (1896–?), born Moncton, New Brunswick; attested October 1915. Son of Viola Lockhart. See entry of 20 February 1915.

55th Can. Bn.
Westenhanger
(Cherry Hinton Hospital, Cambridge)
461462 Pte. Stuart L. Thompson
Sig. Section, 61st Can. Bn.

Sat., Apr. 29:

All available men in Bn. went on work party last night to Kruisstraat
Engineers Dump. Sig. Section sent 12. We went to Pop. station at 7
p.m.; armored locomotive backed our string of 3rd class coaches down
to a mile east of Vlamertinghe; we detrained and marched E. nearly to
Ypres, then southwest along Ypres-Dickebush Road a mile or so. We
were burying cable on both sides of the road until 1 a.m. Returned to
train at 2 a.m. Cars were there, but Germans were shelling line from our
position west to Vlamertinghe (20 shells – 15 minute interval – 20 shells,
etc.) so locomotive had gone up line towards Pop. Shell broke rail just
in front of the coaches. Railway R.E. boys put a 6-ft. piece of wood in to
replace broken piece of steel.[48] Engine did not cross this but drew cars
over with a 50-ft. chain. Germans were shelling line half a mile west all
the while. But we got safely away and were soon back in Pop. and home
to our billet. We considered it a great adventure not to be missed. I wore
steel helmet for first time.[49]

Slept 6 a.m. to 1 p.m. while the town was being bombed and shelled.
Three German planes chased one of ours, riddled its petrol tank, killed
observer, and wounded pilot in leg.[50] But pilot landed safely 2 mi. WSW
of here. Goodwin was out to Div. Hqrs. for phones and wire this morning and saw the plane. It mounted 3 machine guns.

Bombs were dropped at the railway station doing some damage. A
few shells fell in the town square. A girl had her hand and lower arm
cut clean off by a flying piece of shell casing.

---

48 R.E.: Royal Engineers.
49 Steel helmet: The Mark 1 Steel Helmet, aka the Brodie helmet (after John Leopold
    Brodie, designer of the original version), which began to be issued to Canadian
    troops in March 1916. It helped to reduce serious head injuries.
50 Wounded pilot: The machine in question was an FE2b from 20 Squadron, flown
    by Lt. R.D. Sampson and his observer (non-pilot crew member) 1 A.M. (1st Air
    Mechanic) Samuel Cotton, who was killed. The claim that the machine carried three
    machine guns might be inaccurate: the FE2b carried two Lewis guns that could be
    fired from three positions.

This is lovely weather. Apple trees in the gardens are in blossom. Lilac flower buds are bursting. Most of the trees are in full leaf. Birds are nesting everywhere. We see mostly house sparrows here in town just same as at home. The buttercups in the garden are opening and one fine yellow kind has been out full two days. The sky is usually clear with light northerly winds; sometimes there is a quantity of cirrus cloud like a veil over most of the sky, tempering the sun's hot rays a great deal.

Insect life in pools of water is much like that at home. Water striders and whirligig beetles are just as common. Water boatmen are the same, one kind, large, of elliptical shape, the others narrow and oblong in shape. The big predacious diving beetle is just the same as the one in my collection.

Sun., Apr. 30:

At midnight a terrific bombardment started up south of here, becoming more intense every minute. The old boys say they have never heard anything like it. The air was all atremble and the earth shook. Gas alarm came at 12:55 a.m. and soon bells were ringing and whistles blowing everywhere. We all got up, dressed, and stood by our gas helmets ready to don them if the gas should reach us. By 1:45 the cannonade had died down to normal, and the alarm was cancelled, so we returned to bed. We hear the trouble started at our old position at Ploegsteert and worked up this way; so the Canadians had no part in it.

At 3:30 a.m. German aeroplanes bombed Poperinghe with about 12 bombs. Machine guns opened fire and probably drove them off. This has been the most exciting night I have experienced.

Church parade at 2 p.m. in an open meadow on east side of town. About 2,000 men from 5th & 7th Bns. and 1st Canadian Pioneers assembled and heard a good sermon from the Padre.[51] It was a lovely clear day, trees partly leafed out and birds singing. Two of our observation balloons swung in the breeze high above us in the north. Aeroplanes kept flying about here and there.

---

51 Pioneers: The 1st Canadian Pioneer Battalion existed only briefly. Formed in March 1916 it became the 9th Canadian Railway Battalion a year later. Pioneers were both infantry and labour battalions, digging trenches, building dugouts, roads, barbed wire entangles, and so forth.

Mon., May 1:

One Battn. working party to Kruistraat dump on Dickebusch-Ypres road burying cable in 6-ft. trench. Proceeded as on night of April 28. After leaving train on way up, we had to pass along half a mile of road under heavy shell fire. About 25 shells fell near us but none of our party was hit. Met a wounded man being helped along the road at this point by two Red Cross men. Arrived home at 4 a.m.

Tues., May 2:

Battn. proceeded to Bde. reserve position on Vlamertinghe-Voormezelle road north of Ypres-Dickebush road. Left Poperinghe about 8 p.m.; by train to a point between Vlamertinghe and Ypres; marched by road south to our billet. Clements, Goodwin, Mitchell and I are posted to "C" Coy. (Capt. Murdy O.C.) for duty.[52] The night was clear and as light as stars will make it; but it had rained heavily (thundershowers) during the day, so the ground was very muddy. After leaving the cobble road the marching was very heavy – slipping and stumbling on uneven ground, avoiding shell holes which are very numerous and mostly half full of water, jumping ditches and wire trenches, and keeping clear of telephone cables which cross the fields in every direction. We reached C & D coys billet, but were ordered to go to Div. Report Centre (CYAR). Corpl. Willis (scout) guided 2 runners and 6 signallers.[53] We had only half a mile to go, but it took us an hour to find the place, and we were all in (midnight). Found Stowe (32nd Bn. signaller) and a bunch of Div. Sigs. playing French piano and singing songs in their mess room.[54] We could find no accommodation so slept till morning in the Sigs mess room. Very little artillery fire to disturb us. We are about two miles north of the trenches.

---

52 Murdy: Probably Captain (later Lt. Col.) Robert Murdie, DSO (1888–?), born Scotland; attested Valcartier, September 1914. Murdie later commanded the 161st (Huron) Battalion.
53 Willis: Could not be identified.
54 Stowe: Charles James Stowe (1888–?), born England, attested Winnipeg, September 1914.

Wed., May 3:

Coy. sigs found accommodation in Engineer's store in a stable, half cellar, floor 3 feet below ground. Taking messages to C & D Coys at 1:30
pm. Saw 5.9 shell lying on ground by a big shell hole.[55] Someone must
have dug it out and left it lying. Dead shells when they fall on this soft
ground always bury themselves 15 feet or more. The field between our
billet and the road is pitted with shell holes, and more were put there
this forenoon. These buildings have not been shelled, but the 14th Bn.
was shelled out from the farm buildings yesterday where our C and D
coys now are. Our men are kept in the woods and along hedges all day
and only use the buildings at night. There are no civilians in this neighbourhood a mile east of Dickebush.

Thurs., May 4:

Very fine; some cirrus cloud to temper heat of sun.

Met Geo. Leeson's brother, Jim, last evening.[56] He is a signalling officer with 1st Div. Hqrs., working at their Report Centre at present. He
invited me to sit down with him in a quiet place, and we had quite a
chat. He is very informal and cordial; is very popular with all the men
under him. He got his commission recently as subaltern for good work
done out here. He is a very smart looking little officer; extremely mod-
est, and very much resents the article recently published in a Weyburn
paper about him – a real eulogy but all true.

Clements, Mitchell and I returned to "C" Coy last night for billet and
rations, leaving Goodwin on duty at Div. Report Centre as runner for
"C" Coy.[57] Coys were on working party burying cable all night. I slept
in a sandbag shelter behind a tree in the wood north of the house. We
are all in the wood during the day. I am writing, seated at the foot of a
large oak. Aeroplanes of both sides are continually passing overhead.

---

55 5.9: British name for the 150-millimetre (5.9-inch) shell fired by German heavy how-
    itzers.
56 Leeson: James Hubert Leeson (1882–?), MC; attested Valcartier, September 1914.
    Enlisted as a private, Leeson was commissioned as lieutenant in the Canadian Engi-
    neers in February 1916 and subsequently was promoted to captain.
57 Mitchell: Might be John Mason Mitchell (1888–1916), born Scotland; attested Prince
    Albert, May 1914. Killed in action 2 June 1916. Commemorated on the Menin Gate,
    but the "Mitchell" with whom Miller most often associates was still alive as of July.

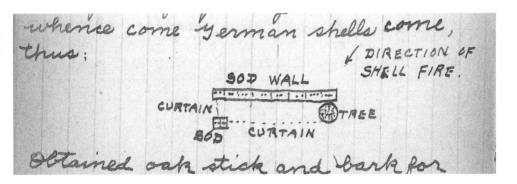

German shells from one battery keep passing on the right and falling over by Report Centre. A 6-in gun is firing from about 40 rods away, giving us quite a shock each time it goes off. Sentries warn us to keep to cover by 3 blasts on their whistles whenever a German plane is in sight. Then the guns cease firing and our anti-aircraft guns open up.

Fri., May 5:

Heavy bombardment away in the south commenced yesterday afternoon and still continues at 9 pm. Guns of every kind have been firing over us all day bombarding the enemy lines. The Germans retaliated feebly with about one shell to ten of ours. This evening they threw 45 heavy shells on a short piece of road in 5 minutes. When it grew dark all guns near here ceased fire and the Germans are not shelling the roads as usual. The rumble in the south never stops for an instant.

Spent yesterday after supper and this afternoon building a bivouac in the woods. Made a wall of sod three feet high facing the direction whence German shells come, thus:

Obtained oak stick and bark for roof from oak tree 3-ft. in diameter shattered by a German shell. Curtains are of sacks.

Thurs., May 11:

Last two days spent at Bde Reserve location H 29 A, were very cloudy, wet and cool; we lived in the house in a small room on third (top) storey. This is a rough plan of the grounds:

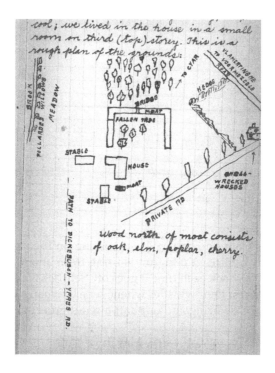

cool; we lived in the house in a small
room on third (top) storey. This is a
rough plan of the grounds:

Wood north of moat consists
of oak, elm, poplar, cherry.

Proceeded to trenches last night, calling at Bedford House to join our
section.[58] This has been a fine chateau and grounds at one time; now
shell-wrecked, though walls and roof are fairly intact. There is a British
cemetery at the rear of the mansion under some large trees. Most of
the large trees that make a veritable park of the extensive grounds are
injured by the shell fire. We crossed Ypres Canal by Bridge 20 to get
to B.H. The canal is now choked with reeds and water plants among
which moor hens or dabchicks may be seen swimming. While we were
at B.H. waiting for darkness to set in, a heavy German bombardment

---

58 "Bedford House" was the name the British gave to the Château Rosendal, a large
   manor home and gardens just outside Zillebeke, south of Ypres. The remains of
   the chateau were used by the British as a headquarters and field ambulance station throughout the war. It is now the site of one of the largest Commonwealth War
   Graves Commission (CWGC) cemeteries on the Western Front.

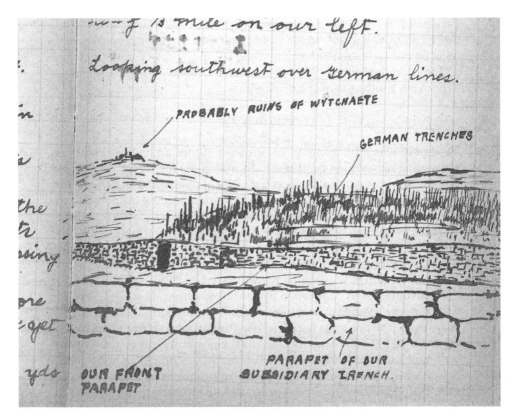

...... ↗ is mile on our left.

Looking southwest over German lines.

PROBABLY RUINS OF WYTCHAETE

GERMAN TRENCHES

PARAPET OF OUR
SUBSIDIARY TRENCH.

OUR FRONT
PARAPET

Ruins of Wytchaete, 11 May 1916.[59]

was in progress on our right front; our fellows were using green flares up at the trenches. We crossed open country until we were almost in the front line, and many stray bullets whizzed about our heads, one passing down through a line of us without hitting a man. This country is more shot-to-pieces than anything I have yet seen. We are on the crest of a low wooded hill facing the Germans 80 yds away across a slight dip on a similar wooded ridge. It seems to be a very uneven bit of country, the ground undulating and partially wooded everywhere. There is hardly a living thing in sight and all that is left of the woods is a wilderness of

59 (Illustration): Wytschaete, Belgium, a fortified town on Messines Ridge.

bare poles. The famous international trench is a 1/2 mile or so away on our right.[60] On our way in we passed the ruins of Voormezeele a mile or so on our right, and at B.H. we could see the Ypres-Comines railway 1/3 mile on our left.

Looking southwest over German lines:

Fri., May 12:

Yesterday was a bit exciting. Lt. Purslow (Blondie) had his bombers registering on German front line with rifle grenades.[61] Fritz came back both morning and late afternoon with rifle grenades and trench mortar bombs. Our fellows had to call up our field guns and use the new Stokes bomb mortar freely to get the affair stopped.[62] Two coy. men and three stretcher bearers were knocked out but none killed; one man, Cpl. Murphy is probably dying with a punctured jugular vein.[63] Howlett of my draft last October, one of the S.B.s had his knees badly smashed.[64] Alex Virtue another S.B. was among the wounded.[65]

I went out with "B" Coy ration party at 10:45 to the ration depot beyond the Engineer's dump. Carrying parties were working there all night, some from 10th Bn., carrying dugout material up to our front line. Nothing must be left there after daylight as the position is quite in the open.

"Stand to" is now 2:45 a.m. as it is beginning to get light by then. Breakfast is at 4:30 a.m. I was on phone midnight to 3:15 a.m., then got mail from Hqrs., water from spring in hillside back there, breakfast,

---

60 International trench: A number of trenches were identified as such, but Miller is probably referring to a length of trench fronting the Ypres Canal that exchanged hands several times over several days of heavy fighting in July 1915.

61 Purslow: John E. Purslow, MC (1891–?), born England; attested Valcartier September 1914. Later received the Military Cross. Transferred to the Royal Flying Corps in March 1918.

62 Stokes mortar: A man-portable British trench mortar invented by Sir Wilfred Stokes (1860–1927). Widely used and adapted, it consisted of the soon-to-be-familiar design of a metal tube, base plate, and bipod. It fired 81-millimetre bombs on a curved trajectory.

63 Murphy: Could not be identified but, remarkably, Cpl. Murphy seems to have survived. Neither the CWGC database nor the Canadian Book of Remembrance includes a Canadian named Murphy who died on or near that date.

64 Howlett: Could not be identified.

65 Virtue: Robert Alexander Virtue (1888–?), born Bowmanville, Ontario, a resident of Margo, Saskatchewan; attested Valcartier, September 1914. Survived having been twice wounded.

BEHIND BEDFORD HOUSE
FRI. MAY 12. 1916:

and had a wash up, so was ready to go to bed by 6:30. Have just found place to wash in brook at bottom of ravine between our right and the international trench which 8th Bn. now hold. 16th Bn. Can. Scottish are on our left.[66]

Very warm weather with uniform layer of stratus cloud and light breezes. Moderately cool nights.

Thurs., May 18:

We are going out to Reserve north of Ouderdom tonight.[67] We have had no serious bombardments during this trip – each day a few whizz-bangs, trench mortar bombs, and rifle grenades. A mortar bomb blew in stretcher-bearers' dugout here in trench 34, wounding Virtue, Howlett

66 16th: The 16th Battalion, Canadian Scottish Regiment, was raised at Valcartier in
     September 1914
67 Ouderdom: Town about five kilometres west of Ypres.

and Ireland.[68] A shell at "C" coy Hqrs. last night wounded Lts. Latter and Smith, Sergt. Biner, and two other men.[69] S.-B. Everett was wounded last night.[70] "Red" Shields, L/cpl. of "B." coy was killed this morning at the front parapet by a bullet through helmet and head.[71] Sergt. Maj. McGlashan has gone to England for his commission.[72]

Very fine warm weather with cool nights.

Relieved by 2nd Can. Bn. about 9:30 p.m.[73] Met S. Emery of old 32nd sigs.[74] Woolley is in England with serious shrapnel wounds in head and arms.[75] Kirk Patrick went on leave and remained sick in England. He is to get a Sergt. Instructor's job in bombing at Shorncliffe. Alexander is still on the job.

The night was quiet save for the usual sniping which scatters bullets all over the area a mile behind the trenches. Walked along Engineers' miniature railway to Ypres-Dickebush Road, thence through Dickebush and up Ouderdom Road. Clements and I separated from the 5 others (Rex, Highton, Goodwin, Lyons, McKenzie) and slept by a hedge at the side of the road 2–5:30 a.m. Had coffee at a house where they had a 4 weeks old kid running around the kitchen, a remarkably cute, nimble creature. The other boys came along at this point and said they had slept in a farmyard for a couple of hours. It was now past sun-up and we proceeded to our cantonment, the Scottish Lines, a mile and a half beyond Ouderdom.

---

68 Ireland: Alexander Ireland (1877–?), born Scotland; attested Winnipeg December 1914.
69 Smith: Lieutenant George Lander Smith died of his wounds 29 May 1916. Buried CWGC Boulogne Eastern Cemetery, France. Later: Lieutenant Ernest Henry Latter, MC (1887–1918), born England; attested Valcartier, September 1914. Died of pneumonia December 1918. Buried Belgrade CWGC Cemetery, Belgium. Biner: Reginald Amsden Biner (1890–1916), born England, attested Valcartier, September 1914. Biner died of his wounds on the evening of 18 May. He is buried in CWGC Lijssenthoek Military Cemetery, Belgium.
70 Everett: Bertie John Everett (1890–?), born England; attested Arcola, Saskatchewan, February 1915.
71 Shields: Actually Hugh Cuthbert Shield (1887–1916), born England; attested Valcartier, September 1914; buried CWGC Woods Cemetery, Belgium.
72 McGalshan: James Stanley McGalshan, MC (b. 1890), born Edinburgh, Scotland; attested Valcartier, September 1914. McGalshan later received his commission and rose to the rank of major.
73 2nd Canadian Battalion: 2nd Battalion (Eastern Ontario Regiment) of the CEF.
74 Emery: Stephen Emery (1890–?), born England; attested Winnipeg, December 1914.
75 Woolley: Could not be identified.

Fri., May 19:

The boys all reached camp by sunrise, had breakfast (the cooks served hot cocoa and fried bacon) and turned in to get some sleep. I had a bath in the horse pond, and by 8:30 am ready to turn in also. It is a perfect morning, green foliage everywhere, and bird music just sublime. This is like a trip home for a rest. We can just hear the guns rumbling away off in the distance.

Wed., May 24:

Yesterday at 3:30–4:30 p.m., Gen. Currie of 1st Div. inspected our Bn. on this parade ground, Scottish lines.[76]

Slept out by hedge last night. On phone duty 4–8 a.m. Very fine warm days and cool nights now. Moon is in last quarter. I am spending spare time studying stars and flowers. Botanizing is good in a small coppice woodlot near camp. Have identified Buttercup, Stitchwort, Herb Robert, Mint, Ground Ivy, Charlock, Bedstraw. Boötes and Corona Borealis are in zenith at 9 p.m.[77]

Fronts about salient have been very quiet for several days. Lively artillery fire towards St. Eloi last night and this morning.

Received a second Flower Guide from Stuart Thompson who is at Shorncliffe. Y.M.C.A. had big sports meet near Poperinghe for all Canadian troops. Many of our boys attended. Bathing parades to Pop. Div'l Baths. I went there with Sigs. parade, thence with two D Mark III phones to Div. Hqrs. where I met Walton of 32nd Sigs.[78] Exchanged phones and returned to camp by Reninghelst and Ouderdom. Spent evening at Botany.

Thurs., May 25:

Showers last night. Uniform stratus clouds much of today, with several light showers. Cool at night but very warm during day.

Duty 8 a.m. to noon. On pass to Pop., noon to 5 p.m. Visited new Canadian cinema in Rue des Chiens. Saw scenes of prairie colonization and fishing on French River, Ontario; a love affair among Alaskan wilds, gold hunting, etc.; a comic keystone film.[79] Poperinghe is still thriving in spite

---

76 Scottish Lines: Colloquial name for a stretch of the front near Poperinghe.
77 Boötes: Northern sky constellation.
78 D Mark III: Portable telephone, carried in a leather case, designed for use in the field.
79 Keystone film: Reference to the Keystone Cops, characters in a series of silent slapstick comedies produced from 1912 to 1917.

of bombs and shells, and everything we require is on sale at reasonable prices. 20th Div. are now established there a week.[80]

Fri., May 26:

Moved to Dickebush huts 8 p.m.

Sat., May 27:

Fine and warm, calm, with uniform light haze of stratus cloud. I gave the signallers their physical drill this morning as Sergt. Rex asked me to do so. Spent day quietly in camp, cleaning up huts and outside, botany, reading, writing; line laid to transport on Ouderdom Rd. where Tibble, McGuire and Coombs are going to take charge.[81]

Sun., May 28:

Fine and warm with gentle breeze. Chaplain held service and preached to us in afternoon among huts under the oak trees; 2nd Bde. Band in attendance.

Mon., May 29:

On phone duty midnight to 4 a.m. It is now quite light by 3 a.m. After duty I did not feel like sleep so walked across fields N.E. of camp until 6 o'clock. Am working hard on plant identification so have a purpose in such walks and derive a good deal of pleasure. Found Shepherd's Needle growing abundantly in a field of rye; scarlet poppies on the banks of a deep ditch; yellow flags in a muddy place where the ditch widened out.

Much aeroplane activity overhead all day long. Germans had three sausage balloons up about the salient by 4:30 a.m. About 9 a.m. one of

---

80 20th: British Army's 20th (Light) Division, one of the new divisions of "Kitchener's Army."

81 Tibble: Herbert Frank Tibble (1894–?), born England, attested Battleford, Saskatchewan, April 1915. Badly wounded in the left leg, September 1916 at Courcelette; returned to Canada April 1917. Coombs: Alfred Coombs (1894–?), born Hamilton, attested Port Arthur, December 1914, transferred to the Royal Flying Corps (see entry of 19 May 1917.) Appointed flying officer in November 1917, he was injured in an accident in December and never flew operationally at the front.

Flowering Plants Identified of Flanders 1916.

1. Brassica sinapis (Wild Mustard, Charlock) — 24 – 5
2. " campestris (common wild Navew) — 26 – 3
3. Tormentilla officinalis (Tormentil) — 24 – 5
4. Raphanus raphanistrum (Wild radish; jointed charlock) — 26 – 3
5. Caltha palustris (Marsh marigold) — 1 – 4
6. Ranunculus sceleratus (Celery-leaved crowfoot) — 28 – 5
7. " aquatilis (water buttercup) — 28 – 5
8. " bulbosus — 16 – 4
9. Geum urbanum (common avens; herb bennet) — 26 – 4
10. Potentilla anserina (silverweed) — 28 – 3
11. Trifolium pratense (Hop trefoil) — 27 – 3
12. Hyacinthus non-scriptus (Bluebell) — 28 – 3
13. Melampyrum pratense (cow-wheat) — 4 – 4
14. Iris pseudacorus (Water flag; yellow flag; corn flag) — 24 – 5
15. Lamium album (white dead nettle) — 28 – 5
16. Primula veris (cowslip; paigle) — 1 – 4
17. Galium aparine (Goose grass; cleavers; catchweed) — 26 – 5
18. Cardamine pratensis (Lady's smock; cuckoo flower) — 28 – 5
19. Capsella bursa-pastoris (Shepherd's purse; pickpocket) — 27 – 5
20. Scandix pecten (needle chervil; shepherd's needle; Venus comb) — 27 – 5
21. Stellaria media (chickweed) — 27 – 5
22. " Holostea (stitchwort; greater stitchwort; white flowered grass) — 26 – 5
23. Bellis perennis (Daisy) — 26 – 5
24. Chrysanthemum leucanthemum (Ox-eye daisy; moon daisy) — 27 – 5
25. Matricaria inodora (corn feverfew; mayweed) — 27 – 5
26. Lonicera album (white dead nettle) — 27 – 5
27. " Tragopogon — 27 – 6
28. Symphytum officinale (comfrey) — 18 – 5
29. Myosotis arvensis (Scorpion grass) — 27 – 5
30. Anthriscus sylvestris (wild chervil) — 26 – 5
31. Carum petroselinum (fool's parsley) — 26 – 5
32. Lychnis diurna (red robin; red campion; red catchfly) — 26 – 5
33. " flos-cuculi (ragged robin; meadow lychnis) — 24 – 5
34. Geranium robertianum (herb Robert) — 25 – 5
35. " molle (cranes bill; dove's foot geranium; dove's foot) — 28 – 5
36. Trifolium pratense (red clover) — 28 – 3
37. Valeriana officinalis (great valerian) — 26 – 3
38. Veronica chamaedrys (Germander speedwell; cat's eye; bird's eye) — 28 – 5
39. Myosotis palustris (Forget-me-not) — 28 – 3
40. Glechoma hederacea (ground ivy; gill-over-the-ground; alehoof) — 27 – 5
41. Ajuga reptans (Bugle; sickle-wort; carpenter's herb; brown bugle) — 23 – 6
42. Nepeta glechoma (ground ivy) — 29 – 5
43. Barbarea vulgaris (yellow rocket; winter cress; St. Barbara's herb) — 29 – 5
44. Polaris gramineus (lesser spear-leaved stitchwort) — 27 – 5
45. Chrysanthemum parthenium (common feverfew) — 29 – 5
46. Papaver rhoeas (scarlet poppy) — 27 – 5
47. " argemone (rough-headed poppy) — 29 – 5

44. Plantago lanceolata (Lamb's tongue; ribwort plantain) — 11 – 5
47. Rumex acetosa (common sorrel) — 11 – 5

Note: An article entitled "The House that Jack Built" appeared in SAT. EVENING POST, Mar. 13, 1915 – a splendid and readable article with detailed description of the process of building and care of material. This was one of a series of three articles appearing in numbers Mar. 6, 13, & 20, 1915.

Note: A teaspoonful of phosphate of limestone in a glass of hot water taken early in morning to cleanse the bowels.

STIMS: Tablets for gas, astringent power, etc.

From childhood, Miller had been a keen observer of the natural world. Even in the midst of war, he kept meticulous field notes, such as this list of flowering plants of Flanders. Credit: Miller family collection.

our battle planes chased a German plane southward over Dickebush, the British being much above the Hun.

Suddenly ours swooped directly down upon the enemy as if to attack him, but passed him, and in a steep narrow spiral dropped down and down until he disappeared head downward behind the trees to the left of Dickebush. I hear that when he swooped to attack his enemy, something went wrong which made it necessary to land at once. This was carried out successfully though the pilot was unconscious and lost two fingers in the engine trouble. We could not be sure whether the unfortunate plane was ours or German, whether he was hit by shell splinters or machine gun fire, and whether he could land safely when coming down so suddenly. It was an astonishing spectacle to see a large plane dive from a height of fully a mile right to the ground in a few seconds.

I learn that a British plane was brought down by German shell fire and wrecked today behind our lines near Zillebeke. A German plane was also brought down behind our lines on the south side of the salient.[82]

After supper I walked across the fields a mile or more north of camp – a warm evening with a uniform grey layer of "stratus" covering the sky. Visited a slough where I found many yellowish green frogs of medium size trilling incessantly; a meadow and choked ditch with a few inches of water under the dank growth of grasses, with Lady's Smock, Buttercups, Ribwort Plantain, Common Sorrel, and a wealth of grasses which I had no means of naming; a hedge and bank with Poppies, Common Feverfew and much White Dead Nettle and Red Campion; a brook and waste field with Avens, Yellow Rocket and Grass Leaved Stitchwort.

A German aeroplane passed right across the salient on a line through Vlamertinghe and Dickebush, shelled all the way by our pom-poms and fired on by a machine gun. None of our planes were near enough to attack it. There was quite a shower of shell fragments and one dead shell fell in the meadow where I was strolling about.

---

82 British plane: Dead was Captain E.W. Barret of 29 Squadron, RFC, flying one of the new De Havilland 2 pushers that would help the British reclaim air supremacy in the summer of 1916.

Tues., May 30:

Frank Gorringe went on leave this morning.[83] Burdon returned from leave on 27th.

Bde. Band provided us with a concert in the open under the trees yesterday pm. This afternoon they gave a concert in the Y.M.C.A. hall. We are confined to the camp area day and night so can appreciate such diversion from the usual monotony. I have just finished reading "The Watchers of the Plains" by Ridgwell Cullum, and am now well into Balfour's "Life of R.L.S."[84]

Wed., May 31:

"Pongo" War, our lineman, went on leave this morning.[85] Bn. moved into trenches S.E. of Zillebeke 8 pm to 12:30 a.m.

Thurs., June 1:

Clements, Goodwin and I are with "B" Coy. in trench 43. We had great difficulty in finding the 10th Bn. Station which we were to relieve. It is a low filthy dugout and we are badly cramped for room. It is in a communication trench 30 yds. from the front line. The Germans from Hill 60 can look down into many of our trenches. At noon, we were heavily bombarded with sausages, many falling near our dugout, wrecking the trenches and parapets. We left our dugout and made our station back near Coy. Hqrs. in a dugout with the two Coy. runners.

An observation balloon, evidently British, appeared at sunset in the south, high in the air behind the German lines, adrift in a light wind from W.S.W. Anti-aircraft guns kept firing at it but failed to make any hits. As it was disappearing in the evening dusk away in the east, an

---

83 Gorringe: Frank Clifton Gorringe (1889 – 1936), born England, attested Valcartier, September 1914. Survived two gunshot wounds; transferred to the RFC in late 1916. He had an outstanding career as a pilot, credited with 14 victories, and earning the Military Cross and the Distinguished Flying Cross. He was promoted to the rank of captain and flight leader in 210 Squadron in 1918.

84 Cullum: Ridgwell Cullum (Sidney Groves Burghard, 1867–1943), British writer of American-style "westerns." Balfour: Graham Balfour (1858–1929), British writer best known for his biography of his cousin Robert Louis Stevenson.

85 War: Should be Warr. See entry 20 February 1916.

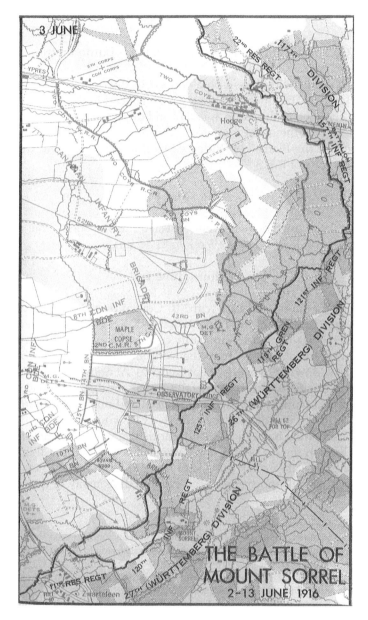

The Battle of Mont Sorel
Note Maple Copse, centre, described in detail by Miller in his entry of
21 June 1916.

aeroplane attacked it, and it soon appeared to be coming down slowly to earth. Its course kept it well within German territory, so there seemed no hope of it escaping.

Gen. Lipsett was in the trenches this afternoon and spoke to several of the boys about the bombardment. No one was injured directly, but Sergt. Rex Lingford of our Section was cut in the head seriously by a fragment of an anti-aircraft shell.

Editor's Note: The Battle of Mont Sorrel

June 2 marks the beginning of the Battle of Mont Sorrel (2–13 June 1916), also known as the Battle of Hill 62, in which two German divisions, backed by heavy concentrations of artillery, launched an attack on the 3rd Canadian Division's positions on the southern flank of the Ypres Salient. Over the coming two weeks the two sides mauled each other terribly, with the Germans initially wresting the high ground from the Canadians and then repulsing a counterattack. In a carefully staged operation, the Canadian Corps, now under the command of Lt. General Julian Byng, supported by the British 20th Light Division, recaptured their lost ground but with heavy loss of life.

Writing from the perspective of an individual soldier, with the inevitable fog of war in his eyes, Miller gives a brief but remarkable account of this often-forgotten battle.

Fri., June 2:

German bombardment of our trenches began about 8 in the morning with mortar bombs, then artillery. Continued all day with a terrific outburst at dark 9 pm. Evidently a mine was put up on our left at 1:10 p.m. for our dugout rocked like a cradle.[86]

Sat., June 3:

Bombardment continued all night with another outburst at dawn. Became weaker towards 5:30 a.m. Reinforcements 7th, 10th and 15th came in between 2 and 4 a.m. Leicester Square became 10th Hqrs. and they took us 3 signallers over as runners. I delivered a message to Bde Report Centre near Battersea Farm at 8 a.m. while a heavy German bombardment was in progress. Goodwin delivered a second message

---

86 Bombardment: According to its war diary, the 5th Battalion, subjected to heavy artillery throughout the day, suffered 10 killed, 32 wounded, and 4 missing.

while Clements and a 10th Bn. Signaller were laying a line from Leicester Square to Bde Report Centre. I attached phone on the earth circuit and we soon had fair communication. At noon Bde ran a metallic line through to us and 7th Bn. took over the station. We went up the communication trench through the wood to find our coy. but learned they had moved to the right on the other coys. of our Bn. hours ago, having been relieved by 7th Bn. We returned to Leicester Square, packed up and made our way back through the communication trench towards Zillebeke. In a hollow behind hedges we found parts of the 16th dug in, so we dug in and remained until night. There was a tile drain with fresh running water opening onto the trench and we had a good lunch with canned food from a parcel addressed to Capt. Pyman who had gone out wounded earlier in the day.[87]

About 8 a.m. parts of the 10th and 7th Bns. assaulted the German positions on our left from which 3rd Div. units had retired on the previous day. Our attack was mostly a failure owing to new wire and heavy machine gun fire. There was a continuous stream of wounded going out across country towards Zillebeke all day and the Germans fired on these with rifles and machine guns as well as the shell fire over the whole area.

At nightfall, rifle fire and flares introduced a terrific artillery battle, but it was impossible to learn what was happening up at the front, whether we or the Germans were attacking. As soon as the German fire had died down, we three crossed to 5th Hqrs. and reported. The boys were pleased to see us as they heard Goodwin and I were wounded and they knew what we had been through. "B" Coy was relieved tonight and has gone out to Dickebush Huts. We three could go too but are remaining at Hqrs. for a while at any rate.

Sun., June 4:

Violent artillery fire at dawn and an attack expected but nothing happened on our front. Steady bombardment on both sides continued during forenoon. I did duty on phone in Col. Dyer's dugout one to six p.m. There was a short bombardment on both sides during evening. Germans frequently put over a few mortar bombs or shells on our position, but by means of heavy retaliation from our field guns, we finally stopped that game.

---

87 Pyman: Captain Pyman (see entry of 16 November 1915) received a gunshot wound to the right hand.

Mon., June 5:

On phone duty in Col's dugout 8 a.m. to 1 p.m. Day passed quietly with light artillery fire from both sides.

Received word last night of a great naval battle in North Sea in which we lost more heavily than the Germans.[88] Wild rumours of every kind are going about among the boys and some are so foolish as to believe them. We believe the naval battle was a substantial victory for us. We believe we have won back almost all the ground which the 3rd Can. Div. lost to the Huns. But it was almost a disaster to us, for had the Huns pressed their advance promptly, they might now be in Ypres and we should be cut off. As it was, ten Saxons separated from their unit, had advanced too far and were caught in Zillebeke village.

Weather cool, windy, cumulus heavy.

Tues., June 6:[89]

At 1 AM our miners blew in a German mine gallery which they had been driving under trench 39 in front of the "Dump".[90] The two galleries ran parallel to each other for some distance and in one place the separating wall was only 7 ft. thick. Our tunnelers could hear the Germans working and shouting and a windlass creaking. As the explosion did not break the surface, it took good effect on the enemy gallery and must have entombed the men who were known to be working there. There was a minute of silence; then a red German flare calling for artillery; but Capt. Bellamy of our "C" coy. sent S.O.S. call and our guns opened simultaneously with those of the enemy.[91] Ours quickly gained command of the situation and within half an hour the enemy

---

88 Naval battle: A reference to the Battle of Jutland, 31 May–1 June 1916. See entry of 8 June.

89 As Miller's diary recounts below, this day saw the 5th Battalion heavily engaged and subjected to a withering artillery bombardment. According to the 5th Battalion's War Diary, it was the conclusion of six days in the line that saw no fewer than 60 officers and men killed and a further 181 wounded and missing.

90 The Dump: Position located just west of Hill 60.

91 Bellamy: George Arthur Bellamy (1876–?) of Abbey, Saskatchewan; attested Valcartier, September 1914. Badly wounded by a bomb fragment to the chest in July 1916 (see entry of 6 July). He subsequently returned to Canada and resigned his commission.

fire had died down. Our guns kept it up some time and gave them a terrible punishment mostly with field guns. Occasional gunfire from both sides during forenoon. At noon two mines went up in the NE part of the salient front and at once S.O.S. were sent in and intense fire opened from both sides from the "Cut" around to Hooge. Continued till 6 p.m. when it gradually died down. Everything in the salient was pounded by the enemy fire, and our artillery all worked at full speed. At our position the trenches on both sides are level, simply blown in and obliterated; the occupants who did not get out to the rear were buried. Men everywhere were blown to pieces or terribly mangled. The machine gun crews in the front line mostly all died at their posts and were buried by the explosion of shells and sausages. Lieut. Purslow ("Blondie", our bombing officer) and Capt. Bellamy went out wounded; Lieut. Taylor was killed.[92]

At 2 a.m. a German prisoner was brought in from "C" coy. Blondie had bombed him out in a party of three from a trench on some disputed ground on our left front. He had run away, but being confused headed for our trench and was taken by Lieut. Conroy. Blondie got his rifle and respirator which he had left in the trench, also a hand grenade which he had thrown at Blondie but which had fallen behind him dead. During this affair, Blondie snatched a burning rifle grenade out of the rifle being fired by one of his men and threw it over the parapet where it exploded and did no harm. Blondie is worshipped and feared by his men, because he is quite devoid of fear himself and leads his men into the greatest danger.

The prisoner was interviewed by Capt. Bellamy with Corpl. Stade as interpreter; then sent to Hqrs. where I was on duty at the Col's phone (3 a.m.).[93] He was a thickset, fat, clean shaven lad of 29 yrs, according to his pay book, but looked much younger. He was a Bavarian from Wurtemburg. I helped Capt. Crombie read the name and printing on the respirator; the name was Zeflr Birke.[94] He was hurried off to Bde. at dawn. The Coy. O.C. had given him rum and food, and the Col. gave

---

92 Taylor: Lieutenant Howard Taylor (1894–1916) of Edmonton, Alberta; attested Edmonton, May 1915; buried in CWGC Larch Wood Cemetery, Belgium.
93 Stade: Corporal (late Captain) Henry George Stade (1895–?), born England; attested Valcartier, 1914.
94 Crombie: Captain William Claude David Crombie (1881–?), born India; attested Winnipeg, December 1914.

him a cigarette and lit it for him before he went away. He seemed terribly frightened.

Wed., June 7:

Relieved by 10th at midnight and came out to camp between Vlamertinghe and Ouderdom.[95] Turned in at 3 a.m. and slept at 2 p.m. Big parcel mail was delivered and I had several of magazines and good things.

Thurs., June 8:

Moved to F camp across the road at 9–10 a.m. Visited camp cinema show in the afternoon, saw Charlie Chaplin and had a good singsong and a laugh; Bde. Band being in attendance.[96] Latest bulletin was thrown on the screen announcing result of naval battle. 28 German ships sunk and 12 interned in Sweden while we lost 16 sunk.[97]

Sergt. Jardine of 32nd Sigs. is here as a Pte., arrived night before last on a small draft of reinforcements and is now taken on the Sig Section.

Fri., June 9:

Spent day quietly being confined to the camp area. Have just heard of Lord Kitchener's death at sea.[98] Canadian mail in, bringing letters from mother and three others.

---

95 10th: The "Fighting Tenth," 10th Battalion CEF, formed at Valcartier in September 1914 from the nucleus of two militia units, the Calgary Rifles and Winnipeg Light Infantry.

96 Chaplin: Charlie Chaplin (1889–1977) was a rising star at the time, having made films only since 1914.

97 Naval battle: The Battle of Jutland (31 May–1 June 1916), a major naval battle fought between the British and German fleets off Denmark's Jutland peninsula. Tactically, the balance of ships lost favoured the Germans. The figures reported by Miller, "28 German ships sunk … while we lost 16," correspond to the number of the battleships that the Royal Navy and German High Seas Fleet *deployed* rather than lost.

98 Kitchener's death: Kitchener was en route to Russia for a series of face-to-face talks with officials when his cruiser, HMS *Hampsire*, struck a mine and sank west of the Orkneys.

Tues., June 13:[99]

The days pass quietly, each one bringing news of further Russian successes against the Austrians.[100] We are on the alert day and night with discussions and prospects of the big attack soon to be made by us from the salient. Guns and munitions and troops are on the move all the time, the roads are full day and night. There must be enough ammunition in this salient to blast a way to Brussels.

Cloudy, rainy weather for the past week has greatly favoured our preparations and there has been no chance for aeroplane work by the enemy. On the only brief occasions when enemy air reconnaissance was possible, the sky was kept full of our planes of all sizes and types. We hear all kinds of wild rumours about what is going on; we do know for certain that a terrible punishment is in store for the Germans behind and around Ypres.

It is 1:15 a.m., cool, windy, raining lightly, a very dark night. The road by camp is crowded with traffic going in both directions. North, east and south the night is torn by the flashes of heavy guns, averaging one every two seconds, some firing from positions not far from our camp.

We lie in camp awaiting orders, eagerly watching to see what Canadian troops are going up to the front. Our Bde went up yesterday and two of our pigeon-men, Pells and Phillips, went up at the same time.[101] We had our semi-annual bath at Reninghelst on Sunday and are kept confined to camp all the time. Visited the camp picture show last evening, our Bde Band in attendance, and had an hour of hearty laughter and most welcome enjoyment.

Our counter-attack on the German positions east of Zillebeke was made about one this morning. It was preceded and accompanied by a terrific bombardment by our guns. All our old trenches from 46 to 59 were carried and on Mt. Sorrel the German trenches were also taken. The 1st and 3rd Bns. are holding the position while the 13th and 16th are consolidating. The official dispatch from Div. says 100 prisoners including two officers, but men from the front line report at least 250 prisoners.

---

99 On this day the Canadians launched a major counterattack, recapturing most of the ground lost since 2 June. In just under two weeks, the Canadians suffered 8,000 casualties, including over 2,500 dead.

100 Russian successes: A reference to the Brusilov Offensive (after Russian general Aleksei Brusilov), a successful but very costly battle fought between the Russian Army and the Central Powers, June to September 1916.

101 "Pigeon-men": Carrier pigeons continued to be used extensively throughout the war to carry messages.

10th Bn. are in E camp and I met Geo. Leeson and Macdonnel; we went to camp cinema in the afternoon.

We moved to Woodcote House into reserve position at night, going by bus and lorries to a point east of Vlamertinghe, and marching from there. It has rained heavily at intervals all day, so marching across the field routes was very heavy.

Wed., June 14:

There were no telephone lines that would work, so we slept all morning. There was a very heavy bombardment by our guns about 1 a.m. to spoil a counter-attack by Fritz. The cannonade has continued fairly heavy all day. We hear our fellows cannot consolidate because of the water and the incessant German shelling. Parties were up last night carrying out dead and wounded. Four wounded Germans passed here in the ambulance at noon.

Weather keeps cool and cloudy with frequent rain.

Returned to F camp at night.

Thurs., June 15:

5th and 8th Bns. occupy this camp, while 10th is in E camp. Macdonnel came over in afternoon to tell me Geo. Leeson was wounded last night in arm and side and is now on way to England.[102] We moved to D camp at night.

Cool, cloudy and showery.

Fri., June 16:

Partly cloudy and warmer. Observation balloons are up and aeroplanes flying about for first time in many days.

Since the attack of morning (of) 13th, our Bn. has supplied work parties every night to the front line. The trenches are deep in oozy mud and full of dead and wounded of both ours and enemy. New prisoners are still being brought in. The last 44 of our wounded were brought out last night. We hear our attack spoiled a German attack which was to have commenced an hour later. Our artillery

---

102 Leeson: Leeson spent the next six months in various hospitals. He returned to front-line service in early 1917.

did terrible execution and upset all their plans. We now hold more than 400 prisoners and more ground than we had previously lost. Sergt. Paton of our Pioneers brought out a great many souvenirs this morning, including a rifle, flare pistol, field glasses, gas helmet, steel helmet, letters, diaries, post cards, paper money, prayer book, etc.[103] Half the boys have more souvenirs than they can carry now. But it has cost us dearly in men.

Sun., June 18:

Went in busses to baths at Pop a most delightful ride.[104]

Tues., June 20:

Weather keeps cool and cloudy. Moved to railway dugouts from D Camp at night. Left our packs at transport. Had a feed on arrival and turned in by midnight.

Wed., June 21:

Woke for breakfast at 8. Lolled about reading and chatting during day. Had chat with Col. Dyer on philosophy and poetry. He has his M.A. in Philosophy. He derives much of his philosophy from men as they are, although giving the literature of philosophy an important place. He keeps a newspaper clipping of a poem by Rupert Brooke and thinks in it is solved the problem of what we are. "A Pulse of the Eternal Mind".[105]

On working party with 6 other Sigs. and coys. to Maple Copse at 10:30 p.m. to 2:30 a.m. Slept 5:30 to 10 p.m. We began to run on summer fast time a week ago.[106] Zillebeke village is little but a heap of debris now. There are still dead Canadians lying unburied up in Maple Copse since the big attack. The whole surface of the ground is a shapeless mess of

103   Paton: Could not be identified.
104   Nickname for Poperinghe
105   Rupert Brooke: British poet and sailor (1887–1915). "A pulse of the eternal mind" is a quotation from Brooke's most famous poem, *The Soldier* (1914), which captures the romanticism and idealism felt by some soldiers in the early years of the war.
106   Summer fast time: Daylight savings.

broken trees, shell holes and ruined trenches. It is by far the worst sight I have ever seen, and the smells are sickening.[107]

Thurs., June 22:

Gould, a signaller, recently attached, was shot through mouth, neck and shoulder this morning on the working party by a German sniper's bullet.[108]

We were working in front line cleaning out trench and building new parades. The Huns must have been suspicious for once in a while they would shoot a flare over us and a sniper would fire a few rounds into our position. They are evidently repairing trenches as fast as us, for there were few flares and little or no fire, especially on our left.

A British plane was brought down by a Hun, and fell midway between us and Ypres at 11:30 a.m.[109]

Weather mostly clear and warm.

Fri., June, 23:

Pongo Warr, Jardine and 2 others last night crossed from left of Mt. Sorrel into a German trench by mistake. They were looking for souvenirs on the ground recently fought over and passed between our 4th Bn. bombing posts where our front line trench has been obliterated, entering the first trench they came to. Jumping down from the parapet, they saw a sign "Der Urinal", entered a dugout in the same bay, struck matches, and finding no occupants but German rifles and equipment, they realized for the first time where they were. Taking the two rifles and equipment, they turned to run. A German was shooting flares from the next bay while a sniper was working beside him. Pongo watched at the turn by the traverse, revolver in hand, while the other three climbed out of the

---

107 Maple Copse: The site of an Advanced Dressing Station, where battle casualties were initially received. As Miller observes, the adjacent cemetery was heavily shelled late in the fighting during the Battle of Mont Sorrel. Today, Maple Copse is the site of one of the CWGC's most unusual cemeteries, in which most headstones include the notation "Believed to be buried in this cemetery …" because most of the dead could not be identified prior to their reburial.

108 Gould: Note that Gould is not listed in the CWGC database as having died at that time.

109 British plane: This was an FE-8 single-seat pusher of 29 Squadron flown by Captain Lionel Herbert Sweet (1893–1916).

trench and started back, Pongo following last. It was every man for himself and they had to flop every few yards when flares were shot over them. Eventually they all got back safely though badly scared, and scratched, with clothes somewhat torn in the barbed wire. Jardine threw his rifle away, but Pongo brought out a Mauser rifle with two sets of belt pouches and bayonet.[110] One of the bayonets is of the saw edge variety so much discussed at one time in the papers. It is all steel handle and blade and the teeth are on the blunt back of the blade but do not extend to within 5 inches of the point. The teeth are arranged rip-saw fashion and are evidently intended for sawing wood, so form a very useful tool.

Heavy bombardment in S.W. beyond St. Eloi all evening.

Sun., June 25:

At 5 p.m. our aeroplanes bombed the German observation balloons around the salient, forcing 5 of them to descend hurriedly, and probably destroying one up the railway S of us. The air was exceptionally clear, and the sky was probably a third overcast with great flat cumulus clouds. A number of our planes flew about at a moderate height to draw enemy fire and observation while the bomb-droppers above the clouds approached their objectives unseen and unexpected. Suddenly incendiary bombs began dropping from the clouds upon two of the balloons which descended on the double. Each bomb left a column of smoke from clouds to earth, and some burst into an umbrella-shaped mass of falling fragments, leaving a smoke formation like a medusa jelly fish hanging beneath the clouds. Our planes dominated the position all evening and apparently had no losses.

Capt. Nash is buried in the field between railway dugouts and ration farm. There are many Canadians in this little cemetery.[111]

I have spent the time reading "La Grande Illusion" and memorizing poetry, for we have had nothing to do except the work party one night; there are eleven of us on one phone station.[112] Woodcote Farm was twice

---

110 Mauser: Probably the Gewehr 98, the standard German bolt-action service rifle. Bayonet: The "sawtooth" or "sawback" bayonet referred to here was a serrated bayonet phased out of service. It created hideous wounds and Allied soldiers threatened retaliation against captured German soldiers possessing one.

111 Cemetery: Now the site of CWGC Railway Dugouts Burial Ground, enclosing nearly 2,500 graves, of which 551 are known to be those of Canadians.

112 La Grande Illusion: Probably *The Great Illusion* (ca. 1910), by Norman Angell (1892–1967), British writer and politician. The book argued that the economic consequences of modern war would be so severe as to deter any country from fighting.

shelled this time in, and our sigs moved thence to Canal dugouts. I met Macfadden [? *Illegible*] of old 32nd who is a 4th Bde sig.[113] Had several interesting chats with Col. Dyer and Capt. Madden, our chaplain.[114] Lieut. Hedley came to the Bn. last night and is posted to "B" coy.[115] I have spent several hours studying the ruins of Ypres through a pair of binoculars. The east side was most visible from our position.

Mon., June 26:

Relieved by 16th, came out to Scottish Lines, arriving at 2 a.m. Marched to Poperinghe to baths 2–4 p.m. Weather very warm, but partly cloudy with few scattered showers.

Heavy attack and bombardment last night from 10 p.m. on Hooge front. We do not know result. We frequently hear incessant rumbling away in the south these days and see the sky all aflash low down on the horizon at night. The booming has been going on all today.

Tues., June 27:

Reported sick to Capt. Brown;[116] taken to 1st Fld. Amb. D.S.[117] Vlamertinghe on march; thence by Horse Ambulance wagon at 7 p.m. to D.R.S. near Abeele, arriving at dark.[118] Rained intermittently all day.

Thurs., June 29:

Time passes quietly. We are well fed here, have little to do, and are left much to ourselves in quiet. There are 14 men in this hut from several Bns.

---

113   MacFadden: Could not be identified.

114   Madden: Captain (later Major) Chaplain Ambrose Madden, DSO (1875–?). Severely wounded in March 1918.

115   Hedley: This is the same Lieutenant Harold Douglas Hedley under whom Miller trained as a signalling officer in Manitoba. See entry of 10 January 1915.

116   Brown: Probably Captain Dr. Harold Ernest Brown (1892–?), Canadian Army Medical Corps, born United States, attested Kingston, Ontario, November 1915.

117   Fld. Amb. D.S: Field Ambulance Dressing Station. "Field Ambulance" was a British and Imperial term for mobile medical hospitals, as opposed to ambulances in the sense of an emergency medical vehicle, typically situated behind the battle zone. Dressing stations were used for applying dressings (bandages, etc.)

118   D.R.S.: Division Rest Station, a unit that cared for the sick, injured, and lightly wounded, but differed from a hospital in that stays tended to be relatively short. Miller was diagnosed with "phernatis," an inflammation of the foreskin, at this time.

of the 1st Div. From noon to four p.m. I walked over to the Bn. for my
mail and returned. Weather bright, partly cloudy, with fresh west wind.
Natives are cutting hay crops and hoeing potatoes and beets. Hops are
up nearly to top of poles. Broad beans are in bloom. Barley is heading
out and rye filling, heads already bending down with weight of grain.
Oats not headed yet. Red clover nearly done blooming.

Fri., June 30:

Heavy bombardment all last night along entire front of Ypres-Kemmel.
Papers say a systematic heavy bombardment of German lines from Ypres
to the Somme has been going on since 24th inst.[119]

Editor's Note: The Battle of the Somme

*Miller's entry of 30 June refers to the bombardment that preceded the Battle of the
Somme, the Anglo-French offensive launched 1 July 1916. Fought where the British and
French armies linked arms astride the Somme River, the Somme was by far the British
Army's largest offensive of the war to date. But Britain's high hopes for a decisive victory
were quickly dashed. The first day of the offensive saw the British Fourth Army suffer
nearly 60,000 casualties, of whom more than 19,000 were killed, the heaviest losses ever
suffered in a single day by the British Army.*

*The Canadian Corps did not join the offensive until its third phase began in September,
but on the left flank of the offensive, near the village of Beaumont Hamel, the Newfoundland Regiment suffered a terrible fate on 1 July. Ninety per cent of the small dominion's
regiment were killed or wounded in an attack that lasted about 30 minutes. Newfoundland
joined Canada in 1949. In the rest of Canada, 1 July marks Canada Day, a celebration
of Canadian Confederation, but in Newfoundland and Labrador 1 July is also Memorial
Day, commemorating the devastating losses suffered by the regiment that day in 1916.*

*The first of July was the worst day but only the beginning of what devolved into
a bloodletting that did not end until the offensive ground to a halt in the November
rains. By then, nearly half a million British and 200,000 French soldiers had been killed
or wounded in exchange for what some critics charged were insignificant advances,
amounting to perhaps eight kilometres in depth in all. But the German forces had suffered enormously, too, in desperate fighting to hold back the Anglo-French advance. The*

---

119 Inst.: Instant, now largely obsolete meaning "of the present month." Heavy bom-
     bardment: A reference to the massive artillery barrage, begun 24 June, against
     German positions along the British 4th Army's front in preparation for the Somme
     offensive.

half-million casualties the German forces suffered, coupled with simultaneous heavy losses at Verdun and on other fronts, strained the German Army to the breaking point.

The Battle of the Somme might more properly be referred to as the Somme Campaign, as it passed through distinct phases and consisted of a large number of sub-battles, several of which Miller references in his entries below. He and the rest of the Canadians observed the first two months of the offensive from the relative quiet of the Ypres Salient, 100 kilometres to the north, but entered the fray directly in September.[120]

Sat., July 1:

Very bright and warm; many wool-pack clouds & a fresh W. wind. Heavy bombardment on this front this morning for several hours about dawn. We hear that our aviators have bombed and burned many of Fritz's observation balloons around Ypres lately. Everybody is optimistic now because all the Allies are fighting and winning successes simultaneously. But few think the war will end this year.

Visited Demols at Berthen 2–7 p.m. and had a very hearty welcome, meeting three 9th D.L.I. boys who had called there.[121] The country there is wonderful for its beauty and the views from the hills are delightful.

Terrific bombardment began at 9 p.m. and continued till dawn over the hills to the south, probably on the Armentières front. The ground here shook with the roar of heavy guns and we could not sleep until the row had abated.

Sun., July 2:

Returned to Bn. transport for duty and ordered to remain there. German planes bombed the salient after dark, but none fell within half a mile of our position. Cpl. Leach, Macdonald, Bill Edwards, and I are living in a tent in charge of the telephone station.[122]

---

120 There is a vast literature on the Battle of the Somme. William Philpott, *Three Armies on the Somme* (New York: Alfred A. Knopf, 2010), presents a balanced overview.

121 D.L.I.: Durham Light Infantry, a British Army regiment.

122 Leach: Corporal (later Lieutenant) Robert Onebye Leach, born England; attested Valcartier, September 1914. Killed in action, 28 September 1918. Buried in CWGC Haynecourt British Cemetery, France.

Mon., July 3:

Very fine and warm. Much aeroplane activity in the salient.

Tues., July 4:

A German plane dropped 2 bombs a mile east of here just after sunset last night. Weather very hot until thunderstorms came up at 2 p.m. and cooled the air.

Thurs., July 6:

Battn. coming out to Scottish Lines tonight. I left transport (F.P.) at sunset and went to Scottish Lines to take over phone.

Fri., July 7:

Battn. arrived about 3 AM., had breakfast and turned in. I was on phone till 2 p.m. Heavy bombardment at dawn towards Neuve Eglise. The air throbbed with the faint rolling of a distant heavy bombardment in the south all day.

Sat., July 8:

Pay and clothing parades in morning. I got a new tunic; got last in Shorncliffe 9 months ago. We are confined to camp, save for the passes issued. The boys are employing the time at baseball, cricket, pitching horseshoes, etc.

Distant bombardment lasted much of day, same as yesterday.

Sun., July 9:

Service on parade ground at ten am. Inspection of Bn. by Brig. Gen. Lomas at 4 p.m.[123]

---

123 Lomas: Brigadier (later Major General Sir) Frederick Oscar Warren *Loomis*, DSO (1870–1937). Loomis rose from the rank of private in the Canadian militia in 1886 to commander of the 3rd Canadian Division by October 1918.

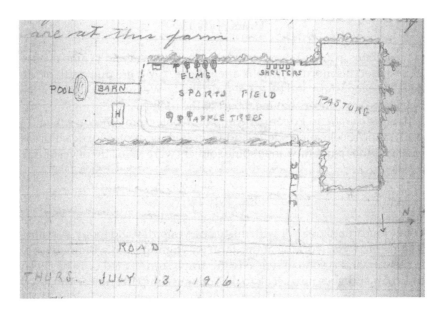

All evening, to the right of Ypres towers, we watched the smoke and flame of a heavy bombardment above the tree tops on the horizon. Mines seemed to go up in the beginning of the fight.

Tues., July 11:

I was taken on Sig. Staff in last night's orders. Lieut. Hedley, formerly 32nd Bn. S.O., who came to France a week ago, is to be our S.O. now.[124] Marched at 2 p.m. via Reninghelst and Abeele to billets near aerodrome.[125] Sigs., Pioneers, Runners, and Bn. Hqrs. are at this farm.

---

124 S.O.: Signals Officer.
125 Aerodrome: The Abeele Aerodrome, located along the Belgian-French border. Now the site of the CWGC Abeele Aerodrome Military Cemetery, which, ironically, does not include any flyers' graves.

Thurs., July 13:

Have phones at A and B coys now. Mitchell, Oswin and I came over to A coy billet this morning to look after phone.[126] We are due north of Mt. des Cats Monastery and by the aerodrome.[127] We live in the attic of the house, the coy officers having a part of the room.

Bathing parade to Poperinghe in p.m. Tibble from "B" coy stn. and I walked to Abeele and rode to and from Pop. on motor lorries. Pop. is shelled quite frequently now; some soldiers were killed there yesterday by shells.

Fri., July 14:

Cool, cloudy and foggy or with misty rain yesterday and today. A young Belgian of 21 yrs. working at this farm was fighting and wounded early in the war, and is soon to return to the army. Another lad of 19 has been called up and goes next week to the training camp in France. The hired girl here is almost an exact likeness of Eunice Forsythe in height, build and features and is 19 yrs old.

Wed., July 19:

Have had a very pleasant 9 days back in this quiet farming country. Have watched the aeroplanes going and coming, starting up and landing, and last night we saw two looping the loop. "Compree" and I have spent several pleasant hours with the three St. Germain girls (Judith, Laura and Margaret) chatting and working with them while hoeing beans.[128] These are three very fine girls in looks, manners, and physique quite superior to most of the farm girls in this district. Judith was a schoolmate of Lucie Demols at Abeele school.

Compree, Bob Reed, and I came to transport station south of Ouderdom to take over from Bob Leach, Bill Edwards, and Macdonald. Pells came down from Mt. Des. Cats hospital and has been telling us about the Trappiste monks there. We three got a ride in a motor lorry from Abeele to Reninghelst and walked the remaining distance.

---

126 Oswin: Bertin Oswin (1884–?), born England; attested Moosejaw, September 1914.
127 Aerodrome: Abeele Aerodrome, mentioned above.
128 Compree: Could not be identified.

British offensive north of Somme R. is going ahead and latest captures are Ovillers and Longueval villages.

Sat., July 22:

Bill Babbington (Runner) and Pongo Warr are living with us three in a tent here at transport.[129]

Last evening I walked to Reninghelst and attended a concert of mostly 26th Bn. given by a civilian English elocutionist in the Y.M.C.A. marquee. He gave us Alfred Noyes' "Highwayman", "The Flight of Emily" from David Copperfield, "The Bolivar" and "Gunga Din" from Kipling, and a selection from Mark Twain. All was well done and very enjoyable.[130]

McGuire was wounded yesterday by a rifle grenade. The Bn. are in front of Hill 60 left of "cut". Rec'd nine Can. letters yesterday.

Sun., July 23:

Bill Babbington and I wheeled to Pop. at 3 p.m. to guide a draft from depot to our transport. These chaps came from 68th Bn. of Regina. I met among them the two Cook brothers of Blackwood, Sask.[131]

Our new observation balloon was installed and tried out a short distance east of Ouderdom this afternoon. A German plane appeared in the clouds above it after its first ascent, but was soon driven off by our guns and planes.

Mon., July 24:

This balloon was shelled by a heavy gun from over St. Eloi late in the p.m. A salvo of two shells as it lay ready to ascend. It rose at once to the clouds. Two more shells came; then the car was moved west of

---

129 Babbington: Could not be identified. Only one Babbington is listed as having served in the CEF, Issac (Ralph) Babbington, who did not arrive in France until 1917. No Babington served in the 5th Battalion.

130 Noyes: Less well known today than Dickens, Kipling, and Twain (the others whose works were read at the concert), Alfred Noyes (1880–1858) was an English poet and author best known for the ballad "The Highwayman" (1906) and some of his later science fiction works.

131 68th Battalion: An infantry battalion of the CEF, authorized in April 1915. Recruited in and around Regina, Saskatchewan, the unit subsequently was absorbed by the 32nd Reserve Battalion. Cook brothers: Could not be identified.

Ouderdom taking the balloon in tow. Two more shells came there, so
the whole apparatus was taken away. Another shell fell in Ouderdom
late at night. There were two killed and 8 wounded, chiefly R.F.C. men,
though some artillery limbers were caught while passing on the road.

Tues., July 25:

Walked to Reninghelst to spend the evening at the Y.M.C.A. reading Ben
Franklin's autobiography. We get the previous days papers at Ouderdom
or Reninghelst by going over on wheel for them.

Wed., July 26:

We four played "500" till midnight yesterday and till 3:30 this afternoon.[132] I have just learned the game. Spades 40, Clubs 60, Diamonds
80, Hearts 100. No trumps 120. Use Joker and all down to the black
fours inclusive. Deal ten each and 3 in Missy. Each player can only
bid once.

   In evening I went to Scottish Lines to take over lines and phone for
our Bn.

Thurs., July 27:

The Sigs. arrived at camp at about one a.m. They report a fairly quiet
time but about 45 casualties of whom 12 were killed. Bill Lyons went
away with a sprained ankle. Sergt. McDougal who was in Paris with
Maj. Page for the Fête July 14 was killed by a 5.9 shell while sleeping
in his booby in the parapet.[133] The Germans put a mine up on the 7th
in trench 29, but our fellows were forewarned and got away with only
2 killed while they laid a trap and caught 50 German prisoners with
machine guns in the crater.[134] So an enemy mine was turned to our
advantage.

---

132 500: A card game derived from euchre and bridge.
133 McDougal: Actually Sergeant John *MacDougall* (1889–1916), born Scotland, attested
     Valcartier, September 1916. Buried in CWGC Railway Dugouts Burial Ground,
     Belgium. Fête July 14: Bastille Day, France's national holiday.
134 Mine: Refers to an action fought by the 7th Battalion 25 July 1916.

Mon., July 31:

Have been in the habit of going to Scottish Lines or to Reninghelst each morning to buy papers. A bulletin in Reninghelst yesterday morning announced the Russian capture of Brody and defeat of the Austrians before Stanislaus.[135]

Weather is fine, clear and very hot, with heavy mists at night. We three lie around the tent minding phone, reading, etc. all day. The boys at Bn. are in a series of baseball games and have just defeated the 13th and 7th Bns.

This front has been unusually quiet for several days. Our planes are busy making bombing raids every day to the E. and S.E. of here.

Tues., Aug. 1:

Bn. moved from Scottish Lines to Victoria Lines west of Reninghelst in the evening. Transport and Q.M. stores moved to new lines 60 rods east of Busseboom. We were busy all evening laying an enamelled wire line to Bde. and putting up our tent.

Fri., Aug. 4:

We now have a short T line on 2nd Bde. transport line. I walked to Reninghelst and Bn. Wednesday and today. The weather is hot and dry. The roads very dusty. Bought a French watch in Reninghelst for thirteen francs.

Sun., Aug. 6:

Compree, Bob Reid and I reported at Victoria Lines, relieved by Haydon, Gorringe, and Lyons.[136] Bn. marched to trenches in evening. Compree, Highton, Phillips and I went with Hq. limber to Transport, thence to trenches.[137] Ration limbers got lost a mile from Transport, then could not find ration depot, drove in by Langhof Chateau and put water cart

---

135 Brody: An additional reference to the Brusilov offensive. Brody is a city in western Ukraine, which included one of Europe's oldest and most important Jewish communities.

136 Lyons and Reid: Could not be identified.

137 Limber: A two-wheeled cart.

in a shell hole where it stuck fast and had to be abandoned for time being. Finally we found our new home and settled in for the night. Don Hay stayed at Transport with a bad knee, so I am to cook for the Hq. signallers.

Tues., Aug. 8:

Very fine weather. Our arty. breaks out frequently with bursts of fire both night and day, but Fritz seldom replies.

Thurs., Aug. 10:

I visited the crater and canal bank and lock areas this morning.[138] This is said to be the largest mine crater on the Western front.

We were relieved by 5th C.M.R.'s at night and came out to Dominion Lines. Phillips and I came out with Hq. limber. On arrival I walked over to Trspt. and got my pack from the Sigs. tent. We had cocoa and bacon before turning in.

Fri., Aug. 11:

Got up about noon and spent the day cleaning up and resting. Compree and Oswin have been cutting hair nearly all day. Moggy Norman is back to us and Ted Veale from hospital. We all know what is ahead of us and we are happy at the prospect of a change. We are tired of Belgium and will be glad to get over into France. Everyone has great esteem for French people and many of us have friends over there. The Belgians are much inferior to the French we have met.

Sat., Aug. 12:

Marched away from Dominion Lines at 6 pm to Connaught Lines where we spent the night. This camp is a large meadow surrounded by a row of tall trees on each side, with one line of tents clear round.

Editor's Note: In the entries that follow, Miller describes the 5th Battalion's redeployment from the Ypres Salient to France, where its men billeted around Houlle, some 60

---

138 Crater: Might refer to the crater left by the German mine referred to on 27 July 1916. Canal: Probably the Ypres-Comines Canal.

kilometres west of Ypres. There they rested, refitted, and trained for redeployment to the Somme with the rest of the Canadian Corps at month's end.

Sun., Aug. 13:

Left Connaught Lines 6:30 a.m. via ABEELE to billets beyond STEEN-VOORDE. We were inspected in column of route by Bde. Gen. Lomas and by former Bde. Gen. Lipsett. Arrived at billet in a farmhouse and barn 10:30 a.m. We are half a mile out from town on the Steenvoorde-Hazebrouck Road. Bearings from this billet:

Steenvoorde spire	48°
Cassel hill	280°
Windmill "A"	291°
Windmill "B"	323°
Bearings from Windmill "A"	
Steenvoorde spire	91°
Cassel hill	272°
Windmill "B"	87°
Terdeghem spire	217°
Mt. Des. Chats monastery	119°
Bearing from Windmill "B"	
A windmill at	52°

Distance billet to Steenvoorde spire judged to be 1/2 mile.

In evening strolled across country to Terdeghem. Binders are being used on many of the farms about here, and much of the wheat and oats is cut. I had interesting chats with three French boys. They said King George is supposed to be at Cassel, where a Hun plane dropped bombs this afternoon.[139] These lads speak French and Flemish, the old people use Flemish, but the boys understood all I said and I understood them. We could see the spires of Winnezeele and Oudezeele in the distance.

Mon., Aug. 14:

Reveille at 4 a.m., marched off at 5:30 and from Bn. rendezvous at 6 a.m. Passed through Cassel, Zuitpeen, Nordpeen and arrived Lederzeele about 1:30 where we went into scattered billets. We Hq. details are at a

---

139 King George V did, in fact, visit France and stayed at Cassel 12–16 August 1916.

As Miller's diary indicates, George V was indeed at Cassel,
depicted here with senior officers, 15 August 1916. Credit: Royal Collection
Trust / © His Majesty King Charles III 2023.

farm on edge of town. Mr. Hedley is very good to us, bought chocolate and gum for us on the march, inspects our feet both before and after each march and sees that we are supplied with iodine. Ted Veale was returned to hospital from Dominion Lines and Bert Honey was sent away with incipient para-typhoid from Steenvoorde billet.[140] Goodwin and I strolled about the village this evening, bought some ripe plums and visited the church and cemetery.

Tues., Aug. 15:

Left Lederzeele billet 9:30 a.m. and marched through Watten to billet between Ganspette and Houlle, arriving at 1 p.m. In passing around brow of hill before descending into Watten, we had a fine view of all the broad valley to the S. and W. where St. Omer lies.[141]

A number of us bathed in a tiny canal in the chateau grounds across the road as soon as we arrived. In the late p.m. we had a fine swim in the ship canal by Houlle brick works.

Wed., Aug. 16:

Flag drill in a.m. in pasture field facing chateau. We are billeted in a small barn behind an estaminet, the Sigs. by themselves. There is a penny-in-the-slot piano in the estaminet which we keep going with our spare pennies during open hours.[142] The people are very nice and treat us well. There are Mme. and M. Ghier and Eugenie and Georgette Ghier of 11 and 1 years age.

Fri., Aug. 18:

Sam Hughes met us and spoke to us in a field 1/4 mile west of this billet at 9 a.m.[143] The 5th and 7th Bns. were together. The ladies from the chateau across the road were there as spectators and met Sam.

---

140 Honey: Herbert A. Honey (1893–1962), born England; attested Valcartier, September 1914.

141 Houlle: Small town (population in 1914 about 300) eight kilometres northwest of St. Omer, France. St. Omer itself was a far more substantial town of about 12,000 and an important logistical hub for the RFC in France.

142 Penny-in-the-slot: A player piano.

143 Hughes: Sir Sam Hughes (1853–1921), Canada's controversial minister of militia.

Sat., Aug. 19:

Parade in the morning as usual. In pm we all went swimming and fishing to the Houlle canal. I caught one nice roach for all my afternoon and evening's work. But we do have lots of enjoyment out of it.

Sun., Aug. 20:

Parades and training in the a.m. In p.m. Bn. sports at canal by HOULLE Briqueterie.

Mon., Aug. 21:

In preparation for Div'l field day tomorrow, the Bde. rehearsed the attack and went over the ground today.[144] We were out 7:30 a.m. to 4:30 p.m., passing through Houlle, Moulle, and Cromette. The training area near the latter comprises some fine open, rolling, almost treeless country, affording some excellent views of wide stretches of country.

Tues., Aug. 22:

Div'l field day. Marched away from billet at 7 a.m. to Leulines E. of Zudausques. Spent day in attack and reached billet again by 4:30 p.m. Bathed in Liette Creek behind chateau in evening.

Wed., Aug. 23:

Duty with Oswin 4–8 a.m. Swim in p.m. in Houlle canal. Goodwin and Pells brought in a nice mess of small fish which Stokes gun bombs on practice blew up in the canal.

Thurs., Aug. 24:

A Bde. field day. 5th and 7th Bns. retired on the southern edge of Cormette valley from a line E. and W. through LEULENE, driven back by 8th and

---

144 Divisional Field Day: Refers to a large, division-level tactical exercise, usually in preparation for an imminent attack.

10th Bns. On our way home we had a fine clear view of Cassel hill and Mt. des Cats, the air being unusually clear.

Goodwin and I went to canal in evening, swam, and helped some Scotties and C.E.'s bomb fish.[145]

Sun., Aug. 27:

Parades have been as usual, but frequent showers spoiled our outdoor work yesterday. Church parade this morning, I am bull-cook today.[146] Bde. left yesterday at 3 p.m. so we have had no phone duty since.

Swam in the canal by Houlle Bricqueterie yesterday p.m. & to-day.[147] We are packing up this evening, expecting to leave Hellebroucq tonight at 2:30 a.m.[148]

Mon., Aug. 28:

Left Hellebroucq billet at 2 a.m. Had tea in the road from Coy. field kitchens as the Bn. was formed up for marching off. Passed through Houlle, Moulle, St. Martins around St. Omer to Arques. Entrained 7 am and proceeded by St. Omer, Watten, Calais, Boulogne, Etaples, Noyelle, Abbeville, to Candas. Detrained about 4 p.m. and marched to billets in Fieffes.

This is a very poor place – the people are mean and have nothing to sell, even coffee is 2 1/2 pence a cup.[149] The billet is dark and filthy and the people look upon us with suspicion. Goodwin, Oswin, and I are living in a half-cave in the hillside in the woods across the road.

Wed., Aug. 30:

Left billets at Fieffes 7 a.m., the entire Bde. marching in column by Montrelet and Belleville to billets in Hérissart. It rained during the whole march: 7–12 noon. This country is all very open and resembles

---

145 C.E.'s: Canadian Engineers. Bomb fish: Refers to the practice of using hand grenades to fish.
146 Bull cook: A soldier assigned to aid the cook and perform miscellaneous chores.
147 Bricqueterie: A brickworks.
148 Expecting to leave: On this day, the Canadians began their transfer to the Somme front.
149 Mean: Miller probably meant this in the sense of "parsimonious" as opposed to rude or unkind.

the Canadian prairies. We are now 18 K. from Albert and can hear the heavy guns firing.[150] We had a good reception, for the dame made us coffee and gave us the freedom of the kitchen and a hot fire.

Fri., Sept. 1:

Left billets at Herissart 11:45 a.m. and marched via Contay 6 mi. to hut camp in a large wood. We are in a hut with the runners and we cook out-of-doors under the tall trees, for the place is clean and open like a park though heavily screened and shaded above by branches and foliage. Weather is warm, often quite cloudy, with light winds. The local soil is shallow and the chalk subsoil crops out frequently, is often at the surface. The land is very rolling and one sees some fine valleys and rounded hills.

Sat., Sept. 2:

Left camp in the woods at 1 p.m. and marched till about five, passing Bouzincourt on our left and bivouacking in the open for the night.

Sun., Sept. 3:

We have been meeting Australians all along our way from Candas.[151] We seem to be relieving them here.[152] Yesterday we passed about 100 German prisoners in small parties under guard working on the roadbed.

An attack was made by our fellows including 1st Bde. on Du Mouquet Farm at dawn.[153] The roar was terrific while the cannonade lasted. A heavy bombardment on the French front south of us has been in progress all morning. We saw a parachute drop from one of our balloons over

---

150 Albert: A French town, strategically situated about nine kilometres (as of September 1916) behind the British front lines on the Somme.

151 Candas: Small town in the Somme region, 30 kilometres north of Amiens. Australians: Since the third week of July, the Australians had been locked in a savage fight for the village of Pozières, a fortified town on high ground along the Albert-Bapaume Road.

152 Relieving Australians: The 3rd Canadian Division relieved the Australians on 5 September.

153 Mouquet Farm: The farm, situated on a ridge northeast of Pozières, was the site of a hard-fought engagement that began during the Battle of Pozières itself.

Albert at 9:30 a.m., slowly drift N.E. as it fell. Something like a man was suspended beneath.[154]

Pongo, Macdonald, Phillips, Highton, and I washed in the Ancre River in Albert this morn. The famous statue of Mary and the Holy Child on Albert Church is leaning over at about an angle of 110° with vertical, and is held fast only by a few bent bracing rods. When this falls the war will soon end as has always been the case with previous French wars.[155]

Church service by the Bns. separately in the open at ten am. Communion service in marquee at 11:15, many of us attended. I took communion first time since joining army. And all the time the guns from Thiepval to Soyécourt bellowed and roared till the voice of the clergyman could scarce be heard. We hear the French have made a big new advance south of us today, while the British have taken Du Mouquet Farm.[156]

Mon., Sept. 4:

Frequent cool driving showers from the west last night and today. Moved to billets in Albert in evening.

Wed., Sept. 6:

Flag and flapper work yesterday morning. This morning at the training area signalling to aeroplane with flares.

Albert has few civilian inhabitants left and is half-wrecked by shellfire. It is seldom shelled now. I am sending Nellie some French school books which I found in a vacant house.

Very heavy cannonade almost continuous day and night.

---

154 Parachute: Parachutes were issued to observation balloon crews but various technical challenges prevented their issue to the pilots of British planes before war's end.

155 Statue of Mary: When a shell struck the Basilica Cathedral of Albert in January 1915, the statue of Mary and the baby Jesus atop the cathedral's spire tipped but did not fall to the ground. According to a legend that arose at that time, when the Virgin fell, the war would end. Over the course of the war, hundreds of thousands, if not millions, of British and Imperial soldiers marched past the cathedral and saw its famous "leaning Virgin." The statue finally fell in April 1918.

156 Capture of farm: On 3 July the Australians took much of the farm but were unable to hold it in the face of the German counterattack.

The British have just taken Guillemont and half of Ginchy. The French have taken Maurepas, Clery, Le Forest, Soyecourt and Chilly with 5,700 prisoners.[157]

Thurs., Sept. 7:

Paraded in back garden at 10 a.m. for inspection of rifles and equipment by Lt. Hedley. Aircraft guns were firing on German planes some distance off at a great height. Our planes came up and, after a short fight, one plane fell, evidently a Hun.

I was called at 2 p.m. to the 2nd Field Coy. C.E. Hq. to translate a German proclamation that had been dropped from an aeroplane this morning. It was entitled HUNGER and dealt with the serious situation in Germany, ending NIEDER MIT DEM KRIEGE! HOCH DIE INTER-NATIONALE SOLIDARITAT DES PROLETARIATS. It was signed as printed in Lubeck.[158]

Bn. went to the trenches to close support tonight, but some of us Sigs. are left here to train and act as reserves, as we are not needed up there.

In the direction of Combles the guns have bellowed all last night and today without a stop.

Fri., Sept. 8:

I took class in physical jerks 9:30–10:30 and map reading 2–4 p.m.[159] On piquet at Q.M. Stores 6–10 p.m. Started to sleep in open but town was shelled about midnight so we took refuge in the cellar. A fine starlit night. Terrific bombardment all evening.

Sun., Sept. 10:

In forenoon, lecture on hand grenades by Mr. Conroy for Sigs., batmen, and draft. Goodwin and I explored military tunnel back of house. In

---

157 Guillemont: Reference to the Battle of Guillemont (3–6 September 1916), a hard-fought Anglo-French victory on the southern end of the British Fourth Army's front during the Somme campaign.
158 German message: "Down with war! International solidarity of the proletariat!" It is remarkable that this pro-revolutionary Marxist statement was dropped into British lines by a German plane.
159 Physical jerks: British term for calisthenics.

pm a bunch of Sigs. explored tunnel supposed to lead to Bapaume.[160] It has three branches, each about 300 yds. in length cut through the solid limestone. But all the passages are choked with fallen rock. In evening, I and Goodwin explored the shell-shattered cathedral.[161]

Tues., Sept. 12:

Bn. returned from front line to billets last night before 12 o'clock. Germans shelled Albert 11 a.m. to noon yesterday, and for over an hour this morning just after midnight. A number of us went down to the chalk tunnel in the back yard to sleep.

Parties of German prisoners pass thru town every day. Our boys have brought back many souvenirs, including respirators, papers, and a new combination binoculars-range finder periscope.

We can buy the Paris papers, including Continental Edition of London *Daily Mail*, in town every night. A Frenchman drives up from Amiens each afternoon with them.[162]

Sent five French books to Nellie in last night's mail.

In afternoon, Frank Gorringe and I went out on left of Pozieres road to see our new Machine Gun Destroyers: H.M.L.S. Cordon Rouge, H.M.L.S. Creme de Menthe, and others.[163] Preliminary bombardment for our next advance commenced at 8 pm.

Wed., Sept. 13:

This Bde. left billets in Albert about 1:45 p.m. and marched to Warloy, arriving at billets about 3:30 p.m. This is a fine little village of considerable size and has some good native stores, and an army Y.M.C.A. marquee.

Leave opened today and L/Cpl. Austin left for his on our arrival at billet. I am next from the Sigs. Sergt. Rex L. called on us this evening. He is in the entrenching Bn. which reinforces this Divn.

---

160 Tunnel and Bapaume: The tunnel in question certainly did not lead to Bapaume, some 18 kilometres northeast of Albert and behind German lines.

161 Cathedral: Albert Cathedral.

162 Amiens: The capital of the Somme region. The city of Amiens had transformed into an important logistical hub sustaining the British Army on the Somme front.

163 Machine Gun Destroyers, H.M.L.S.: "His Majesty's Land Ship," a reference to the first tanks, of which roughly 60 were available for action by mid-September.

Thurs., Sept. 14:

Left Warloy billet 7 a.m. I could not sleep well so rose at 4 a.m. and made the fire for breakfast. It was a clear cool morning with a light fresh breeze from the west. We marched to our former billet at Herissart, and have the blacksmith's fat wife once more looking after our welfare. Arrived here 9:30 a.m.

Editor's Note: The Battle of Flers-Courcelette

This is Miller's first reference to the Battle of Flers-Courcelette (15–22 September 1916), a major action that marked the beginning of the third phase of the Battle of the Somme. The battle was notable for several reasons: it saw the first use of tanks (described by Miller in his entry for 16 September) in battle; it marked the entry of the Canadian Corps and the New Zealand Division into the Somme; and despite some 30,000 casualties the battle was a significant victory for the British. The Canadian Corps, now three divisions strong, spearheaded the attack in and around the village of Courcelette itself. New artillery tactics, such as the "creeping" barrage that aimed to suppress the enemy until attacking infantry was upon them, and the support of seven tanks aided the successful Canadian assault. As always, the cost of victory was very high: over 1,000 Canadians were killed on 15 September alone and, as Miller's account goes on to show, Canada's participation on the Somme had only just started.[164]

Sat., Sept. 16:

Yesterday forenoon practice in visual signalling. In p.m. a lecture on gas and care of helmets by a 16th Bn. Sergt. We heard of a big British advance that morning, taking Thiepval, Courcelette and Martinpuich. The 2nd & 3rd Can. Divns are said to have taken part.

Left billets this morning at 10 and marched by Contay to take motor busses at Vadevillers, thence to brickfield outside Albert. Very fine day, tolerably warm, but a fresh N.E. breeze. Was unloading shells with C.F.A. at their depot this evening.[165] Shells are being rushed up to the front as fast as the limbers will take them, and the bombardment has been continuous all evening. Our fellows are said to be still advancing very methodically and we are all in high spirits over it.

---

164 The best recent account of Canadians in the Somme campaign is Tim Cook, *At the Sharp End: Canadians Fighting the Great War 1914–1916* (Toronto: Viking Canada, 2007).

165 C.F.A.: Canadian Field Artillery.

Sun., Sept. 17:

We made rough shelters of shell boxes to sleep behind last night. But that was none too warm, for the night was clear and cool with a heavy dew. Very heavy artillery fire all night long. We hear that our fellows are continually making new advances, both night and day. Our turn at it will come soon.

No church service for us this morning, though some other units had services. This area is black with troops, horses, and traffic. One would wonder how it is all managed and where it comes from. The troops here would have to be reckoned in the tens of thousands, and we only see a small part of all that are operating on this front.

Splendid reports come in of the work done by the new TANKS, how positions were mastered and the Germans demoralized. The Sucrerie at Courcelette was a machine gun stronghold.[166] A tank circled completely around it and destroyed or silenced every gun with the 6-pound shells. The infantry followed and took the place easily. A German machine gunner, now prisoner, tried his gun on one tank but confessed that every bullet fell dead and only made a spurt of blue flame against the armour of the car. A bombing party tried to approach one but were annihilated by M.G. fire. In some cases a tank stopped on a trench and enfiladed it both ways. The occupants of the trench could neither fight nor run away.

Mon., Sept. 18:

Rained during last night and most of today. We broke camp about nine am and moved into our old billet in Albert.

Tues., Sept. 19:

Cool and showery, clearing in the afternoon. As soon as the clouds had broken and visibility had improved, our observation balloons went up and the artillery commenced hammering away again. Just after sunset, a German gun or two began shelling the town from the direction of Thiepval. We retired to the cellar and tunnels to spend the night.

---

166 Tanks: The tanks, of which six supported the Canadians, had mixed success at Courcelette. In some places, they overawed and overcame German opposition, as Miller described, but they were slow and mechanically unreliable. Sucrerie: Sugary refinery located just outside of Courcelette.

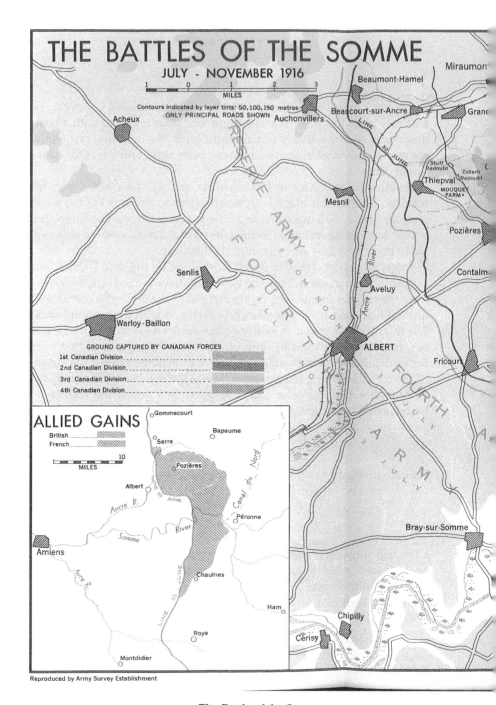

The Battle of the Somme

Overview of the Battle of the Somme, July to November 1916. Just above centre is Courcelette, seized by the Canadians in hard fighting in mid-September. Far left on the map is Warloy, where Miller was billeted as the Canadian attack began.

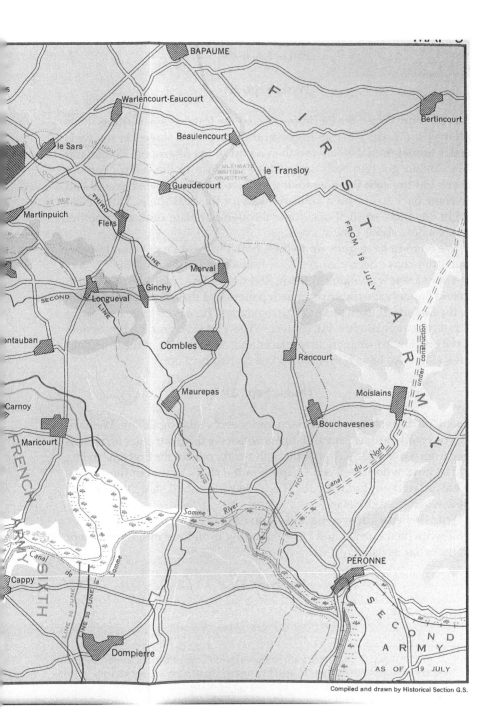

BAPAUME

Warlencourt-Eaucourt

Beaulencourt

le Sars

ULTIMATE
BRITISH
OBJECTIVE

le Transloy

Gueudecourt

22 SEP

Martinpuich

Flers

Morval

Ginchy

Longueval

Combles

ntauban

Rancourt

Maurepas

Moislains

Carnoy

Bouchavesnes

Maricourt

Somme   River

PÉRONNE

Cappy

LINE 30 JUNE

Canal   de   la   Somme

Dompierre

FRENCH   ARMY

SIXTH

FIRST   ARMY   FROM 19 JULY

THIRD   LINE

SECOND   LINE

31 AUG

19 NOV

Canal   du   Nord

under construction

SECOND   ARMY   AS OF 19 JULY

Bertincourt

Wed., Sept. 20:

Just after breakfast, the Germans shelled the town again, putting shells all over our area, 3 in one house in this street. We stayed in the wine cellar tunnel until dinner, and then a part of the afternoon. Pongo and Macdonald got two beds and a stove fixed up in the cellar chamber there, but the 49th Bn. are moving in there tonight, so we have all had to come back to our own attic and wait for the next shells. During last night one piece of shell case came through our slate roof, and another made a hole above Oswin's bed.

We were to have gone up to the Chalk Pits reserve position tonight, but orders have been changed so we stay here for the present.[167]

There are few civilians in town, and only a few small shops. We can get no papers save the Paris French papers and the Continental Edition of the *Daily Mail*, even these very irregularly. There is no large Exp. Force Canteen and only a few Bn. canteens. The Y.M.C.A. and the Boy Scouts have good marquee recreation places and canteens out at the brickfield area where we have been bivouacked on two occasions.

Thurs., Sept. 21:

Spent the day at billet with usual parades and visual signalling. We have just received the new canvas flappers which we fix to our rifles for signalling from cover. Read a flapper through a periscope for the first time today.

The boys who have been sleeping in the chalk tunnel in the garden were ordered out today by the R.E.'s. So we must all stay in our billets now when Fritz shells us.

Fritz shelled us in evening and set on fire a big ammunition depot east of town which burned and kept exploding until near midnight. I slept in the cellar as usual.

Fri., Sept. 22:

Visual signalling all day.

---

167 Chalk Pits: Located just under a kilometre south of Pozières, Chalk Pits was a reserve position with dugouts located in a former chalk mine. One of Miller's contemporaries, Sergeant Leonard McLeod Gould of the 102nd Battalion, described it as "a muddy depression honeycombed with inadequate shelters." (www.102ndbattalioncef.ca/warpages/102chap4.htm)

Sun., Sept. 24:

Very fine, clear, warm. Left billets at Rue de Boulan, Albert, and marched to Chalk Pits at 3 p.m. We Sigs. are living in a deep German dugout at Bn. Hq. These positions have all been taken from the Germans since July 1. In the hillside behind us is a smashed battery of their field guns. They have been wrecked by our shell fire and the Huns have blown them up, bursting the barrels near their centres.

During the evening we were sitting about on the ground outside our dugout. A battery of 4.7 guns was firing nearby and other batteries of heavy guns all about.[168] The roar is almost deafening when these guns are in action, but they do not all fire at once. The ruins of Pozieres are just north of us on the ridge. The main road from Albert is opened up there and traffic runs up into the village continually day and night. Fritz shells over this area every day, but he cannot observe on it. Our aeroplanes are passing overhead all the time and rarely is a Hun plane seen except at a great height where observation is impossible.[169] I counted 17 of our planes at one time on a small sector north of Pozieres. We see no enemy balloons from here, but a whole swarm of ours hangs high in the air south of us. From Fricourt south to the French front by Peronne we can count 22.

Norman, Goodwin, and I had a swim in a pool in town last night. Afterward we passed the Canadian Corps prisoners' cage and saw about 30 Huns there who had been brought out from Courcelette. Today at noon, Goodwin and I took them some tobacco, cigarettes, a pipe, and a cap, had a chat with 4 of them, and got some German money as souvenirs. They are all Prussians, some quite young; all were agreeable and fairly cheerful, especially at the prospect of getting to England till the end of the war. They said they are well fed at the cage.

Editor's Note: The Battle of Thiepval Ridge
   No sooner had the Battle of Flers-Courcelette ended than the Canadians were hurled into action again. While the British had secured Courcelette, Thiepval Ridge to the west

---

168   4.7: The Q.F. (quick firing) 4.7-inch gun, a naval artillery piece also used as a long-range field gun.

169   Hun planes: This is not the first time Miller has noted the absence of German aircraft. It was the RFC's policy to try to engage German planes on their side of the line.

remained in German hands, forming a salient in the British line. On 26 September,
elements of the British Reserve Army, including the Canadian Corps, assaulted the
heavily fortified ridge.

   The short battle ended in victory for the British, but serves as a reminder of how
annihilating First World War combat could be. Although supported by heavy artillery
and large numbers of machine guns (alluded to by Miller, below), the Canadian Corps
suffered nearly 1,000 dead, including approximately 740 on 26 September alone, mak-
ing that day one of Canada's bloodiest of the war. Nor did the fighting end there, as
follow-up operations by the Canadians against the notorious Regina Trench met a grim
fate in the face of uncut wire and heavy machine gun fire.[170]

   On the evening of 25 September 1916, the 5th Battalion relieved the 7th and prepared
to take part in the attack, its first major assault of the war. "Everyone is keyed up," the
Battalion War Diary records, "for it is what many have put in 18 months waiting for."
Over the next two days, before being relieved, the 5th Battalion suffered grievous losses:
52 killed, 291 wounded, and 122 missing. This amounted to nearly half the battalion
in all. Miller spent much of the first day signalling from headquarters, but this was
only marginally safer than joining the assault itself, as his account below of the fate of
the 13th Battalion HQ indicates. In the coming days, Miller himself narrowly avoided
being killed on more than one occasion.

Mon., Sept. 25:

Left CHALK PITS at 6 p.m. and marched to trenches between Courcelette
and Monquet Farm. Hqrs. is in a support trench 200 yds in rear of a
freshly dug front line from which we are to advance. The Sigs. with Bn.
Hq. are Temp. Sergt., L/cpl. Pedley, Goodwin, Coombs, Pongo, Highton,
Phillips, Jardine and McGuire and I.[171] Gorringe and I have aeroplane
signals to manage, Phillips has the pigeons; Temp and Pedley have the
phone. The others are spare runners. Pickup and Edwards are at Bde.[172]
The others are left at the Chalk Pits to do whatever work is required.
Things are quiet at the front, so we are settling down in fair comfort after
digging good shelters for ourselves under the parapet.

---

170 Here, too, see Cook, *At the Sharp End.*
171 Pedley: Private (later Sergeant) James Alexander Pedley (1892–?), born England;
     attested Valcartier, September 1914.
172 Pickup: Private (later 2nd Lt.) William Hayes Pickup (1885–1918), born England;
     attested Valcartier, September 1914. Transferred to the RFC, April 1917. Killed in a
     flying accident, 12 March 1918, buried CWGC Accrington Cemetery, Lancashire,
     UK.

Tues., Sept. 26:

About midnight trouble began on our right in front of Courcelette. After a little bombing and M.G. fire, Fritz sent up S.O.S. (a red flare bursting into two) and the artillery on both sides opened up. Shells fell thick all round us and we expected to go up any instant. A heavy British shell twice fell short at Bn. Hq. and killed one of our scouts (Bell) wounding another.[173] Our artillery soon dominated and the cannonade died down to normal i.e. a little German fire and quite heavy British. Our heavy guns have fired steadily now on all the German positions in front of us for 2 days and nights.

At 12:35 p.m., our attack began. The boys went forward in six waves. As the first wave left our jumping off trench, a terrific fire was opened from our supporting field guns and machine guns. We had some hundreds of M.G.s behind our support trench and they poured a hail of indirect fire on the German lines. The German artillery and M.G.s opened almost at once. Our fire was astonishing for its volume, but the Hun fire was heavy too. The 5th led with 8th on the left and 15th and 14th on right. They took the enemy front line (Zollern trench), then the 2nd line (Hessian trench) and the 3rd Bde even reached his 3rd line (Regina trench).[174] All Germans who had not been killed surrendered as soon as our chaps entered their trenches. There was little or no man-to-man fighting. We lost heavily, chiefly in wounded. But the 8th Bn. suffered worst from M.G. fire in their flank and rear from Zollern redoubt.[175] The mopping-up parties found 2 Hun M.Gs. in Mouquet Farm at 5 p.m. and cleaned them up. We sent back about 350 prisoners from this Bde., chiefly Saxons and Prussians.

The artillery fire moderated at dark, though ours was intense all night. After dark, a party of us, mostly sigs., took flares, water, and ammunition up to Capt. Mahaffy in the new front line (Hessian trench).[176] It was quite

---

173 Bell: William Alan Bell (1892–1916), born England; attested Sewell, Manitoba, June 1915. Commemorated on the Vimy Memorial.

174 Zollern, Hessian, Regina trenches: British names for heavily fortified German trench lines that were the Canadian objectives.

175 8th Battalion: 8th Battalion casualties for the two days were 42 killed, 233 wounded, 171 missing, or 446 casualties total, according to the battalion's war diary.

176 Mahaffey: Captain Kenneth A. Mahaffey, MC, DSO (1892–?) of Bracebridge, Ontario; attested Valcartier, September 1914.

dark and the Huns were shelling the whole area apparently at random. Luckily we made the trip without hurt or loss. A wounded 8th Bn. man called to us from a shell-hole; he had a shattered leg and we had no stretcher, so could do nothing for him but leave him for a stretcher party to find. On the return trip I brought out a wounded officer of the 15th Bn. He had a leg injured and a slight wound in the side, but was able to hobble on slowly with a little assistance. I took him to our dressing stn. in Sunken Road. He was very grateful for the way I had stuck to him and he wished me the best of luck. I think it has come to me.

Wed., Sept. 27:

Reached dugout about 2 a.m. and had a little sleep. On phone duty in Hq. dugout 4 to 8 a.m. Our Bde. made a bombing attack on the left this morning, cleaning up Zollern redoubt and putting some enemy M.G.'s out of action.

About 9 a.m. we spare Hq. men went out carrying in the wounded. We first got a chap in a shell hole between Zollern and Hessian Trenches. He had shrapnel in the lower back and his legs were paralyzed. But he was as patient and cheerful as a man could be. After we had seen him safely to the dressing stn. and returned to Bn. Hq., we rested a while. All this time prisoners were being brought out in twos and threes, and stretcher parties were out all over the open right up to our new front line. It may have been the white flags which they carried that protected them, for the day before we had let a German party cross right in front of us carrying the white flag. But by noon, our carrying parties were bringing up supplies and the Huns started firing on everything without distinction. We heard that Mr. Wilson, intelligence officer was up in Hessian trench seriously wounded, so Pongo, Jim Pedley, I and 2 others volunteered to bring him.[177] We crossed to Zollern trench under machine gun fire, and could not get beyond, for Pongo and Jim, as soon as they emerged from the trench with white flag and stretcher, were met by a burst of M.G. fire and twice driven back. Just then an H.E. shrapnel shell burst above us and we thought we would end our careers right there. Our scout guide got the heavy driving band on his head and staggered groaning, "I'm hit". The band fell at my feet and kicked up the dust. But it had

---

177   Wilson: Probably Lieutenant M.P. (Major Percy) *Willson* (1883–1916), died of wounds 30 September 1916. Born England; attested Prince Albert, Saskatchewan, April 1915. Buried in CWGC Etaples Military Cemetery, France.

struck the chap's helmet a glancing blow and only dinted the metal; he was quite all right in a minute. More shells burst above us and the Hun M.G. raked the trench savagely. We worked down to our right and took what cover the parapet afforded. The trench was well manned by our fellows in preparation for counter attack. German equipment was lying everywhere and there were several dead Huns and a wounded one. We found a wounded 5th man with a broken leg. We bound him up, using a German shovel as splint, then went back to Hq. for a stretcher on which we took him out.

At the dressing stn. I had a chat with a young Wurtemberger shot through the leg. He was very frightened and anxious to get back out of shell-fire.

Two young Saxons were taken past Hq. and had a stretcher to carry out. One was very nervous as if suffering from shell shock, for when B.S.M. Haydon asked him for a button from his tunic as a souvenir, he started to whimper and finally cried like a scared child. There were Saxons, Prussians, Badeners and Wurtembergers among the prisoners.[178] Most of them were fairly cheerful and agreeable, and all who could do so helped carry out our wounded men.

We lost about 460 men in all, mostly wounded. Maj. Williams of old 32nd was killed and Capts. Findlay, Crawford, and Lts. Wilson and many others wounded.[179] Sergt. Simpson of M.G. section was killed in his dugout near Hq. just before the attack began.[180] Bde. S.O. Norton was killed.[181] The 13th Bn. lost all their Hq. staff by having a heavy shell blow in front of their dugout and set some gasoline on fire, making escape impossible.[182]

Relieved by 8th Bde. about midnight.

---

178 Saxons, Prussians, etc.: Miller seems more aware of the regional differences among Germans than many of his comrades, perhaps because of his own German heritage.

179 Williams: Major Alman Clare Williams (1876–1916), born Port Hope, Ontario; a lawyer from Portage la Prairie, Manitoba; attested Winnipeg, 14 December, buried CWGC Albert Communal Cemetery.

180 Simpson: Thomas Nesbitt Simpson (1890–1916), born Vancouver; attested Valcartier, September 1914. Buried Courcelette British Cemetery, France.

181 Norton: Glen Norton (1891–1916), born Ireland; attested Valcartier, September 1914; buried CWGC Bedford House Cemetery, Belgium.

182 13th Battalion HQ: This horrific incident is recounted in the 13th Battalion War Diary, which survived the conflagration. The battalion's commanding officer, Lt. Col. V.C. Buchanan, and most of the headquarters staff were killed or wounded by the fire.

Thurs., Sept. 28:

Arrived at billets in Albert, had breakfast and turned in till noon. Bn. marched off at 4:30 p.m. to billets in Bouzincourt village. Saw Eadie again in "A" Coy 8th Bn.; we were in same class at Regina Normal 1914.[183]

Fri., Sept. 29:

Left billets at 8:30 a.m. and marched by Warloy and Contay to former billets in Herissart. It has been misty with a drizzling rain all morning. A heavy cannonade has raged all last night and today along the front, apparently north of Thiepval.

We read in yesterday's paper that both Thiepval and Combles have fallen to the British with many prisoners and much equipment.

Sat., Sept. 30:

Left Herissart billet at 8:45 a.m. and marched to billet in Montrelet, in a barn on north side of the road. An ideal day for marching with cloudless sky, warm sun, but cool air and fresh breeze from the north. Had our packs carried by motor lorry all the way. Found Fieffes and Montrelet as wet and muddy as last time, but we have a far better billet.

Sun., Oct. 1:

Fine and clear, calm and warm. Gen. Lomas of Bde. spoke to us after church parade and thanked us for our splendid work.[184] The Pres. Chaplain held the service at noon and is conducting a communion service in the Y.M.C.A. marquee at 8 p.m. Gen. Currie of Div. came to review us this p.m., but most of us had gone nutting and berry-picking so avoided the parade, as no notice was given until the parade was called. He must have found a very small Bn. to review.

It is the height of blackberry season and the fruit is quite abundant. We got quite a few walnuts and filberts, still a bit green, and the apples

---

183 Eadie: Sergeant Nelson Burns Eadie (1894–1917) of St. Joseph's Island, Ontario. Attested Sewell, Saskatchewan. Killed in action 28 April 1917. Commemorated at the Vimy Memorial.

184 Lomas: Loomis. See entry of 9 July 1916.

are not all picked yet and beyond our reach. We get what fruit we can and stew apples and blackberries together or separately. Black elder-berries same as at home are plentiful and I have stewed them with apples, making a fine sauce. This is a great change from tinned jam and so much meat.

Mon., Oct. 2:

Last night's mail brought my first birthday present – a book, "Night and Morning" by Lytton, sent by F.M.W.[185] I appreciate it very much, for it has rained all day, we have had few parades, so I read most of the time. Frank Gorringe was 27 on Sept. 30 and he got a nice cake last night which he divided among the boys. Goodwin will be 27 on Oct. 28 so three of us are of same age.

Had bathing parade to the travelling steam fumigator this morning. The machine forces steam into a tank of cold water dipped from the creek, and this, when hot, feeds the spray baths.

Pay parade at 5:30 p.m.

Tues., Oct. 3:

Rainy and misty in morning. Left billets about 10 a.m. and marched to camp (new canvas) near Val de Maison on road to Herissart. Weather cleared in p.m., still quite warm. Have good Y.M.C.A. marquees with canteen here and are very comfortable. In this tent are Pongo, McGuire, Leach, Gorringe, Moggy, Pedley and I.

Wed., Oct. 4:

Left Val-de-Maison camp at 1 p.m. and marched via Herissart and Contay to huts in woods above Vadencourt, arriving at 5 p.m. Cloudy and dull, fairly warm and calm. Heavy rain began just after our arrival at the huts.

By last night's orders, all details were put into a Hq. Coy.

---

185 Book: *Night and Morning* (1841), by Edward Bulwer-Lytton (1803–1873), English novelist and politician (served as secretary of state for the colonies). He was a popular novelist in his day, but is perhaps best remembered for the opening line of his 1830 novel *Paul Clifford*: "It was a dark and stormy night."

No photo is known to exist of Arthur Currie's disappointing review of the 5th Battalion on 1 October 1916. By the time this photograph was taken in September 1917, Currie, centre, was in command of the entire Canadian Corps. Credit: William Rider-Rider, "General Currie, and General MacBrien at a Practice Attack, September 1917." Department of National Defence/Library and Archives Canada/PA-001478

Thurs., Oct. 5:

Very fine with a fresh breeze. Autumn is in the air, the trees are just tinged with brown, but already the leaves are falling in light showers and dotting the ground among the bushes or making the mud look a little less slippery and disagreeable. Spent day quietly in camp with only a rifle inspection to bother us. I am reading "Night and Morning" by Lord Lytton.

Fri., Oct. 6:

Left billets at 8:30 a.m., marched via Warloy, Senlis, Bouzincourt, Aveluy to chalk pits. The Huns had just been shelling the road on east side of Aveluy and some mules were lying dead.

I was on a carrying party up to midnight, but we accomplished nothing – went through shellfire up to Courcelette sugar refinery where we lay in shell holes an hour and returned to chalk pits. We sigs have some dugouts together by an old Hun battery.

Sat., Oct. 7:

Very fine, but fresh wind from north. Fixed up my dugout in forenoon. Frank Gorringe went to Albert to see G.O.C. about commission in R.F.C.[186]

On carrying party at night with most of the sigs. and others. We took cans of water from 1st Bde. Hq. by sugar refinery and through Courcelette to 1st Bn. Hq. in gully on right of Courcelette. Returning to sugar refinery dump we took bombs and Stokes ammunition to the same place. Fritz was shelling the whole area heavily with field guns, and with a 5.9 on the entrance to the gully from Courcelette sunken road. It was marvellous how we came through it safely.

British took Le Sars this afternoon.[187]

Sun., Oct. 8:

Reached dugout at 2:30 a.m. It was near full moon but partly cloudy and showery all the night. We were wet and the mud was so bad and the paths so slippery that we were quite worn out when we arrived. I directed a wounded 1st Bn. man to the Fld. Amb. dressing stn. near our dugouts, so had my fill of hot cocoa before turning in. We had orders to be ready at 5 a.m. to move up the line for an attack was made on all our fronts this morning. But we hear the affair was a success, and we are left here yet. We have seen parties of prisoners going out.

---

186 G.O.C.: General Officer Commanding, that is, 1st Canadian Division commander Arthur Currie. Gorringe successfully transferred to the RFC. See footnote for the entry of 30 May 1916.

187 Le Sars: The 23rd Division captured Le Sars, a village on the Albert-Bapaume Road, on 7 October 1916, an important preparatory step in the subsequent renewed assault on Regina Trench.

A dugout caved in at noon and partly buried one of our S.B.'s but he was dug out alive and taken out on a stretcher.

Mon., Oct. 9:

Changed places with 14th Bn. last evening but were ordered back again within an hour. No working parties for Sigs. last night or today.

Tues., Oct. 10:

10th Bn. with us in CHALK PITS last night and today, moved up to front this evening. Met Pete Brown as "B" Coy Sergt. Maj.,[188] Vic Macdonnel and Douglas Maxwell as cpls., Lem Gavil as coy. runner.[189] Stewart, former principal of King Edward School Regina, is their M.G.O.[190]

A British biplane fell just behind our position this morning, and a monoplane out of petrol landed in the p.m. without breaking a stick.[191]

Wed., Oct. 11:

In evening we moved from Chalk Pits 400 yds. N.E. where we are in dugouts on open ground. 10th Bn. come out here and join us tonight.

Austin, Mitchell and Oswin returned from a pigeon course at Warloy.

4th Can. Div. is moving into this sector.[192] They came to Ypres when we were leaving.

---

188 Brown: Milton Peter Brown (1888–1916), born England; attested Winnipeg, December 1914. Formerly of the 32nd. Killed in action 11 October 1916. Buried CWGC Albert Communal Cemetery Extension.

189 Maxwell: *Dougald* McTaggart Maxwell (1881–1956), born Scotland; attested Winnipeg, December 1914. Gavil: Lemuel Hobbs *Gavel* (1886–?), born Nova Scotia; attested Winnipeg, December 1914. Also spelled "Gaval" on his service file.

190 Stewart: Captain Stanley Peter Stewart (1889–1917), born Ontario; attested Valcartier. Killed in action at Vimy Ridge, 9 April 1917. Buried CWGC Ecoivres Military Cemetery, St. Eloi, France.

191 Biplane: This day saw several combats and losses over the Fourth Army's front. The most likely candidate for the plane that fell behind Miller's position, however, is a 32 Squadron DH.2 flown by the extravagantly named Lieutenant Maximillian John Jules Gabriel Mare-Montembault, MC (1895–1917), who survived the crash but was killed in action the following year.

192 4th Can. Div.: The 4th Canadian Division was established in England in April 1916 and deployed to France in August of that year.

Very violent attacks occur twice or 3 times a day at one point or another on the line in front of us. The artillery fire is always fierce on both sides. From Courcelette to Thiepval seems to be the hottest part of the line.

Thurs., Oct. 12:

In afternoon we dug ourselves in or built dugouts another 400 yds. N.E. on the right of Pozieres. In the evening we moved up to this new position. Fritz shells all around ahead of us continuously with shrapnel and percussion heavies, but seldom touches this spot. There is a wrecked aeroplane and a shattered "Tank" just ahead of us up the valley.

Fri., Oct. 13:

Weather has kept cool and cloudy without rain for several days.

Bn. moved to "Candy" trench between Martinpuich and the Courcelette sugar refinery. Some of the Hq. details are left behind to do working parties. Of the Sigs., there are L/cpls Leach and Pedley, Cpl. Burdon, and Haydon, Reid, Highton, Phillips, Jardine, Lyons, Gorringe, Edwards, Pells and I.

Sat., Oct. 14:

Last evening we moved back to former position, then to Chalk Pits this morning for breakfast. We carried water to Bn. last night, then returned to Chalk Pits and took up their rations, getting back to turn in by 3 a.m.

Weather keeps cool and cloudy with light winds, but full moon makes the nights agreeable.

Goodwin went sick yesterday to Hospital with 103° temp. Clements is at transport.

At night we made one trip with rations and water to the Bn. in support trench on right of Courcelette, 600 yds. from the front line. We were out 10 p.m. to 3 a.m. This is a long trip, at least 3 1/2 miles each way. We go up the miniature railway, then off half-right on the tape line to the Candy trench and Le Sars road, whence a communication trench leads up to the front. There is German material strewn all over the ground from Candy trench up and one could pick up thousands of souvenirs. Fritz shells this area with bursts of fire all night long. Rarely can one get across without being shelled.

Sun., Oct. 15:

At night, 8:30 to 11 p.m., we carried water from mule [?] trench up tape line to Bn. (I to D Coy). We were caught in a heavy burst of shellfire by the Le Sars road and had to take shelter in shell holes for a while, but ran as fast as we could as soon as there was a lull so as to get out of the area. There were violent artillery duels on the redoubts north of Thiepval at 8:30 and 11 p.m. The first was an "S.O.S." from our infantry, but the second was evidently our counter-attack. But the trouble did not extend to Courcelette and our Bn. front. We hear the Huns have made seven attempts to recapture the Stuss Redoubt, but were always repulsed with heavy losses.[193]

Mon., Oct. 16:

Left Chalk Pits 11 a.m. and marched by Albert and Bouzincourt to Transport Lines, then back to our Q.M.'s in Bouzincourt for supper then back to our billets on Rue de Carnot (Aveluy Rd.) in Albert. On our march out to Albert at noon, we saw a Holt Caterpillar bringing out a 6 inch naval gun and another taking up a six inch howitzer.[194] Bn. came out to these billets about midnight. Very fine cool autumn weather with a touch of frost in the air.

Tues., Oct. 17:

Left Albert billets 1 p.m. and marched as a Bde. to a new camp on east side of Warloy where we are under canvas for the night.

Editor's note: Over the next several entries, Miller recounts the 5th Battalion's movement 40 kilometres north, to the foot of Vimy Ridge, where the 1st Canadian Division and eventually the entirety of the Canadian Corps will train in preparation for the assault on Vimy Ridge itself, in April 1917.

---

193 Stuff Redoubt: Located northeast of Thiepval and west of Courcelette, the Stuff Redoubt was a strategically important and heavily fortified German position bitterly contested in a series of actions in late September and early October 1916.

194 Holt Caterpillar: A "caterpillar" (tracked) style agricultural tractor, manufactured by the American firm Holt Caterpillar Company. These were used extensively in the First World War as artillery tractors.

Wed., Oct. 18:

Left camp 8 a.m. and marched by Warloy and Herissart to camp at Val-de-Maison.
Weather cool and a little showery in the morning, but fine later.

Thurs., Oct. 19:

Spent day quietly in camp. Rained nearly all last night and there were frequent showers during the day. Ted Veale joined us yesterday from the rest camp across the road.[195]

Fri., Oct. 20:

Left camp 9:30 a.m. and marched to billets in Candas, arriving about 11:30 a.m. Weather clear and very cool with fresh easterly wind. Brigadier Lomas was with us, and Gen. Currie had us march past him. There is a good R.F.C. canteen in town.[196] The billets are very good and we are very comfortable.

Sat., Oct. 21:

Left Candas billets at 9 a.m. and marched by Hem-Hardinval where there is a waterpower grist mill on the river and a splendid grove of tall poplars and where we saw the factory chimneys and roofs of Doullens, 3 kilometres on our right, Occoches, Outrebois, Mézerolles, and 1 K. 5 to the right to Remaisnil where we are billeted in a shed at an estaminet. The weather is just like Indian summer at home, with a fresh easterly wind, splendid for marching. This is beautiful rolling country with small woodlots scattered profusely, especially in the valleys, and wide spaces of pasture and cultivated land. There are fine old chateaux here and there in commanding positions, usually with spacious grounds and grand driveways, all laid out as a complete work of landscape art. One sees here what wonderful beauty can be created by careful tree planting. But

---

195 Veale: Edward John Veale (1883–?), born South Africa; attested Valcartier, September 1914. At the time Miller wrote, Veale was recovering from a foot injury.

196 RFC Canteen: Candas was the location of the No. 2 Air Depot, a major logistical hub for the RFC.

the village houses are poor and conditions very unsanitary. The house we were at last night would surely have done service without a change for any generation right back to the dark ages. There was an old wooden loom in one room of a type used certainly since weaving has become a human art. There is too much difference here between the homes of the rich and the poor. I am glad it is not so pronounced in Canada.

First frost last night. There was a thin coat of ice over the pools this morning. Our blankets have gone astray and we are spending the night with just our greatcoats to protect us in a half-open shed under freezing conditions.

There is a very fine old chateau with extensive grounds including some splendid woodlands and sylvan driveways adjoining the village.[197] The officers are all billeted there. The estate is said to have changed hands once in its history through a game of cards. It seems to me that most of the beauty and attractiveness about these chateaux-estates is in the woodlands and wooded driveways. Careful tree planting has done it all. Of course, the chateaux themselves are very fine and especially inside. This one is steam-heated.

Sun., Oct. 22:

Left Remaisnil billets at 9 a.m. Marched through Barly, a little village in a deep narrow, well-wooded valley; Neuvillette; Bouquemaison on the main Doullens-St. Pol Road; thence NE between the railway and main road, to the right across the railway and down through Rebreuviette, and Etrée-Wamin, to Lienval and thence to billets in Magnicourt. We are passing 14 kilometres to the right of St. Pol.

Weather is mostly clear with some cirrus cloud, but very cool with a fresh easterly wind. The country we passed today is well wooded, but the villages are very poor. The country is just grand but it is too bad to see people living in such conditions as they do here.

Mon., Oct. 23:

Left billets in Magnicourt-sur-Canche at 7 a.m.; marched through Maizières, Averdoingt, up the road to Ligny-Saint-Flochel, but turned

---

197 Château: Château de Remaisnil, described by the French Ministère de la Culture as an elegant eighteenth-century residence.

off to the right before reaching the station; at right angles across a Route Nationale that runs west into St. Pol 8 kilometres away; across the railway about 100 yds. farther on; northwards through Bailleul-aux-Cornailles, on road towards Houdain through Magnicourt-en-Comte, and Houvelin to billets in Bajus off on a road to the left one kilometre.

The natives are taking up the potato crop and the mangols. Turnips are still green and growing in the fields. Grain is mostly in stacks. The work is being done by women, a few old men, and an occasional soldier on leave. This is fine country, quite level for the valleys and ravines are fewer than on yesterday's march.

Tues., Oct. 24:

Rained gently all day. We remained in billets.

Cpl. Bert Burdon received his papers for Lieut's commission in a new Bn. in New Brunswick tonight. He is leaving us tomorrow and will take this with him to post in Canada. I will buy a new book and continue from this date.

Second Diary

No. 81593[198]

Pte. Leslie H. Miller

Signals

5th Canadian Bn.

B.E.F.

Next of kin: –

(father)

Mr. Wm. Miller

Milliken

Ontario,

Canada.

---

198 Miller wrote this on the cover of his new diary.

Fri., Oct. 27:

Weather keeps very cool and continuously cloudy with a few showers. This is a fine-looking agricultural district. The land is very rolling, well wooded, with many orchards, hedges, shade and ornamental trees. The farmers are busy plowing, sowing and taking up root crops.

We have buzzer practice during the mornings and are free the remainder of the day.

Sat., Oct. 28:

Left billets in Bajus 9:15 a.m., marched back through Houvelin, off to the left through Frévillers and Bethonsart, passed Aubigny in the bottom of a valley a mile or more on our right, conspicuous by its church spire and single tall factory chimney; Mingoval; Villers-Châtel, where there is a fine chateau occupied by the Mission Militaire Francaise, and just outside the park-like grounds a French military cemetery with several hundred graves, one cross bearing the inscription of a "Médecin Militaire Auxiliaire" killed Jan. 11, 1915; Cambligneul; to huts in Camblain l'Abbe, arriving about 1:30 pm.[199] This is a fairly large village with a church. We have good quarters, and there is a Chaplain's Assn. canteen and cinema hut and several French stores.

Met Lieut. J. Leeson in the street this afternoon. He says George is in England unfit for further service. He caught pneumonia when he was wounded June 15, and one of his lungs is gone. I hope to see him when I am in England on leave.[200]

Thurs., Nov. 2:

We have spent the last four days quietly in camp with rifle inspection and buzzer practice in mornings and free remainder of the day. Had a bathing parade day before yesterday. A cinema has been opened at the Chaplain's Assn. huts, and Monday night we all went to the pictures.

---

199 Camblain l'Abbé: Small town in the Pas-de-Calais, France, about 15 kilometres northeast of Arras. Editor's note: Over the succeeding pages, Miller mentions so many towns that it was impossible to write entries on all of them. I have referenced a select few to give readers a sense of the Arras sector in late 1916.

200 Leeson: George Leeson did not, in fact lose a lung, although he suffered a shrapnel wound to the chest. He returned to service and was wounded again in September 1918.

It has rained nearly every day of late; and the weather keeps mild.

Left huts in Camblain l'Abbe one pm and marched to billets in Villers-au-Bois about 3 kilometres away. This is on the south side of a valley that runs east to Souchez and Lens. The soil is chalky, roads good, and the land wooded here and there. We have a good view towards the east where the country is open and bare, blasted by shellfire. We are in the line of our own observation balloons, and we can see some of Fritz's observers low down in the east. A few civilians are working in the fields north of the village, but there are very few living here, and east of here the country is dead and wild.

Mon., Nov. 6:

Left billets 9 a.m., marched through Carency by Hospital Corner and Redoubt Rd. communication trench to a position on ridge south of Souchez.[201] Carency is wrecked, but not demolished, by shellfire, for most of the walls are standing in whole, or in part. This village extends some distance along south slopes of valley and reaches down into the valley bottom where the little Carency or Souchez creek flows eastward towards Lens.

I am with Jim Pedley and Moggy on "C" Coy. stn. We are down in the chalk about thirty feet below the surface in a chamber off a tunnel made by the French. From the entrance to the tunnel we have a fine view towards Lievin and Angres, northward towards Loos and La Bassee where slag heaps and mining buildings dot the land. None of the buildings appear to be much damaged by shellfire and the mines and factories are running both night and day. We understand that the Germans are employing French civilians and prisoners of war in these places which no civilians have been allowed to leave. Therefore our fellows are leaving this Hun industry which lies so close under our guns that we could destroy it all in a few hours.

We are told that Souchez, now within our lines, is a prohibited area for all troops. The French government is preserving it as a monument of Hun cruelty for the inspection of impartial tribunals after the war.

---

201 Souchez: Town in the Pas-de-Calais, France, about three kilometres northwest of Vimy Ridge. Population in 1914 about 1,500. Like most towns near the front, Souchez was essentially destroyed during the First World War.

There the dead have lain for 18 months just as they fell, the French soldiers attacking, the Germans facing the charge, and between the two French civilians driven ahead by the Huns as a shield for their cowardice. It is almost impossible to visit such a place to verify rumours of this kind for the ground is flat and in plain view of the enemy observers all day long.

Little shelling is done here, save by our artillery. Trench mortars on both sides do most of the fighting. We are using a great many of these machines of several types. It is interesting to stand in an open trench and watch the bombs of various sizes going and coming, from the little Stokes cylinder bombs to the 60 lb pippin of spherical shape on an iron tail-rod, and the 200 lb aerial torpedo which does terrible damage.[202] Fritz comes back with about one bomb to our 5 or 8.

Fri., Nov. 10:

Relieved by 8th Bn. 5:30 p.m., came out to Hospital Corner and the companies to Carency. Very muddy underfoot, but the weather is fine during the day and chilly at night with full moon.

Yesterday I was standing in a trench watching when Fritz put over two "rum-jar" mortar bombs. Our chaps instantly replied with eight 60 pdrs. and about 30 Stokes bombs which discouraged the Hun.

Yesterday a British plane over our right front attacked two Germans behind their lines, drove one down under control, but was forced to come back and land himself on the high ground north of Carency. Our planes were busy all today far back over the Hun territory, scouting and directing artillery fire. In the pm a large squadron of bombing planes returned from behind the enemy lines on our right.

Tues., Nov. 14:

Returned to same trench positions on right of Souchez. Jim Pedley, Moggy and I have the telephone stn. with the 60-lb. trench mortar battery (Imperials) where Haydon, Reid and Oswin were last time in.[203]

---

202 The term "aerial torpedo" does not, in this context, refer to torpedoes of the naval variety dropped from airplanes. Rather it was a generic term for non-standard munitions, often those which protruded in part from the artillery tube prior to being fired.

203 Mortar: Probably the BL 60-pounder gun, a heavy field gun used by the British Army.

Sat., Nov. 18:

Relieved by 14th Bn. and marched back to huts in Camblain l'Abbe, where we arrived about 4:30 p.m. During this trip to the front, we had one heavy bombardment over us and on our left, which was reported in the papers as a British bombardment of trenches in front of Loos. The Huns took it all meekly and made little reply. That night, one of our heavy guns dropped some shells short, almost on top of us, giving us a bad scare. Fritz shelled us in our position behind the ridge very cleverly at times, but doing no damage. He cannot drop a percussion shell on the back of our ridge, for if they miss the crest they cross the valley before striking and exploding.

During this period, the British have made a new attack on the Ancre taking Beaumont-Hamel, Beaucourt, and St. Pierre Divion, and obtaining a footing in Grandcourt, taking 6,000 prisoners.....[204] Weather mostly very fine and cool, but rainy last night and today.

Tues., Nov. 21:

A case of diphtheria was discovered in our hut yesterday morning.[205] We were placed under quarantine after dinner, moved into another hut at night, and inoculated at noon today. No more cases have appeared.... A number of us Sigs. went to Bde. yesterday p.m. for a lecture on the Fuller phone.[206]

Fri., Nov. 24:

Attended cinema in evening and stayed to hear the band, and Canon Scott speak to us. He told jokes about his experiences in marrying people, then turned to speak of some questions relating to the war. He was very jolly and certainly infused a happy feeling of comradeship into his

---

204 Ancre: Refers to the Battel of the Ancre (13–18 November 1916), the last major British operation in the Battle of the Somme, in which the Fifth Army pushed into the Ancre River valley, meeting with considerable success against exhausted German opposition.

205 Diphtheria: A highly contagious bacterial infection that can cause severe flu-like symptoms.

206 Fuller Phone: Named for its inventor, Captain Algernon Fuller (1885–1870), the Fuller Phone was a field telephone/telegraph whose messages were less vulnerable to interception.

audience. One would not have guessed that he had just lost a son killed on the Somme a few days ago. Another son has lost an eye. Both were officers. But he told one of our boys in a private conversation that he had another lad "coming on", as if that were real consolation to a bereaved man. He closed his talk by reciting one of his own poems "What is the Blue in our Flag, Boys?" It was fine. I hear he has written some excellent poetry which is well worth reading.[207]

Sat., Nov. 25:

Attended Gas School west of here this morning where we were all issued with the new gas helmets, and put through some lachrymatory gas to test them out.... Baths in p.m.

Sun., Nov. 26:

Left huts noon and marched by Villers-au-Bois to reserve position at Berthonval Wood near Cabaret Rouge.[208] We are about a mile from Mont St. Eloi which shows up well on a low rounded hill. I walked out there and to Villers-au-Bois one morning to buy candles. Many civilians live in Mont St. Eloi as it is little damaged except the big church which has suffered from shells.[209]

Cpl. Leach, Honey, Coombs, Pongo and I have a very comfortable dugout below the surface. We have all wire screen beds, and have a good fireplace in the clay wall where we keep a wood fire burning most of the time.

Sat., Dec. 2:

My leave to England for a holiday has come at last, so I miss this trip to the trenches Dec. 4 to 12. We eight left our dugouts at 8 a.m. and marched

---

207 Canon Scott: Major Frederick George Scott, GMG, DSO (1861–1944). An Anglican priest and one of the "Confederation Poets," Scott attested at Valcartier in September 1914 at the age of 53. He was senior chaplain of the 1st Canadian Division. His son Henry was killed on the Somme on 21 October 1916.

208 Cabaret Rouge: British position four kilometres west of Vimy Ridge, now the site of Cabaret Rouge CWGC Cemetery, from whose burials Canada's Unknown Soldier was chosen in May 2000.

209 Big church: Probably the Abbey Mont St. Éloi, destroyed by revolutionary violence in 1783, not by First World War shelling as commonly thought, even today by passers by.

out to Transport Lines at Grand Servins, where we spent the day getting new clothing, bath at Gouy Servins, pay, etc. Busses came for us 9:15 p.m. and took us to Bethune in about an hour. Spent a couple of hours in Y.M.C.A. hut by the stove, drinking tea and eating cakes. Train left after midnight and reached Boulogne at daybreak. We spent an hour in a large shed where there was a canteen selling hot tea and rolls. Boat left at 9:30. We had an uneventful trip across as the weather was calm. The channel seemed full of boats including mine-sweepers and destroyer escorts and patrols. A Dover patrol airship passed overhead as we neared England. How we strained our eyes for the first glimpse of the familiar white cliffs, and when they came slowly out of the mist, a murmur of suppressed joy went round among those on deck.

On arrival at Folkestone, we disembarked at once, had a cup of tea, and took train to Victoria Stn., London. We had free tea, cake and sandwiches on the station platform, changed our French money into English, were met by representatives of the Overseas Club and guided or directed to the places we sought. I went with a party to the Maple Leaf Club, 31 Elizabeth St., where I had my cheque cashed, left my kit, engaged a bed, had a hot bath and changed to new underwear, shirt and sox free.[210] As it was late afternoon Sun. Dec. 3, I had tea at the Club and decided to spend the evening at Charlie Cornish's home in S.E. London.[211] I had a little difficulty in finding the place, but forgot that in the warm welcome I received from those at home. Mr. and Mrs. C., Maud, Edie, Grace, Mabel, Harold, Alfy, and Dorothy. I felt so pleased to be in a nice home again with people of my own race and language that I hardly knew what to say, and when they realized all I had been through, they hardly knew what questions to ask first of the hundreds of things they were curious about. We were all embarrassed at first but all the happier for that. I did not stay late as I had planned to see them several times again.

Mon., Dec. 4:

The beds at the Club are soft and warm, and oh, the comfort of clean sheets and pyjamas once more. As I was tired and sleepy, I did not get

---

210 Club: The King George and Queen Mary Maple Leaf Club, established in 1915 by Canadian philanthropist Lady Julia Drummond for Canadians serving overseas.
211 Cornish: Miller's friend of the 32nd. See entry of February 22, 1915.

up until nearly ten o'clock. Bought a few things in the stores nearby and at Gamages in Holborn St., where I met Mr. Hobday who is on leave from our Bn.[212] Arrived back at Club too late for dinner, so took bus to Queen's Hall where I bought tickets for tonight's and Wed. night's concerts.[213] Went to Polytechnic Institute Cinema across the street and saw British official film of the Somme Battle and French official film of the Allies at Salonika.[214]

The Somme film told the truth as far as it went in showing the first attacks, and I have been in many similar events and situations. Had supper at Verrey's in Regent St. and paid eight shillings for a two shilling meal, being served by young chaps who looked as if they ought to be in the army.[215] In evening, attended a concert in Queen's Hall by the London Symphony Orchestra, conducted by M. Wassili Safonoff.[216] The numbers given were (1) Overture..."Tannhauser"...Beethoven, (2) Aria..."Ocean, Thou Mighty Monster"...Weber ...Vocalist, Miss Edith Evans, (3) Enigma Variations...Elgar, (4) Symphony in A major, No. 7 ...Beethoven.[217] I have never heard this kind of music before, so it was all a new experience to me. I suppose I could not enjoy and appreciate it as those do who are musicians themselves and understand operatic music. But I did like it very much. There were some light ethereal parts which simply carried one right away into the world of dreams and fancy and relieved all mental strain and worry.

212 Gammages: Famous department store founded by Arthur Walter Gammage in 1878. Hobday: Lt. Leonard Stanley Hobday (1884–1955), born England 1884, a resident of Winnipeg; attested Valcartier, September 1914.

213 Queen's Hall: London's leading concert hall, opened in 1893. It was destroyed on 10 May 1941 by the Luftwaffe.

214 The Polytechnic Institute Cinema: A West End stage and motion picture theatre; site of the first commercial film presentation in London in 1896. Somme film: Refers to the 77-minute documentary *The Battle of the Somme*, which debuted in UK theatres in August 1916. The film was seen by 20 million people in the UK. Salonika: Refers to a newsreel film presumably depicting Anglo-French actions on the Macedonian front against the Bulgarians, August–November 1916.

215 Verrey's: Café Verrey, a French restaurant in the West End.

216 Safonoff: Vasily Ilyich Safonov (1866–1918), Russian pianist, composer, and conductor.

217 Beethoven: Here Miller seems to have confused his composers. *Tannhaüser* is an 1845 opera by Richard Wagner. Evans: Edith Evans (1880–1919), a well-known English/Welsh soprano.

Tues., Dec. 5:

I have written to Charlie Cornish to come home for the week-end, so that we can spend a couple of days together. Also wrote to Miss Holbrook at Nottingham arranging to go there Thurs. morning, and I wired Highton of 5th Sigs. (who is on leave and visiting Brighton) to meet me at St. Pancras Stn. on Thurs. morning, as he is going to Derby on the same train.[218] Looked up St. Pancras Stn. this morning: this is the London terminus of the Midland Ry. Visited Mme. Tussaud's wax works museum noon till six o'clock. This collection of images is very interesting and educative for it is almost like meeting the living people. Some of the new people of interest there are John Cornwell, V.C., Capt. Fryatt, Nurse Cavell, Admiral Jellico, Count Zeppelin.[219] The Chamber of Horrors is not a place to frighten even a child. The best sights are the tableaux, such as King John signing Magna Charta, Cinderella, Queen Victoria at Kensington Palace receiving the announcement of her accession to the throne. I had supper at Victoria League Club in Charing Cross Rd. where Charlie Cornish and I dined in July 1915. Went to Duke of York's Theatre in evening to see "Daddy Long Legs". Miss Renee Kelly as Judy Abbott was wonderful.[220] She just carried the audience away with her and forced us from laughter almost to tears again and again. As I had read the book, I enjoyed it fully and followed every detail with closest attention and keenest appreciation. Miss Pritchard and Jervis Pendleton were delightful, and Sally McBride was full of the proper spirit, just bubbling over with girl's fun.[221]

---

218 Miss Holbrook: An English schoolteacher who was a cousin to Marion Wallwin, a classmate of Miller's at Regina Normal.
219 Fryatt: Charles Algernon Fryatt (1872–1916), British civilian sailor who, as captain of the ferry SS *Brussels*, attempted to ram a German U-boat in 1915. Captured in 1916, he was tried and executed by the Germans. Cornwell: John (Jack) Cornwell (1900–1916), a 16-year-old British sailor posthumously awarded the Victoria Cross at the Battle of Jutland. Cavell: Edith Cavell (1865–1915), British nurse executed by the Germans in occupied Belgium. Jellico: Admiral of the Fleet John *Jellicoe* (1859–1935), commander of the Grand Fleet at Jutland (1916) and First Sea Lord as of November 1916. Zeppelin: Ferdinand Graf von Zeppelin (1838–1917), airship pioneer.
220 *Daddy Long Legs*: Play adapted from the 1912 novel of the same name by American author Jean Webster (1876–1912). Kelly: Renee Kelly (1888–1965), English actress.
221 Pritchard, Pendleton, McBride: Names of characters in the play.

Wed., Dec. 6:

Bob Reid, Mitchell, and I visited the Tower of London but did not stay to see more than the White Tower.[222] Went to a cinema in Charing Cross Rd. Bob Reid and I had supper at the Victoria League Club.[223] I had a ticket to concert at Queen's Hall, so went alone and heard the New Queen's Hall Orchestra conducted by Sir Henry J. Wood, and Miss Carrie Tubb, the popular soprano vocalist.[224]

The numbers were (1) Overture... "Coriolan"... Beethoven, by the Orchestra, (2) etc. songs in English, French and Italian by Bach, Handel, Mozart, Rachmaninoff, Verdi, Lalo, Beethoven, Tchaikovsky. The singing was marvellously sweet, pure, and the words so clearly enunciated that I could easily follow the Italian words on the program. The soloist received tremendous applause and many beautiful flowers, both large bouquets of cut flowers, and potted plants in full bloom. The Sunday Times complimented the soloist on her splendid achievement but added that the expensive flowers were quite unnecessary and out of place in War Time. The Orchestra closed the program with "Brunnhilde's Closing Scene from Die Gotterdammerung", illustrating Siegfried's death and descent into Valhalla.[225]

Thurs., Dec. 7:

Feeling rather used up with a dose of influenza which I brought from France with me. Spent the day 11 to 4 p.m. at Zoological Gardens. I did not see all the specimens, but was absorbed so much during the 5 hours that I forgot all about my illness. The wild squirrels in the park are so tame that they come to you to take nuts from your hand. I saw the Lions and Tigers fed on fresh meat in the afternoon. Returning to the Club early in the evening, I wired to Nottingham not to look for me, then reported to the Army Doctor who visits the Club. He said my temp. was 100 and I was not fit to be going about. He sent me to bed and gave me a note of information and orders to report to hospital in morning.

---

222 White Tower: The White Tower is the keep at the Tower of London.
223 Victoria League Club: Branch of the Victoria League for Commonwealth Friendship, a voluntary association promoting imperial cooperation founded in 1901.
224 Wood: Sir Henry Joseph Wood (1869–1944). Prominent British conductor, most famously associated with the Proms (Promenade Concerts), a feature of musical life in London, aimed at all audiences.
225 Closing scene: From Richard Wagner's 1876 opera *The Twilight of the Gods.*

Fri., Dec. 8:

Entered King George Military Hospital near Waterloo Stn., and went to bed at once. A Tasmanian occupies next bed to mine and he loves to tell of the attractions of his country. He thinks it far better than any part of Australia.

Sat., Dec. 9:

Mr. Cornish and Charlie called on me a few minutes in the afternoon and left some fruit for me. I told them I would try to get out tomorrow, though I am in bed all today.

Sun., Dec. 10:

Felt better this morning, so was discharged from Hospital at noon. Went to Cornish's at once after leaving my kit at the Club. We had a jolly afternoon and evening together, though Charlie had to leave early for Shorncliffe. Stayed all night at Cornish's.

Mon., Dec. 11:

Bought a few things and left order for Weekly Times at W.H. Smith's in Kensington. Mitchell and I met for supper at the Victoria League Club and in the evening went to the Playhouse to hear Miss Gladys Cooper in "The Misleading Lady."[226] She is very clever and handled delicate situations with marvellous skill. But we had seats in the Upper Circle and could not observe details, so were a little disappointed. I have visited the Canadian Pay Office and had my leave extended two days, so that it now expires December 15.

Tues., Dec. 12:

Did some buying in the morning. Had dinner at Cornish's and spent the afternoon with Harold and Alfy seeing the Somme film and visiting Mme. Tussaud's. Spent evening and stayed for night at Cornish's.

---

226 *The Misleading Lady*: 1913 play by Charles Goddard and Paul Dickey, subsequently adapted into two films. Cooper: Dame Gladys Cooper (1888–1971), British actress.

Wed., Dec. 13:

Said "Goodbye" to the Cornish's, finished my buying, and took 1:48 p.m. train from Charing Cross Stn. to Folkestone. Got off at the Central Stn. and walked to "Luton" Y.M.C.A. hut on the Leas where I left my rifle and equipment. Took bus to Sandgate and called on Jack Smythe's wife and family for an hour, but Jack is up at barracks and not at home. Walked to St. Martin's Plain to 4th C.I.T.B. Signal Base. Charlie Cornish was downtown, but I met Jack Smythe, now a Sergt., and Sergt. Mattingly and spent the night in their hut.[227]

Thurs., Dec. 14:

Met Charlie this morning. He loaned me a bicycle with which I wheeled to 32nd Bn. at East Sandling where I met Geo. Armstrong of 68th Regina Bn., now a drummer in the 32nd Band, once a pupil of mine at Blackwood, Sask.; Cpl Birch with the 5th when wounded December 15, 1915; several old 32nd Bn. boys, including Capt. Mackay of Stoughton, Lieuts. Beet, Wilding, and Moon, Sergt. Macintyre, and Holmberg who enlisted with me at Weyburn.[228] Capt. Mackay offered to get me a fortnight's extension if I wished it, but I did not see him again and was not keen for it anyway. Charlie and I spent the evening at the Pleasure Gardens Theatre in Folkestone. I slept on the floor in the Q.M. Stores.

Fri., Dec. 15:

Rose at seven and left camp at 8. Walked to White Lion in Cheriton and took bus to Folkestone.[229] Joined "Leave Party" at the harbour and took boat about one o'clock. The sea was calm and the air clear, so we could see land all the way across. On arrival, our party was marched up to the rest camp to spend the night. But we two of the 5th skipped over into the previous day's party which was coming out to take train to Bethune. So we left Boulogne at four o'clock and reached Bethune by midnight

---

227 Smythe: Could not be identified.
228 Beet: Harry Churchill Bert Beet, VC (1874–1946), born England; attested Winnipeg, December 1914. A veteran of the Boer War, Beet had received the Victoria Cross while serving in South Africa with the Sherwood Foresters.
229 White Lion, Cheriton: A public house (pub).

where motor lorries were waiting for us. We were at our Q.M. Stores
at Grand Servins by two, received a whole stack of mail and turned in.

Sat., Dec. 16:

Reported to Paymaster and rejoined Bn. at Camblin l'Abbé. Soon settled down again to the ordinary routine, but not without many a sigh
of regret at having to leave such a comfortable life. O for the day when
we can return to it again!

Mon., Dec. 18:

The 1st Can. Div. is being relieved by the 4th which is moving in here from
the Somme. We are going to Houdain and that district for a month's rest.
Left camp at 9:30 a.m. and marched to billets in Houdain where we took
over billets from 44th Can. Bn. of 4th Div.[230] Stuart Thompson has just
joined their Signallers with a draft of reinforcements. He saw Clements and
Phillips of our section who are at Houdain since Dec. 4 taking a course at
the Corps Signalling School and they told him where I am. We are billeted
in the attic above an estaminet, up under the slates in the dark and cold.

Tues., Dec. 19:

Had a pass 10 a.m. to 8 p.m. to visit Stuart at Camblin l'Abbé, but I got
there over an hour after the 44th Bn. had left for the trenches, so I missed
him and must wait 16 days more for another opportunity to see him.[231]
Before returning to Houdain, I went to 44th Bn. Q.M. Stores at Grand
Servins and left a message for Stuart with one of their signallers.

  This has been the coldest day yet this season, frosty, with a fresh easterly wind, and snow falling lightly in the afternoon.

Wed., Dec. 20:

Mr. Hedley, McGuire and I came to the Bruay aerodrome to take a 3-day
course in signalling, to commence tomorrow.[232] We were to live in the

---

230 Houdain: Mining town, population roughly 2,000 in 1914, about 22 kilometres
     northwest of Vimy.
231 Stuart: Reference to Stuart Thompson. See entry of 10 January 1915.
232 Bruay: Important British aerodrome, 10 kilometres northeast of Houdain.

upper storey of a brewery, but did not like the prospect of such a cold place. Jack Fudger, McGuire and I made enquiry and secured a private room with two beds in a French house at 1 franc per bed each night.

Thurs., Dec. 21:

This is a mining town and lies in a large coal mining district. Coal is cheap and the houses and buildings all have electric light. The family with whom we live are very nice and clean, quite different to so many of the French working classes. The Stepfather, Parlier Leon, works in the mine 3:30 a.m. to 3:30 p.m. The mother is Mme. Delveaux of 50 years, well preserved, very kind to us, grieving over the loss of her married son Victor of 30 years, reported missing since Oct. 28 at Sailly-Saillisel on the Somme. Aline of 18 is helping her mother, but is going to Paris as a maid soon, where her sister of 14 is already in service. André of nine is at school every day but Thursday which is a school holiday like Sat. in Canada. Albert of 3 years is the grandson whose papa was missing on the Somme since Oct. 28.

Sat., Dec. 23:

Rain and wind have prevented aeroplane work, so we have done little signalling. A French biplane of 60 ft. wing landed here on Thurs. in a gale and shower.[233] He remained until yesterday when he set off for Paris again. We returned to billets at Houdain in the evening, though we are to return and try the signalling tomorrow if the weather is good.

Sun., Dec. 24:

Signalling training at aeroplane all day. R.F.C. officers went up and took our flip-flap signals, replying with Claxton horn and lamp.[234] During the morning class, a German aeroplane threw two heavy bombs on Bruay and an adjoining mine-head. We thought at first that they were shells from a gun. But Bruay is much too far from the lines to be shelled. The course of instruction is finished and we returned to Houdain.

---

233 French biplane: Might be the Caudron G.4, a French bomber with a wingspan of just under 60 feet.

234 Claxton horn: Probably a reference to a Klaxon horn.

At night we sat up till after midnight singing songs, eating and drinking.

Mon., Dec. 25:

This is a holiday for everyone in this area – British soldiers and French civilians. It is a French national holiday, "la Fête de Noël". We had quite an ordinary dinner except for the contents of Pongo's and Jack Pells' parcels. In the afternoon, I went to Bruay, walked about a while, then spent the evening at Mme. Delveaux's where McGuire and I were living last week. Everybody seems to be half-intoxicated, for the Frenchmen have been drinking all day, and the soldiers are doing their part. I met a French couple with their three little children, all dressed in their best, carrying two baskets of bottled wine, going to the home of a neighbour or relative to spend a merry evening. Their means of enjoyment are chiefly wine, dancing, and song. Many of the men have beautiful voices and they sing with great spirit and expressive movements of arms and body. "La Marseillaise" is sung a great deal on these festal occasions.

Tues., Dec. 26:

Our half of No. 5 Coy. had their Xmas dinner at 7 this evening. We had roast turkey, vegetables, soup, pie, nuts, etc., quite a complete menu. Col. Dyer made a spirited speech in reply to the toast "Our Bn.". Dr. Brown made a touching reply to the toast "Canada". Charlie Haydon recited from Drummond and I gave them "The Revenge" again as on the same occasion at Bulford Camp a year ago. The musical part of the program was poor. Everybody enjoyed themselves.

Wed., Dec. 27:

Very fine bright weather. We had signalling practice on the hillside above the village this morning and it was a pleasure to be out without gloves or overcoat working in the warm sunshine. Some of the Sigs. reported to Corps Hqrs. at Rebreuve this morning to try for places there as operators and linemen.

Editor's Note: On 28 December 1916, Miller requested a transfer to the Canadian Corps Signals Service. While battalion signallers were charged with maintaining lines of communication between companies and their battalion HQ, corps signallers had the responsibility of sending communications from corps HQ to divisions, adjacent corps,

Miller later captioned this photo in his own hand: "Me – on Xmas morning.
Hope you received plenty of parcels." Credit: Miller family
collection.

*the Royal Flying Corps, and heavy artillery. Corps signallers also worked to intercept
enemy signals, which gave Miller the opportunity to demonstrate his proficiency in
German. On 16 January 1917, Miller's transfer from the 5th Battalion was formalized.
His first posting within the Corps Signals Service was to the British Expeditionary
Force General Headquarters Wireless School, where he underwent training in corps-
level signalling procedures and equipment. In the entries that follow, Miller gives the
names of many signallers he served with who were British or Imperial troops from other
Dominions, many of whom could not be identified. By the Battle of Vimy Ridge in April
1917, British units made up nearly a third of the Canadian Corps' order of battle, which
helps to account for the presence of many British signallers at Canadian Corps HQ.*[235]

---

235 On British units in the Canadian order of battle at Vimy, see Gary Sheffield, "Vimy
Ridge and the Battle of Arras: A British Perspective," in *Vimy Ridge: A Canadian
Reassessment*, ed. Geoffrey Hayes, Andrew Iarocci, and Mike Bechthold (Waterloo:
Wilfrid Laurier University Press, 2007), 15–30.

Thurs., Dec. 28:

Walked over to Corps Wireless Hq. at Rebreuve and made enquiry about chances of my getting on that work. Found their O.R. Cpl. to be Johnston of C.M.R.'s who was in one of my classes in Shorncliffe.[236]

Fri., Dec. 29:

Interviewed Corps Wireless and Intelligence Officers for my proficiency in German language. Was favourably reported on and returned to Bn. to await orders. Goodwin and I spent evening in Bruay where we visited a French picture show and several shops.

Sun., Dec. 31:

The boys bought wines, etc. and during the evening we remained in billet dancing and singing until midnight when we joined hands to sing "Auld Lang Syne" and wished New Year greetings all round. The one wish of everyone was "May we see 1917 end in God's country, Canada".

---

236 Johnston: Probably James William Johnston (1886–?), born England; attested Niagara, June 1915. Killed in action at the Battle of Passchendaele, October 1917. Commemorated on the Menin Gate.

1917

Mon., Jan. 1:

Best of New Year's Day surprises, Stuart Thompson walked up from Estrée Cauchie and dropped in to see me just as I was packing up to go and report to Corps Wireless, for orders came through to that effect today and I obtained Col. Dyer's sanction yesterday for my transfer on probation. Stuart and I chatted all the remainder of the day, we walked down to Corps, back to Houdain for supper and the evening, then I accompanied him part way back to his billet. I slept in Rebreuve.

Tues., Jan. 2:

Reported to officer this morning and ordered to fill in time until a new course begins at G. Hq.[1] Left in car at 1:30 p.m. for No. 6 Listening Post on the right of Neuville St. Vaast.[2] Arrived about 8 p.m. This station is manned by L/cpl. Loveday, Sprs. Holyman and Gibson, interpreters, and Sprs. Lewis, Cook and Ernie —, linemen.[3] Spr. Douglas, the cook, went on leave tonight. We have a deep dugout beside a new "flying pig" bty. about 250 yards behind our front line.[4]

---

1 New course: That is, at the Canadian Corps Signal School.
2 Neuville St. Vaast: Neuville-Saint-Vast, a town 3.5 kilometres south of Vimy Ridge, population in 1914 about 800.
3 Holyman: Only one Holyman served in the CEF, Thomas Henry Holyman, a clerk who never served in France.
4 "Flying Pig": Nickname for the British 9.45-inch heavy mortar. The Canadian Corps Wireless Section War Diary indicates that the firing of this heavy battery was so loud that it forced No. 6 Post, to which Miller was attached, to shut down intermittently.

Mon., Jan. 15:

I have had a good time in the past two weeks and learned much about
the listening post work, the working of the instrument, and all that is
likely to be required of me. We have lived well, for there is a splendid
Y.M.C.A. canteen among the ruins of Neuville St. Vaast. Spr. Douglas
returned from leave tonight, and I packed up, came out to No. 5 post,
took car back to Rebreuve, Corps Hq.

Tues., Jan. 16:

Signed my transfer paper this morning, which puts me permanently on
Corps Wireless as soon as it has gone through all the necessary channels.
Went to Houdain for a bath, and met all the boys of the 5th Sigs. once
again. In evening, Goodwin and I walked to Bruay, called on Madame
Delveaux, and visited several stores in town. Have walked many miles
today through the brisk, cold air, and am feeling better than ever. Two
weeks confinement in a deep dugout needs a break and change like this
or one's health would fail.

Wed., Jan. 17:

In afternoon went by motor car to amplifier station in Cité Calonne.

Fri., Jan. 19:

Went out over the loops this morning, up through front trenches and
mining tunnels under No-Man's Land. Car came up to this station tonight
and Mr. Manson paid us.[5]

Sat., Jan. 20:

The 2nd Div. are moving out to Corps reserve and the 1st Div. are taking
over this front. Danielsen and I walked out to Bully Grenay this morning, found our Bn. and saw the boys, saw that our transfers are going

---

5 Manson: Lieutenant (later Captain) John Cormack Manson (1889–1954), born
  Scotland; attested Toronto, December 1914, then officer commanding the Canadian
  Corps Wireless Section.

through, then spent the day in town, returning to Calonne in evening.[6] Wireless message summons us to Corps Hq. in morning.

Sun., Jan. 21:

Danielsen and I started out to walk to Rebreuve, but met car in Hersin. Mr. Manson took us to Camblin l'Abbé and left me there while they went on to Neuville St. Vaast at night. Dan has gone up to his station on Vimy Ridge. We arrived Rebreuve about 7 p.m. after having considerable trouble with the lights on the car.

Mon., Jan. 22:

After dinner, Stuart, the chauffeur, brought Sergt. Skinner and four of us new men to G.H.Q. Wireless School through St. Pol and Hedin to Campagne-le-Hedin. Sergt. Skinner is going to England in a week to take his commission in the Can. Corps Wireless.[7]

Wed., Jan. 24:

I am waiting for the last class to be passed out and next course to begin. Was free yesterday and am so today also, so spend my time writing letters and reading. The weather keeps quite cold but fine. The ponds are frozen hard enough to bear one and the ground is white with snow but the roads clean and hard.

Fri., Feb. 2:

Our class has not commenced yet, as we are waiting for a draft of interpreters to arrive from England. Meanwhile we are filling time usefully with route marches, buzzer practice, and German dictation on the phone. I have been on guard at the main entrance one night. We are paid each Fri. afternoon. We are free after midday Sat. and Sun. and lights must be out by 10 p.m. Of four of us who came together from Can. Corps, Coates of 10th Can. Bn. has been sent to England and will likely go on to Canada

---

6 Danielsen: Lauritz Frederick Libercht (1885–?), born Denmark; attested Prince Albert, January 1915.

7 Skinner: Charles Skinner (1890–?), born Scotland; attested Vancouver, February 1915.

as being too young, only 17 yrs, though he is fully 6 ft. high. Dixon and Wilson of 58th Bn. are to take the lineman's course. Hilsendeger of 58th Bn. is an interpreter like myself. An Alsatian by name of Charlie gives us the German dictation on the telephone. He is now on parole and has a great deal of personal freedom, being a prisoner who gave himself up to the French by coming over from the German lines one night. Sergt. Skinner went to England tonight on leave. I have had no mail since coming here, as it must come through both 5th Bn. and Corps Wireless. But I find my days so full that I have no time for writing letters.

Editor's Note: Miller's previous sentence may go some ways towards explaining the two-month gap in the diary that follows.

Fri., Apr. 6:

I was in close quarantine in No. 3 hut for measles Feb. 12 to March 1. The whole camp was under quarantine and out of bounds to other troops until we left last Sat. I completed my course and passed all tests last week. Petersen and I took train from Beurainville Saturday afternoon, the first train over the new double line from St. Pol to Étaples. Spent night in St. Pol rest camp. Left Rudy, Brand, Albrecht and Sonina there with 3rd Army. Came on to Bethune and spent a night there in the Belfast Boy Scouts hut. To Lillers next day by train and then by motor car to Choques where we spent two nights at Army Wireless. Came to Camblain l'Abbé on Wednesday by motor car. Walked over to Bn. in evening at Cambligneul and saw most of the 5th Sigs. and Mr. Hedley. Yesterday morning, we were warned to proceed to No. 6 post and we came up in early afternoon, so here I am again in the old place with Cpl. Loveday in charge and Spr. Holyman on the staff also. Gibson went out yesterday.

We have had much bad weather of late, a month of clouds, cool damp weather with rain, sleet and snow, some very heavy gales. The ground was white with snow on Tuesday morning. There was frost last night. Yesterday was very fine and the mud began to dry up. Today has made a good beginning.

In hut No. 3 at Campagne-le-Hesdin, I made the acquaintance of:

Jno. Dutton of Cheshire Regt., did a spell of duty at Gibraltar in 1914–15; fought at La Bassee in 1915, wounded, now permanent base, cookhouse fatigue.

West and Belcher, the two camp gardeners.

Brown of Worcester, a fitter in R.E. motor shops.

Frank Gribble of London, SE near Cornish's place. Amos Collyer
(Happy), wash house fatigue.

Johnson of R.E.

Buckley on fatigue red cross hut.

Fred Thrower, Tom Lloyd, Sid Wood, Arnold, Maher, Smith.

We all enjoyed our 2 months or more together in spite of the quarantine and good-will ruled in the hut until we were broken up and
sent up the line.

Some of the interpreters were Cpl. Behrmann, L.cpl Cobb, Jackson,
Grimsey, Mazzier, Borrow, Julman, Chisholm, Baines.[8]

Petersen of 1st Can. Bn. and I left Campagne Sat. Mar. 31. Took train
at Beurainville 8:30 pm and proceeded to St. Pol where we spent night
in rest camp, etc. Duties went on at No. 6 post as usual until

Sun., Apr. 8:

when we moved our instruments over to the cave and tunnel in preparation for the attack next morning.[9] On the way under heavy shell fire, we
had to free a man stuck in the mud in the trench.

Editor's Note: The Battle of Vimy Ridge, 9–12 April 1917

*Part of the larger Arras offensive of April–May 1917, the Battle of Vimy Ridge saw
all four divisions of the Canadian Corps in action together for the first time, albeit
still under the command of a British officer, Lt. General Julian Byng. A strategically
important seven-kilometre-long German stronghold, Vimy Ridge was attacked by the
Canadian Corps on Easter Monday, 9 April 1917, after weeks of preparation. That day,
the Canadians seized most of the ridge, including the highest point, Hill 145, where
Walter Allward's famous memorial was unveiled in 1936. It was a significant victory,*

---

8 Mazzier: Probably Klaas Massier (1888–?), born in the Netherlands; attested
  Haileybury, Ontario, April 1916.

9 Miller's entry is somewhat confusing here, with the date both continuing the
  previous sentence and marking a new entry. Cave and tunnel: The region around
  Vimy Ridge consists of soft chalk, conducive to extensive tunnelling. Thousands of
  Canadians lived in tunnels facing the ridge in the weeks before the attack.

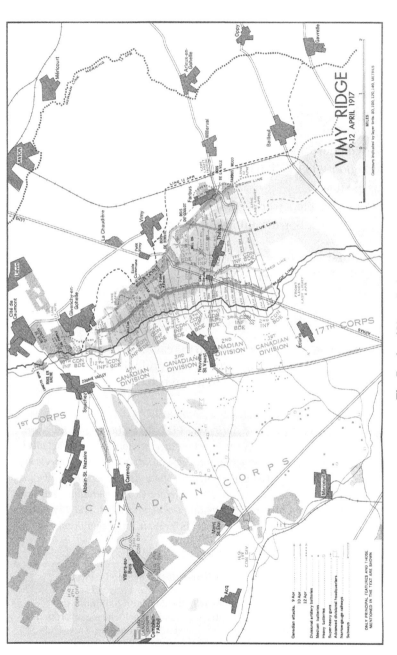

The Battle of Vimy Ridge

While Miller wrote little about the defining battle itself, his diary includes many references to the sector immediately before and after the Easter 1917 engagement. Note Mont St. Eloi, left of centre, from whose monastery tower Miller viewed the region on 15 April 1917.

but one earned at an immense cost in blood: nearly 11,000 Canadians were killed and wounded, most of them on the first day of fighting. Although it is often remembered as a Canadian battle, vital support for the attack on Vimy Ridge was provided by the British 5th Division, the Royal Engineers, and by a huge weight of British artillery attached to the Canadian Corps. Vimy Ridge was recognized as an important victory at the time, albeit in the context of yet another offensive that failed to meet its objectives. Surprisingly, Miller writes fewer than a hundred words about the battle, but as was the case for many Canadians, it subsequently assumed great significance in his sense of self.[10]

Sun., Apr. 15:

Great attack was made last Monday morning 5:30 a.m. and Vimy Ridge taken by Canadian Corps. I was in charge of inst. to pick up power buzzer from 4th and 6th Bdes.[11] Next day I was out over the top carrying wounded and I was up as far as Thelus village.[12] It is utterly destroyed by our shellfire. It is reported we took 12,000 prisoners and 150 guns from the Huns in this battle.[13]

The weather is infernally bad since the attack with snow and rain every day save yesterday, which was fine.

Friday I visited dentist at Houdain to have a nerve killed. Last evening I was at Mt. St. Eloi and climbed the ruined tower of the monastery. It affords a splendid view of all Vimy Ridge, Arras and the high ground south and east of that town. There was only a little artillery fire at one point on the eastern skyline. We hear that our fellows are closing on Lens.

It has rained lightly all today.

Today, Mr. Manson, Sgt. McClellan, Petersen, and I took small gadget and went up to Willerval and Mt. Forêt Quarry corner to test lines.[14] Returned by Vimy Village and Neuville St. Vaast to Camblain soaked through by the rain that set in in the afternoon.

---

10 On the battle and its somewhat overblown role in shaping postwar Canadian identity, see Tim Cook, *Vimy: The Battle and the Legend* (Toronto: Random House Canada, 2017).

11 Power buzzer: Refers to passing a wireless signal through the ground using induction rather than a cable. A receiver could be attached to a metal spike to transmit the message. Such messages were, like those transmitted through the atmosphere, vulnerable to interception.

12 Thélus: Small town (population in 1914 about 400) located just southeast of Vimy Ridge.

13 Prisoners: The actual number of German prisoners was approximately 4,000.

14 McClellan: Actually *MacLellan*. See entry of 29 July 1917.

Thurs., Apr. 19:

Visited Canadian dentist at Houdain yesterday morning and had tooth filled. L/cpl. Loveday and I went on to Bruay and saw "The Very Lights" at the Grand Theatre in the evening.[15] I spent night with Leon and family and this morning we returned by motor lorry to Corps. On 9:30 parade warned to proceed up line. Car broke down before we reached Neuville. Walked with a party to Vimy and Petit Vimy, but this was a mistake so we returned to stns. near Neuville.

Mon., Apr. 23:

Spent Fri. at J. Wireless stn. On Sat. guided an operator to Petit Vimy to relieve Will Laurie, returned to L. stn. Yesterday proceeded to A stn. and helped move to Lievin where we established wireless stn. and I came on to Amplificateur stn. This 5th Div. made a local attack this morning and we were to read power buzzer for 95th Bde. but were not needed as it happened.[16]

Tues., May 8:

George Hydes and I were relieved at 3 p.m. and came by the light car back to Corps, arriving at tea time. During our fortnight on the station, we have had lovely fine summer-like weather which has brought back the summer birds and set everything agrowing. Last night's shower has made a wonderful change. It is warmer than ever now, and all the buds are bursting. The tree tops and hedges are all veiled in green and plum and cherry trees are in blossom. From Villers-au-Bois to Camblain l'Abbé the country is as pretty as many places over in Kent, and apart from the signs of war, it reminds me very strongly of scenes in England.[17]

---

15 "Very Lights": A popular British Army musical review. "Very Lights" were flares which took their name from the inventor of the flare gun, Edward Wilson Very (1847–1910).

16 5th Division: The British 5th Division (to which the 95th Brigade was attached), still attached to the Canadian Corps, launched a subsidiary attack about five kilometres north of Vimy on 23 April, part of the ongoing Arras offensive.

17 Now site of the Canadian Corps headquarters.

It seems that a touch of green and a few flowers will make a paradise of any place at this season.

Thurs., May 10:

Had a bath yesterday and spent the day lying in the grass, drinking in the spring sunshine and writing letters. Today we had parades and instruction. Dixon, Wilson, and others arrived from Campagne and Choques this morning.

Mr. Skinner received a Blighty in Lievin yesterday.[18]

Sat., May 19:

I am still at Headquarters at Camblain l'Abbé and have been having quite an easy time for the past 10 days.[19] We parade twice a day, at 08:45 and 14:00, and each time we generally have an hour or two of buzzer and code practice. I had a pass and spent one day in Houdain with my old Battn., the day of their Bde. sports at Hallicourt. I met Mr. Hedley, Sergt. Clements, Goodwin, Mitch, Moggy, Boates, Willis, J. Pells, and Bob Reid. Most of the boys have gone away for commissions, Highton, Phillips, Coombs, to the R.F.C. Pells and Bob Reid are in Orderly Room. McGuire is a L/cpl.

I met Stuart at Chateau de la Haie and we have spent two evenings together. Yesterday, we went to Estrée Cauchie for supper together. We met Garnet Macklin one night at some sports near Gouy Servins.[20] He does not seem to have changed a bit tho' he looked strange in the kilt....

We are having fine weather for the season, not so hot as it was a week ago, because there are plenty of clouds and an occasional shower these days...

---

18 Blighty: Lieutenant Skinner was seriously wounded in the thigh. He returned to France in March 1918.

19 Headquarters: Canadian Corps headquarters, although Miller's service file indicates that he has been attached to the British First Army Wireless Company as of this day. In mid-1917, the First Army comprised the Canadian Corps and two British army corps. This, in turn, explains Miller's subsequent temporary attachment to various British units (see, for example, entry of 23 July 1917).

20 Macklin: Lt. Garnet Ernescliffe Macklin, MC (1892–1975) of Miller's hometown, Milliken, Ontario. Macklin served with the 15th Battalion, raised by the 48th Highlanders of Canada regiment, hence the reference to his kilt.

We see quite a number of triplanes these days.[21] They have only become common since the first of May. They are the best, fastest and most successful plane made now. They beat the German fast planes nearly every time....

I am writing in a meadow on the edge of the village. An old lady has just been along and we had a little chat. Her only son of 34 years has been a prisoner in Germany since Aug. 14, 1914. She is quite bent and crippled and seems to always have that one grief on her mind, for I have met her before. She receives letters from her son regularly and he seems to be always in good health; he works in a small factory. I showed her my snaps and she took quite a keen interest in all the ones of home, and she asked my age and the ages of all the folks at home. She shook hands warmly and called me "Mon garçon" when she turned to hobble back to the house. These people are wonderfully brave and sympathetic.

Leave to England has opened again and Cpl. Johnston went today.

Wed., May 30:

Came to establish station in brick piles between Petit Bois and railway with Corporal Rognowsky, Danielsen, Wilson, Kloepfer, and Murray; by car to railway bridge in Angres, then walked up, carrying our outfit.[22]

Fri., June 1:

Set up instrument and put out lines last night. This afternoon the Hun bombarded us with heavies for hours, cut all our lines to pieces, and made several direct hits on our brick pile and the concrete gun emplacements, while we lay safe in the tunnel under the edge of the brick pile.

---

21 Triplanes: Sopwith Triplane, flown by squadron of the Royal Naval Air Service, the Royal Navy's counterpart to the RFC, which deployed squadrons to the Western Front in early 1917.

22 Rognowsky: Could not be identified. Miller spells the name in more than one way in the coming pages. Kloepfer: Gregory Kloepfer (1889–?) of Chepstowe, Ontario; attested Mildmay, Ontario, March 1916.

This photo, of Miller's sister Nellie and brother Carman posing in front of the family home in October 1914, was apparently one of the "snaps" Miller shared. Credit: Miller family collection.[23]

Sun., June 3:

At midnight May 31–June 1, we put over 500 gasbombs and another hundred last night when this 10th Bde. went over the top to take the electrical station.[24] Objectives were gained in some cases, but later our chaps had to fall back on their former positions. We are said to have taken over 200 prisoners, and apart from that, casualties are heavy on both sides.

---

23 The Miller family farm was at Lot 28, Concession 4, Milliken. Miller's great-grandfather Henry, the first member of the Miller family to be born in Canada, purchased the land in 1838 from his in-law James Kennedy.

24 10th Brigade: In late May and early June 1917 the 4th Canadian Division launched a series of set piece attacks northwest of Vimy Ridge in the region south of the Souchez River. The 50th Battalion took the electrical station in question but was unable to hold it in the face of German counterattacks.

Both sides have been busy today getting out their wounded, and the white flag and red cross armlet are being respected. One of our stretcher bearers told me that both Canadian and German S.B.s are working over the same ground, and that German S.B.s bandaged some of our wounded and beckoned to our fellows to direct them where to go with their stretchers.

This fight appears to have been a bloody mix up, and nothing but butchery. Some of the 50th Bn. have come out with their nerves and morale completely gone.[25]

Four young German prisoners, acting as stretcher bearers for our fellows, passed by here and stopped a while in our tunnel. Three were farm lads from Thuringia and the fourth from Mainz. They were very fine, intelligent-looking young chaps, were eager to talk, and were quite frank and unreserved in answering questions. They were afraid they would be kept here in the line to work for us. They say they are all on short rations, both the army and the people at home. There is no one left at home to work the land except the women, children, very old men, and prisoners, and as a result crops are bound to be very poor. They claim their prisoners are well treated, get more food than the German soldiers, and have a good deal of freedom where they work on the farms. They wish heartily the war would end at once, but they say the soldiers on both sides are quite powerless to stop it.

When word came that there were no more wounded to be carried and that they would now go back away from the shelled area, they were certainly pleased, and they all shook hands with Kloepfer and me, for we were the only ones who had been able to talk to them in their own language. One of them said he was 20, but they all looked younger than that.

Mon., June 4:

Mr. Jones and the Sergt. came up this morning, brought us some mail and paid us. This evening I went out with L/cpl. R. to Kings Cross to get our rations at Bde. We got no rations but we enjoyed our walk, for

---

25 50th Battalion: Regiment authorized November 1914 and raised in Calgary. The 50th Battalion War Diary recounts ferocious fighting over the course of the day with its "D" company suffering 75 per cent casualties. In all, the 50th suffered 200 casualties in the brief action.

Canadian official war photographer Ivor Castle took this
photograph of Miller for the *Canadian Daily Record*. On the reverse, Miller later
wrote, "Souchez Creek, back of Vimy – May 1917 shell hole bath place fixed
up by Engineers near Callonne Trench." Credit: Miller family collection / Ivor
Castle, "Comfort and Safety," June 1917. Department of National Defence /
Library and Archives Canada / PA-001478.

it was a quiet evening after a very fine hot day; the full moon rising in a cloudless sky just after sunset. Crossing the Pimple on the Vimy Ridge one gets a good view of all this area on both sides of Hirondelle wood and ridge, even of Lens, though there was too much smoke this evening all over the battle line, so only a few towers and tall chimneys were distinguishable.[26] It only gets dark at ten o'clock now. On our return after that time, the flares were going up and the flashes of bursting shells marked out the firing line far in front and below us. It was hard to take the war seriously on such a beautiful night; yet all the way we walked over shell-torn ground, stretchers were being taken out with their burdens, and outside the dressing station lay a silent object sewed up in a blanket and labelled Pte. Oikari of the 50th Bn. What strange fate it was that brought him from his far away island home in Japan to die on the field of honour as a Canadian soldier![27]

Fri., June 15:

We are still in the brick field with the same gang, but we are getting no results for our work. Fritz tried once again day before yesterday to blow us out of our position with more shells than last time, but he did no more damage than to get a heavy shell in the gun emplacement at our doorway. I missed it all by leaving early in the morning and going to Camblain l'Abbé for a change of clothes and canteen stuff, then to Neuville St. Vaast for our mail, and back to Souchez for a bath on the way back to the dugout. An officer photographed me sitting in the swim with my steel helmet on, for the Canadian War Records pictures. I suppose that picture will be circulated on post cards and printed in books, though it will most likely prove a failure.

We have had continued fine hot weather so far this month with only a few thundershowers. I have never seen such a fine spring season anywhere.

---

26 Pimple: The nickname for a fortified German position at the northernmost point of Vimy Ridge.

27 Oikari: Some two hundred Japanese Canadians served in the First World War, but Miller's assumption about the nationality of the private was incorrect, perhaps based on a misreading of his name or a misprint on the label. Victor *Oikar* (1882–1917), a resident of Three Hills, Alberta, was born in Finland. He is buried in the CWGC Villers Station Cemetery, France.

Sat., June 16:

Danielsen returned to Corps this morning for a rest as he has been in the line almost continuously this year. The 85th Bn. is in the line here now.[28] They say they lose more men holding the line than when making attacks. Fritz has made it hot here for three days past, so that it is very dangerous to go for water or rations and movement during daylight is quite impossible. Weather very fine and hot.

Mon., June 18:

For three days the Hun had two whizz-bang batteries trained on our path leading up beside the railroad to the spring in the angle where we get our water, and he almost got Greg Kloepfer and me going up there one evening. But those guns have all been quiet the last two days, probably put out of action by our guns, for our planes have been back over his lines every day.

Our planes have complete mastery on this sector and are doing wonderful work, back and forth over the positions all day long. We hardly ever see a Hun plane, and when our planes are not on hand to oppose them approaching our positions, the anti-aircraft usually succeed in turning them and driving them back.

A triplane of ours brought down two enemy planes on this sector front day before yesterday.[29] Yesterday three enemy planes chased one of our contact scout planes down almost to earth over the trenches in front of us, ripped off several hundred machine gun bullets, and seemed to have disabled our fellow. But it was only a ruse for escaping. He fluttered and nose-dived until about 300 ft. above ground, when he straightened up and flew away, unsteadily as it seemed, over the electric station, along Hirondelle Wood and ridge, rising over Angres and Lievin and returning to the front once more. He must have done some valuable observing.

This morning our heaviest guns are booming away, shaking the ground here from miles behind us, the big shells roaring overhead

---

28 85th Battalion: Authorized in September 1914, the 85th Battalion (North Nova Scotia Highlanders) played a decisive role in April 1917 in the capture of Hill 145 during the Battle of Vimy Ridge.

29 Triplane combat: No victories were recorded for triplanes on 16 June, but several were recounted for the 15th, which may be what Miller is referring to.

and going far back into the enemy territory to burst out of range of our hearing. Our heavies are very busy thus nearly every day and often at night, occasionally varying it by putting a few into his trench positions........

This is strawberry and rose season. We usually have a bouquet of fine red, pink, and white roses on the table in the dugout these days. The boys find quite a lot of strawberries in the abandoned gardens in Petit Bois, Lievin, and Givenchy. I went over to the former place last evening, but found nothing save a few roses. The place is shelled to pieces and is still under direct observation from a fosse in the enemy lines, so one has to be very careful in moving about....[30]

Wilson of the 50th Bn. has been telling me this morning of his experiences in Canada.[31] His home is in England; all his time in Canada he worked for Ellis, a big fruit grower and market gardener in the western Ont. peninsula, in Essex county near the edge of Kent, 20 mi. from Chatham, 30 from Windsor, and 3 from the shore of Lake Erie. He received two dollars a day the year round and had a car of his own for both business and pleasure. Their farm was small, all taken up with fruit orchard and greenhouses; they have one of the biggest greenhouses in Ont. which they can work with horses and plow right inside under the glass. They spray all the orchards very systematically several times each year, prune carefully, keep the soil worked, and grow no undercrops. Wilson says the job is open for him when he goes back, he likes it very much, and intends to settle in that district, as his boss will assist him in starting up. I strongly urged him to stay with it and never let the West lure him away from such a life with such good prospects. Few British boys find such congenial conditions in Canada, and take up with the occupation they try first as he has done.

Tues., June 19:

Weather hot with scattered thunderstorms. A part of this Bn. and the Tommies on our left made a local attack at 2:30 p.m. to straighten the

---

30 Fosse: In this case, a ditch or defilade in the enemy line.

31 Wilson: Could not be identified. Miller's comment on the conditions experienced by British boys may be a reference to the British Home Children, impoverished children sent to Canada as indentured labourers. Several thousand – perhaps as many as ten thousand – subsequently served in the CEF, a majority of those who were eligible.

line on this front.[32] It is reported they had no casualties because the Huns left their front line and ran as soon as our chaps went over.

Heavy artillery fire developed later and losses became heavy.[33] The Hun counterattacked repeatedly, and has just repeated the attempt now at 10 pm. The shelling has been incessant, at times violent, for nearly 8 hours now.

An original 13th Bn. officer has just gone through here with a broken forearm. He was out with the 1st Div. over two years ago, wounded and discharged, but since rejoined and on his first trip up the line this 2nd time......

Mr. Jones and Sergt. McClellan called and paid us at noon. We had a cold supper because of shell fire. Bn. relief tonight.

Wed., June 20:

Station was relieved 4:30 p.m. and instruments returned to Corps. L/cpl. Rognosky, Wilson, and Kloepfer went in the car to Corps, Murray and I to Sturdy's Listening Set, relieving Dixon and Johnston.

Thurs., June 21:

Showers last night: cooler with fresh breezes since. Our people gave Fritz several hundred gas mortar bombs this morning at 2:30 a.m. on this front.[34] He came back with lively shell-fire for a time and the 50th Bn. suffered quite a number of casualties. With this new gas of ours the German respirators are supposed to be useless, while ours is proof against it.[35] Yet through the mismanagement of someone, our fellows always have casualties when gas is put over. In nearly every case the end is death.[36]

---

32 This Battalion: That is, the 85th, the North Nova Scotia Highlanders. See entry of 16 June 1917. Tommies: The 5th Battalion, Lincolnshire Regiment of the 46th Division.

33 Casualties: 85th Battalion War Diary records 5 killed and 30 wounded in the counter-attack.

34 Gas mortar bombs: The 50th Battalion War Diary notes "2 tons of gas and 500 Stokes shells" were used, – an important reminder that gas continued to be widely used throughout the war by all sides.

35 New gas: Might be phosgene or diphosgene, a highly toxic choking agent in use for over a year, but "new" in the sense of replacing chlorine gas. It is untrue that German respirators were powerless against it, but it was colourless, unlike chlorine, giving the enemy less time to don their gasmasks.

36 Casualties due to own gas: The 50th Battalion War Diary notes some "70 to 80 casualties" when some gas shells fell short in front of an adjacent unit. Two men of the 50th itself were killed and eight were wounded by "friendly" gas.

Sat., June 23:

Sturdy relived by Savage this afternoon while I was out at Bde. having a bath. We have had abundant rain last two days; the mud has become a bit troublesome and the weather is cooler; but the plants have freshened up again. Everywhere you find the rank growth of June in herbs, grass, and foliage. Many herbs are in bloom including buttercups & the tall crimson weed same as at home.

Tues., June 26:

It was discovered today that the Germans have abandoned their forward positions on this Bn. (50th) front and on the left on Hill 65 and Fosse 3, held by Imperial troops. A daylight advance was made to occupy certain trenches, and this evening the 10th Bde. made an attack and took further trenches.

Wed., June 27:

We read 11 messages for 10th Bde. in their attack and they relied on us for their communication. Moved station to 12th Advanced Bde. to-day to prepare for scheme in attack on Avion tomorrow morning. Bayliss of 18th Bn. is with us in place of Savage.

Thurs., June 28:

38th, 72nd, & 85th Bns. went over this morning at 2:30 and took all objectives, got into Avion, met the 10th Prussian Guards, and took some prisoners.[37] We were not used.

Returned to former position in afternoon by 85th Bn. dressing station. Had difficulty in getting our outfit carried and were not able to set up this evening. Attack by 46th Imperial Div. in evening over Hill 65 and into Cité du Moulin to align their position with that of the Canadians.[38]

---

37 Avion: On 28 June 1917 the 3rd and 4th Canadian Divisions advanced in order to keep contact with German forces retreating in their sector, south of the Souchez River, taking the German trench line in front of the occupied French town of Avion and then most of the town itself.

38 46th Imperial Division: A British Army division. The 46th advanced on the Canadian left, north of the Souchez River.

A heavy thunderstorm broke at the commencement of the attack, rain poured down for over an hour and thunder added to the roar of the artillery. The attack was a complete success.

Fri., June 29:

Weather a little fresher, breezy and partly cloudy. Front comparatively quiet until evening; our artillery busy moving up into this area.

Sat., June 30:

I made last trip to 12th Bde. Advanced Hq. this morning and brought back remainder of our equipment. The Hun was shelling La Coulotte and this side of Avion....

I was relieved this afternoon by Griffiths and came out by car to Camblin l'Abbé. The weather is cooler, cloudy, and with fresh winds. Wheat is headed out. Growth has been rapid of late since the heavy rains; all crops look well and the growth of weeds and grass is quite rank.

Sun., July 1:

Our troops took Cité du Moulin and advanced 700 yds. into Lens this morning. The Canadians hold most of Avion now; Fritz is out of it, except a bit of the east side which is no-man's land. There has been a continuous rumble of heavy artillery all day in the direction of Souchez, i.e. probably on the Lens front.

Special service in Chaplain's Ass'c'n hut this evening. Chaplain said "Keep the printed programs as souvenirs, boys; they will be valuable in a few months time". Everybody is wondering what he meant; hoping that it is a prophecy.

Mon., July 2:

Big sports here at Corps Hq. all afternoon and concert in evening by the "Rum Jars" concert party. Flags flying and refreshment booth running as at such a celebration at home. The booth even sold bottled ginger beer. They do try hard to make army life pleasant for us.

Tues., July 3:

In afternoon, Dixon, Bierworth and I walked or stole rides back to Rancicourt quarries for a swim; returning we had supper in Estrée Cauchie and got back to the hut by seven.[39] Weather is cooler with clouds, showers and fresh winds.

Wed., July 4:

Made a bed for myself this afternoon. Canadian mail was in yesterday and I have many letters to answer.

Russian victory in Galicia with capture of over 17,000 prisoners announced today.[40]

Sun., July 8:

The wireless personnel is now all handed over to Divisions, the last of the boys leaving us this evening.

After tea, Wilson, Kloepfer, and I walked by Cambligneul to Villers-Chatel where we strolled all through the Chateau grounds and park, returning by Aubigny and Agnières to camp after nine.[41] The Chateau woods are remarkable for the great number of fine old trees of many kinds: beech, oak, elm, birch, poplar, and kinds I did not know. One wide path or promenade which leads right across the grounds from front to rear is lined on each side for 200 yds. with magnificent beeches 3 to 4 ft. through with 50 ft. bare trunk and interlaced branches above. The remaining 500 yds. is done with blue beeches, as in the diagram (2).

When walking through this promenade, we found it so calm while a strong wind was blowing outside, the light so strangely softened and diffused, and the gentle rustling of the leaves so soothing a sound that the place seemed like a bit of fairyland. There is a grotto shrine in the grounds also, built of rocks and cement on top of the ground among the trees. Several candles were burning in the shrine and, as we passed it,

---

39 Bierworth: John Henry Bierworth (1891–1959) of Elmwood, Ontario; attested Walteron, Ontario, 30 March 1916.

40 Russian victory in Galicia: A reference to the Battle of Zborov, fought in Galicia (then part of Austria-Hungary) 1–2 July 1917 as part of the Kerensky Offensive, Russia's last major offensive of the war.

41 Villers-Châtel: Village in the Pas-de-Calais, 20 kilometres due west of Vimy Ridge.

some young girls came along and went in to trim them. This is the Hqrs. of a reserve imperial Div. but the French owners still live in the Chateau and farm house. The crops in the surrounding fields are as fine as any I have seen. There is one patch of 2 or 3 acres of poppies.

We have had new potatoes in rations for a week. Cherries are ripe on the trees in the village orchards. Fresh onions and tomatoes are being sold in the stores....

It is announced that since Jan. 1, the British have spotted 5,000 German battery positions, obtained direct hits on 4,000 of his guns, of which 1,280 were destroyed by this counter battery fire.[42]

Fri., July 13:

Day before yesterday, I was sent up to Z.Q. station between Vimy and Farbus, but found the station already withdrawn & the instruments at 3rd Bde. Hq. at Thelus Cave.[43] I slept at a dugout by some concrete gun emplacements on the east slope of the ridge with Hilton and

---

42 Counter-battery fire: Refers to locating enemy artillery and directing fire on it. The figures Miller reports for German guns destroyed are greatly inflated.

43 Z.Q.: The Morse code call sign of the wireless station.

Gelfond. The car brought us out to Corps again yesterday afternoon. Danielsen, Demme, Savage, Kloepfer and Wilcox (Whizz-bang) left us to go to the base tonight, to Aubigny by car, then by train to Etaples. First Division are marching by today on way out to new position on left of Can. Corps....

There is much talk now of the events in Germany, the summoning of the Crown Council, the Russian offensive with 30,000 prisoners in two weeks, and our coming big offensive on this front.[44] Everyone is a bit optimistic.

Mon., July 16:

Weather has been cooler with showers, though very hot at times. We have had few duties of late. After morning parade, Cpl. Wrognoski gave us an hour at German conversation; then we spent the time till noon in the hut reading, writing and chatting or out strolling or playing games.[45] In the afternoon, Cpo. W. gave me an hour at French conversation and reading. After tea, we would get our mail and then go to the cinema or walk to Villers-Chatel or Aubigny where we could always buy the morning French papers and get the latest news. We usually get back to camp by 9:30 and turn in soon after.

Hilton, Blaikie and I came to Lieven this evening to open a stn. on 4th Bde. front; car left Camblain at 9:45 pm.[46]

Thurs., July 19:

We have set up shop in three cellar rooms, kitchen, bedroom, and instrument room. We have gathered in a complete stock of furniture, ornaments and utensils, everything we need or fancy, for the ruined houses nearly all have wreckage of their furnishings strewn about the cellars and first-storey rooms. The top storeys and roofs are usually

---

44 Events in Germany: In July 1917 a coalition of parties in the Reichstag passed the Peace Resolution, calling for a negotiated settlement to the war. Crown Council: Kaiser Wilhelm summoned the council to discuss electoral reform. Russian offensive: Refers to the Kerensky Offensive. See entry of 4 July. Big offensive: The British summer offensive in Flanders, known as the Third Battle of Ypres (July–November 1917).
45 Wrognoski: See footnote 269.
46 Liéven: Mining city in Pas-de-Calais, five kilometres north of Vimy. Population in 1914 about 25,000.

gone. Some rooms are crammed from floor to ceiling with everything imaginable, usually broken stuff. We got tables, chairs, paintings, cupboards, beds, mattresses, glassware, pots, pans, pails, tubs, dishes. And we only got the few things we fancied. Thousands of dollars worth of stuff is destroyed or being destroyed in every group of houses. It makes us sad to see such awful ruin of so many homes. There is nobody here save the few soldiers, which only makes the town more like a city of the dead. The line is a mile ahead of us, but the Hun shells around here in searching for batteries.

Sun., July 22:

Received wireless message to report at Souchez at noon with kit. Went out alone while Fritz was shelling our batteries and I had to make a detour to the left to get by the danger zone. A staff car brought me from east of Souchez to the Mont St. Eloi Rd. to Camblin l'Abbé. Walked in and had dinner at Corps, took light car to advanced army, Rancicourt, in afternoon. Sent on by car after tea to 10th Corps at La Buissiere. Billeted here for the night in a loft. This is a fine rural village, attractive for its many trees and chateau.

Mon., July 23:

Went by motor lorries by Bethune to Sailly Labourse where I reported to 6th Div. Hq. Sent to Philosophe to report to 71st Bde. and proceed to Observation Post on Fosse 3. Went on duty at night.

Wed., July 25:

Moved our billet to a house on the Vermelles side of Philosophe because our billet is being usurped by one of our big guns. Walked in to Mazingarbe last night, took washing and saw some of the 16th Bn. Can. Scottish who are on our right.

Thundershowers all afternoon.

Sun., July 29:

Wheeled by Mazingarbe, Les Brebis, Bully Grenay and Sains-en-Gohelle to Hersin-Coupigny to our Corps Hq. to get my mail and tell them what I am doing.

Sergt. McClellan was killed day before yesterday on a motor cycle trip up the line forward of Lievin.[47] A shell hit him just as he had left his cycle to proceed walking to one of our stations. He was rushed out to the dressing stn. unconscious, and only recovered consciousness long enough to dictate a letter home. His going under has cast quite a gloom over the section. He is the first casualty of a serious nature since I joined the section in January.

Mr. Jones gave me a pass to proceed back to my post and told me he has applied to have me recalled to Can. Corps. The 5th Bn. was in Hersin-Coupigny with their transport at Les Brebis. I met Mitchell in the street so went over to see the sigs a while. Mr. Hedley is now a Major and in charge of next operations. The boys are all very hopeful of the coming attack.

There is a Chinese labour unit working in Hersin-Coupigny, the first I have seen. They wear a loose-fitting blue overall and smock when at work and a peculiar brownish-grey cloth cap.[48]

Sun., Aug. 5:

The war is now entering its 4th year and the opinion prevails here that it will continue through much or all of another year until America is in a position to take France's place in the offensive. We know that all is well with Britain, even though everyone hates the thought of another winter here in misery. We can endure it much more easily than the Germans. We believe that they will make another big retreat this fall or next spring so as to delay our offensive operations and keep up the failing spirits of their men. We expect rot to slowly destroy their morale, and we hope revolution will appear in Germany. Intelligence gained by us has revealed signs of both these.

We have had a week of very unseasonable weather, cool, with fogs and nimbus cloud, rain and Scotch mists and never a bit of sunshine. The ripening wheat is badly lodged; there has been considerable wind

---

47 McClellan: In fact Sergeant Edwin Raymond *MacLellan* (1891–1917) of Nova Scotia; attested New Westminster, British Columbia, March 1915. Buried at CWGC Noeux-Les-Mines Communal Cemetery.

48 Chinese labour unit: Refers to the Chinese Labour Corps. At least 140,000 Chinese workers served on the Western Front, carrying out critical rear-echelon labour for the British and French armies. See Dan Black, *Harry Livingstone's Forgotten Men: Canadians and the Chinese Labour Corps in the First World War*. Toronto: Lorimer, 2019.

with the excessive rain. Roads and trenches are in a terrible condition. We have spent our time reading and sleeping as we are very comfortable in our cellar and dugout.

I did not go up to the post for 3 days because visibility was so poor, even on fine days I only watch from 6 to 10 each evening. I have read Stephen McKenna's new novel "Sonia" and am reading French nearly every day for self instruction at that language.[49] A.J. Wooldridge, an undergrad of Oxford, is one of the observers on the post, a chap of 23, very bookish and keen on argument.[50] History and politics are his favourite topics of reading and discussion. We get on splendidly together. He reads my French books which I picked up in Lievin, and I am reading one of his college texts on English Constitutional History.

Mon., Aug. 6:

Wheeled to Hersin-Coupigny to get my mail for past week. Found I had been made an acting corporal during my absence.[51]

Tues., Aug. 7:

Stuart brought car for me at noon and I returned to Can. Corps. I am to work with Sergt. Smedley.[52]

Wed., Aug. 8:

Made evening trip to Loos amp. stn. with car. Spent morning learning to ride motor cycle.

---

49 McKenna: Stephen McKenna (1888–1967), British novelist. *Sonia* (1917) was his best-known and best-selling work, subsequently made into a film.

50 Wooldridge: Probably Arthur John Wooldridge of the Royal Engineers, commemorated on the Oxford University Roll of Service. Wooldridge was killed in action just two weeks after this entry, on 21 August 1917. He is buried at Mazingarbe Communal Cemetery.

51 Corporal: This is the only reference to promotion that Miller makes in his diary, although he subsequently will be made acting sergeant and then promoted from the ranks to lieutenant.

52 Smedley: James Smedley (1878–?), born England; attested Toronto, August 1916.

Fri., Aug. 10:

Went up to St. Pierre amp. stn. yesterday and stayed overnight. Came out in light car this p.m.

Wed., Aug. 22:

Am now at Canadian Corps Rest Camp at Fresnicourt with poisoning in hands and left foot.[53] Came here on Monday from the Field Amb. at Coupigny where I had reported on Saturday and was kept for treatment. Had been very busy of late making trips up to stations nearly every day. Sergt. Adams and I went to St. Pol one day on motor bikes, my first long ride in that way.[54]

Mon., Sept. 3:

Have spent a fortnight now at the rest camp and am going back to my unit tomorrow. This has been a real holiday to me, for we are very comfortable, about sixty of us in this ward, a big French hut. We sleep on the board floor on straw palliases with three blankets each. The food is good; in addition to the usual rations we get rice and tapioca puddings, jellies, and sealed fruit in glass jars put up by Hamilton church women especially for the Red Cross. An old Frenchman and his two boys come along every day with a cart of fruit which we can buy – tomatoes at 2 1/2 D each, etc. – too dear for most of us. Boys sell papers to all the wards nearly every morning, both the English papers and the Paris *Daily Mail*. The hills on the north of the village are covered with woods which are intersected by many paths – a very pleasant place to stroll and one which I have made good use of. Twenty minutes walk through the woods and across a field brings you to the north side of the ridge where you have a magnificent view from Lens on the right to Bruay and Marles on the left right across the great plain over Bethune and La Bassée to the horizon which lies partly in Belgium, and bears three slight humps. Kemmel (60 K. distant), Mt. des Cats, and Cassel. One afternoon we saw the Lille signal light working on the horizon, though Lille would only be visible

---

53 Miller's medical file notes he was suffering from "ICT" or "inflammation of the connective tissue" in his hands and left foot. He had been at the rest camp since 18 August.
54 Adams: Could not be identified.

through a glass. Several times I walked down into Coupigny to see how things were going with the Wireless and to get my mail.

The late August weather has been very wretched, cool, strong westerly winds, with driving squalls of rain every day and night. Several whole days we remained in the hut without venturing out into such weather. But it is full moon now and today is fine and warm, quite seasonable... The French harvest has been greatly delayed and considerable cutting remains to be done, though stacking is also in progress.

Wed., Oct. 10:

We have had much rain and cool weather of late, but last full moon of a fortnight ago gave us a long spell of perfect weather.

The big British attacks at Ypres have been following one another in quick succession, giving us possession of Poelcapelle and Zonnebeke....

We have had two stations in the line lately, one at Eleu-dit-Leauvette and one on the Arras Ry. on the edge of Avion. Sturdy and I dug out a blocked German dugout for the latter, after Sergt. Smedley and I had made a trip to locate it. I went up today on the bike to warn both stations to come out tonight by railway from Brewery Dump in La Coulette to Lens Jct. in Ablain-St. Nazaire, where a lorry is meeting them.

We are all busy packing up stores and getting ready for the next move, as we suppose, to Reninghelst in Belgium. We are all debating with ourselves how to accommodate our packs to the requirements of a long march.

Tues., Oct. 16:

Moved by lorries to Ecquedecques a kilometre west of Lillers on Sat. morning.[55] Sergts. Adams and Smedley and Cpl. St. Louis and I had a nice billet over an estaminet where we met Leonine, the Roamer. Proceeded by lorries yesterday to Poperinghe.

We are billeted in the old hop barn by the railway station. A German plane attempted to bomb us last night, but the searchlights spotted him, 4 of them converged on him, making him look like a silver moth overhead, and the shrapnel barrage drove him off. He dropped his bombs outside the town.

---

55 Ecquedecques: Small village, population about 300 people in 1914. Lillers: Much
   more substantial town with a prewar population of about 8,000.

There is a tremendous concentration of troops here and every part of the empire is represented, besides Belgians, French and Chinese labour units.

Fri., Oct. 26:

We have settled down at TEN ELMS camp on the north edge of Poperinghe. Sergt. Smedley is running a depot up in Potijze Wood while I am staying at Corps to do the car trips. I have been forward nearly every day to Potijze, or to YU on the canal bank where we put up a high aerial yesterday, or to Vlamertinghe where we have established a station in a tower of the chateau.[56]

Patmore, Beisel and Davidson had their forward "pill-box" station demolished by shellfire and had to be withdrawn....

The weather is bad, tho moonlight at nights and often bright during the days. It rains every day and nearly every night. Our camp was shelled by a naval gun last night and a heavy shell fell in the field by the officers' huts. We were up till after midnight wondering where the next one was going to drop. German planes were over dropping bombs also.

Wed., Nov. 14:

Have been very busy of late making daily trips with the car to forward station at Potijze Wood, Dead End, Capricorn Keep, Gallipoli Farm, and Vlamertinghe Chateau. After the Canadians took Paschendaele, we established a C-W Wireless station in Mosselmarkt.[57]

For the past fortnight, we have been sending a relief and carrying party up there every third day. I led one party of men one morning, leaving Capricorn Keep at 3 a.m. and returning at ten. We were held up by barrage fire on Bellevue Ridge and lay three hours in a shell hole at Metscheele cross roads under as heavy fire as I have yet experienced. But we delivered our supplies and returned safely.

---

56 YU: Again, the morse code call sign of the wireless station. Canal bank: The Ypres Canal.

57 Passchendaele: During the final phase of the Third Battle of Ypres, the Canadian Corps took the Belgian town of Passchendaele on 6 November 1917. In all, some 16,000 Canadians were killed or wounded in the battle, fought in horrific conditions. CW Wireless: Continuous Wave Wireless, a wireless set using electromagnetic waves of constant amplitude and frequency. Its adoption resulted in less interference with transmissions on other frequencies than earlier transmitters.

Sergt. Smedley came out from the Potijze station yesterday to don a lieutenant's uniform and become a Wireless officer. He goes to Blighty tomorrow on special leave.

I spent most of yesterday roaming around the country on foot and by motor lorry. Visited Kruisstraat, Shrapnel Corner, Trois Rois, Woodcote Farm, Bedford House, Voormezeele, Cafe Belge, and Vlamertinghe.

Found Ernest Hooper's grave about 31 yds. east of the NE corner of Bedford House.[58] This is an uncared-for cemetery of troops from every part of the Empire. The spot has been shelled heavily a long time since, many crosses have been destroyed and identification of graves lost. But Ernest's grave is unharmed and both the large white head cross and the smaller foot cross are intact. There is a large shell hole near the foot of Ernest's grave just to the left side. There has been no shelling of the cemetery for a long time.

Sun., Nov. 18:

Left Ten Elms Camp at 9:30 a.m., J. Miller, Sturdy and I by motorbike and the others by lorries and busses. Half the wireless personnel left yesterday in the same way. J.M. and I lost Sturdy in Poperinghe so came on alone by Reninghelst, Locre, Bailleul, Merville, Bethune, Hersin-Coupigny to Camblain l'Abbé. We had a good lunch in Merville at a French restaurant. Arrived at our destination by 4 pm. and found everything in confusion. Could not find a bed, so applied at my old friends, the Boudart family. Received a very warm welcome, supper of chicken, apple dumplings, etc. and went to sleep in a big French four-post bed of feathers and clean sheets. I never realized the value of friends so keenly before. It pays to make friends in this country. I doubt if any officer or man had so good a bed as I his first night in Camblain.

Editor's Note: No explanation is given for the six-month gap in the diary that follows. Miller's service file contains what seems to be a plausible answer at first glace: that he spent January 1918 to April 1918 in hospital, having been wounded in the shoulder and thigh. But a closer examination reveals a clerical error: the casualty card refers to Lt. Leslie H. Millar of 5th Canadian Mounted Rifles, and appears to have been accidentally inserted into the file of Leslie H. Miller of the 5th Canadian Battalion.

---

58 Hooper: See notes following entry of 28 April 1917.

1918

Sun., May 5:

Corps moved to Pernes. Mr. Johnston as billeting officer. I helped as his interpreter.

Fri., May 10:

IT section and other spare troops moved to Ourton to form a Corps Signals depot.[1]

Fri., May 24:

Cool and rainy for Victoria day.[2] Sports planned at Pernes had to be postponed.

Sun., June 16:

Left Ourton Thursday morn with Cpl. Craig to join Sgts. Mills, Bruce, and Rayment at Pernes;[3] by car to St. Pol 8 p.m.; spent night on platform awaiting

---

1 IT: Instructional technique.
2 Victoria Day: Canadian holiday celebrated since 1845 in honour of Queen Victoria's birthday.
3 Craig: Joseph Albert Craig (1892–?), born Edinburgh, Scotland; attested Toronto. See also entry of 22 June 1918, as Craig accompanies Miller on his trip to Scotland. Corporal (later Lieutenant) Rayment, Victoria Claud (1886–1972), born England; attested Victoria, BC, November 1914.

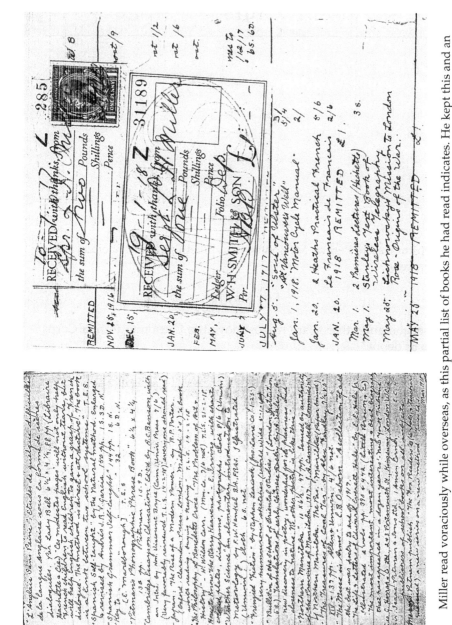

Miller read voraciously while overseas, as this partial list of books he had read indicates. He kept this and an old W.H. Smith's receipt tucked into his diary. Credit: Miller family collection.

train. Left by train morning 14th to Boulogne, by boat to Folkestone 12:30 to 3 p.m. and train to Victoria Stn. London. Spent night at Cornishes. Yesterday reported at Argyle House, saw Hippodrome show (Harry Tate & Shirley Kellog) in p.m., by train in evening to Seaford, Sussex.[4]

Tues., June 18:

Obtained leave this morning to Edinburgh and took 9 a.m. train to London.

Sat., June 22:

Have been waiting here while Joe Craig made a visit to Crayford in Kent. I visited Tower of London, Houses of Parliament, Buckingham Palace Stables, and Kew Gardens. Lived at Eagle Hut (American Y.M.C.A.) and Aldwych Hut (Australian).[5] Left King's Cross Stn. 10:15 p.m. for Edinburgh, with Joe Craig as company.

Sun., June 23:

Attended service in St. Giles Pres. Church in morning and walked about remainder of day.[6]

Mon., June 24:

Visited Royal Scottish Academy Gallery exhibition of recent paintings, and Edinburgh Castle, Forth Bridge.

Tues., June 25:

Left Edinburgh 9 a.m. by Caledonian Railway, spent an hour in Stirling, then to Callander; thence by coach westward by Loch Venachar and Loch

---

4 Miller is on leave once again. Hippodrome: Probably the Royal Hippodrome Theatre in Eastbourne, midway between Folkestone and Sussex. Shirley Kellog: *Kellogg* was an American-born actress, born ca. 1887.

5 Eagle Hut: A complex of temporary buildings that opened in Aldwych, central London, in August 1917. It provided American and other overseas soldiers with beds and meals. To the delight of Canadians, it also served "authentic" pancakes with maple syrup. Aldwych YMCA Hut was its Australian counterpart.

6 St. Giles: St. Giles' Cathedral, located on Edinburgh's famous Royal Mile.

Achray to dinner at Trossachs Hotel. By coach on to Loch Katrine, by S.S. Sir Walter Scott to the west end of Loch Katrine, Stronachlachar; thence by bus past Loch Arklet to Inversnaid on Loch Lomond.[7] By S.S. Prince Edward 5:15 p.m. down Loch Lomond, making 4 stops on alternate sides of the lake, to Balloch at the southern end. Thence by train to Glasgow and on to Edinburgh at 10:30 p.m.

Wed., June 26:

Visited John Knox House and Holyrood Palace, and came to Glasgow at 2 p.m.[8] In evening, went to White Inch Burgh Hall to hear Cmdr. Simson give the account of his motor gunboat expedition to Lake Tanganyika.[9]

Thurs., June 27:

Visited Beardmore's Howitzer Works in morning and Stewart and Lloyd's pipe and tube works in afternoon, entertained to tea after latter visit.[10] Cheapest tram fares in the world here; we can go anywhere for 1/2 D.

Fri., June 28:

In morning, visited David Rowan's shops, makers of marine engines and boilers. They are making engines for standard ships; it takes three weeks to complete one. In afternoon, we visited the factories of the Scottish Cooperative Wholesale Society.

Sat., June 29:

I took the trip down the Clyde to Dunoon and Lochgoilhead by S.S. Lord of the Isles. Leaving Bridgewharf at Jamaica Bridge 10:45 a.m., returning

---

7 Scott: SS *Sir Walter Scott,* launched 1900 and still in service in the early twenty-first century, is a 100-ton steamship that cruises Loch Kartine in the Highlands.

8 Holyrood: The official residence of the British monarch when in Scotland. Knox House: Popular tourist attraction in Edinburgh, reputedly the home of John Knox (1513–1572), the founder of the Presbyterian Church.

9 Simson: Captain Geoffrey Basil Spicer Simson, DSO (1876–1947). Simson commanded a tiny British flotilla that defeated a superior German force on Lake Tanganyika, one of the African Great Lakes, between December 1915 and July 1916.

10 Beardmore's Howitzer Works: William Beardmore and Company was a Glasgow-based heavy manufacturing and shipbuilding company.

at 8 p.m. One sees all the ship-building yards in passing down the Clyde. I counted 73 ocean-going ships on the stocks in course of construction, besides destroyers, submarines, mine sweepers, and a new floating aerodrome.[11] On the trip I saw one of the new rigid dirigibles bearing three gondolas underneath.[12]

This makes a very fine trip right into the Highlands of Scotland. Nearly all the land along the Clyde is tilled, and forms a rich pattern of green fields, but up Loch Goil the land is all wild rocks covered with brown heather.

We left Caledonian Central Stn. 9:45 p.m. for London. In Glasgow we have lived at the Overseas Club in Buchanan St. The Y.M.C.A. Hospitality League is at 140 Buchanan St. In Edinburgh we lived at Ramsay Lodge, The Mound, run by the Victoria League Club.

Sun., June 30:

Arrived Euston Stn. 8 a.m., came to live in Eagle Hut. Attended service in St. Paul's Cathedral in morning.

Editor's Note: Miller spent the following ten weeks in training at the Canadian School of Military Engineering in Seaford, England, as an officer cadet in the school's No. 3 Company, OTC (Officer Training Corps) Wing. While Miller was training, the endgame of the First World War began. What subsequently was called the 100 Days Offensive began 8 August 1918 and concluded with the Armistice of 11 November. The Canadian Corps played an important role in the decisive victory of Allied arms in this period, though at immense loss of life. Preoccupied, it seems, by training, Miller has nothing to say about the beginning of the Allied counteroffensive.

Mon., July 1:

Left London 3:20 p.m. for Seaford, arriving 5:15 and reporting to Cdn. School of Military Engineering. My leave trip has cost me 12 pounds – about 4 pounds spent on Kit and such things.

---

11 Floating aerodrome: Almost certainly a reference to HMS *Argus*, the world's first real aircraft carrier, then under construction at Dalmuir on the River Clyde.

12 Rigid dirigibles: Possibly R27s, constructed by William Beardmore and commissioned that day, or one of the 23 Class airships, built by Beardmore and which also had three underslung "gondolas" or "cars."

Sun., Sept. 29:

Did an eight weeks course in General training July 1 to Sept. 8, and two weeks equitation, to Sept. 22, along with Ashford, Bennet, Butterfield, Bruce, Craig, McCausland, Lee, Mills, Rayment, Rutherford, and Allen. Received kit leave Mon. to Sat. the past week, and we are now preparing to start for France tomorrow.

Mon., Sept. 30:

To London by morning train, spent day and night there.

Tues., Oct. 1:

From Victoria Stn. by 6:40 a.m. train to Folkestone. Lt. Topping, a returned casualty Sig. Opr. for 4th Div. with Mills, Ashford, Craig, Rutherford, and me.[13] By 3 p.m. boat to Boulogne, arriving after dark, by lorry to Ostrahove Camp east of the town, where we spent night in tents.

Wed., Oct. 2:

By train to Etaples in the morning, into camp there.

Fri., Oct. 4:

By train from Etaples at nine to Agny-les-Duisans, Corps rear, arriving after dark.

Sat., Oct. 5:

By Napier boxcar to Corps near Quéant, thence to 3rd Div. Hq. west of Bourlon Wood and village.[14]

---

13 Topping: Ernest Topping (1893–?), born Scotland; attested Toronto 1915. Wounded February 1918 and, as Miller notes, returned to France in October.

14 3rd Division: Miller is now a junior officer with the 3rd Canadian Division Signals Company. It will be his final posting of the war. Bourlon hill: On 26–27 September 1918 the Canadian Corps crossed the Canal du Nord and captured Bourlon Wood. It is now the site of the Canadian Bourlon Wood Memorial, commemorating the Canadian Corps in the 100 Days Offensive.

Oct. 30, 1918

Dear Carman:

I wonder what you are doing to-day, picking potatoes, or turnips, or spy apples? Or are you at school learning 7×8=56 and how Wolfe captured Quebec 159 years ago? I suppose you don't like school so well now since Louisa is no longer your teacher. What kind of a teacher have you now? some big girl with red hair and freckles who bosses you around, a sort of Miss Broadbottom who can sit on your boys all at once when you are bad? Tell me all about it when you write next time.

We have a scheme nearly every day now as part of our training. Three of us take a set of wireless instruments in a motor car away off to some little country village and set up a station for the day. Other stations go out to other villages and set up their instruments. Then we send messages from one station to another. That is for practice in setting up instruments and sending and receiving messages. It is very interesting work and I know you would like it too.

Do you still keep the wing wood up from the bush. It would be nearly all cut down now and burned up. Soon there won't be any squirrels or chipmunks left if they've no wood to live in. You'll have to let the grass grow up until so the wild things can live there. So you see our chipmunks or even my oak wood are these days.

I suppose you'll soon be having snow when the juniors will go coasting and the wind will cut cold. Are you going to skate this winter? I haven't skated for over a year and may have forgotten how. I'm going to write more this evening.

Ken

Miller's letter to his younger brother, Carman, describes his work testing wireless equipment and returns to his favourite subject – the natural world. Patricia Sinclair believes that this period afforded Miller the opportunity to collect acorns from Vimy Ridge. Credit: Miller family collection.

Tues., Oct. 8:

Have walked over and around Bourlon hill twice, looking down on Raillencourt, Fontaine Notre Dame, St. Olle, and Cambrai which burns day and night.

Two British planes collided above us and crashed, killing both pilots.[15] Cambrai taken this morning by 8th Bde., 2nd Div. on the left.

Wed., Oct. 9:

Moved back near Quéant.

Sun., Oct. 13:

Came to Abbeville in car with Capt. Leeson to take a four weeks' wireless course, sparks and C.W.[16]

Sun., Nov. 10:

Course finished and exam written at noon. Have had a useful and enjoyable time and made many new acquaintances. Had a dinner last night at the Club in town to celebrate the breakup of our class.

Editor's Note: The Armistice
   At 11 a.m. on 11 November 1918 the armistice signed between the Allies and Germany came into effect. The other Central Powers had already withdrawn from the conflict. Formally a cessation of hostilities, the Armistice essentially constituted Germany's surrender. However, the formal end of the war did not occur until after the signing of the Treaty of Versailles in 1919 (the treaty came into effect January 1920). While 11 November would subsequently be commemorated as Armistice or Remembrance Day, fighting in much of Eastern Europe went on as revolutionary violence continued. The end of the war seems to rejuvenate Miller, and perhaps give him more free time, as he devotes more time to his diary at war's end than he had in the year leading up to it.

---

15 Collision: These were Sopwith Camels of 209 Squadron flown by 2nd Lt. R.G.A. Bingham and Capt. D.G.A. Allen.
16 Course: At the Central Wireless School, Abbeville.

Mon., Nov. 11:

Armistice was signed by Germany this morning and hostilities ceased at eleven. Everyone takes it calmly; there was very little celebrating last night and today. By train to Etaples on return journey to the front.

Tues., Nov. 12:

By train Etaples to Raismes by Arras and Douai.

Wed., Nov. 13:

Arrived Raismes, Canadian railhead, at 5:30 this morning. By lorry through Valenciennes to Mons to 3rd Div. Hqrs.[17] Refugees were pouring back to Valenciennes along the main road from all the way to Mons. It was a pitiful sight to see people of all ages pushing and pulling carts loaded high with household effects along the rough road in the chill misty morning. Yet everyone who looked up greeted us with a smile or a friendly nod.

Mons is full of people and is gaily decked with Belgian flags of all sizes. The people are all very friendly and will do anything to oblige us. The Boche only left last Sun. night. A woman showed me a fine brass lamp she had hidden in her fireplace to keep from the Huns. The eight 3rd Div. soldiers who were killed in the taking of Mons were buried this afternoon with great ceremony. The square (Grande Place), where the procession formed up, was packed with people. All the windows and balconies were crowded with onlookers, and every bit of masonry facing the street was covered with flags. British aeroplanes kept flying overhead.

Really these are times worth living for and it thrills one with pride to be here. Priests and old men lift their hats to us, and they are greatly pleased if we salute them in turn or speak to them in French. We are making our Divisions mobile for the march to the Rhine, supposed to commence this weekend.[18]

---

17 Mons: Belgian city, population about 27,000 in 1914, occupied by the Germans throughout the war and liberated by the Canadian Corps on 11 November 1918.
18 March to the Rhine: The victorious Allied armies occupied the left bank of the Rhine and four bridgeheads on the right bank at war's end. The region remained under occupation until 1930.

Newly commissioned Lieutenant Miller, 3rd Canadian Division Signals, in a portrait photograph taken in Belgium sometime in late 1918. Credit: Miller family collection.

Thurs., Nov. 14:

The Div. is making all necessary preparations for a month of marching. Stores are being reduced to a minimum and got into perfect condition. Men's equipment and dress is being brought to the necessary standard of completeness and smartness.

Visited the Mons Church where sick civilians are being cared for. Conversed with French chap from St. Quentin who had been in a Hun punishment Labour Battn. for refusing to work voluntarily with the other evacuees impressed for labour.

Attended 3rd Div Party's (Dumb Bells') show in the theatre in La Grande Place this evening.[19] Half the audience was civilian. At end of program, orchestra played "La Brabanconne", "Marseillaise" and "God Save the King", which brought everyone to their feet and made the civies cheer with great enthusiasm: "Vive La France" "Vive l'Angleterre".[20]
Weather very fine like Cdn Indian Summer.

Sat., Nov. 16:

Night before last, the 3rd Div. officers gave tea to the prominent civilians of the town in the Hotel de Ville.[21] This afternoon from 4 to 6, the courtesy was returned by the civilians and I attended. An orchestra and baritone soloist gave a short musical entertainment in one of the large council chambers, rendering the national anthems of England, France, Belgium (in French) and last of all the music of "O Canada". The room where this was held was the most perfect piece of interior furnishing I've ever seen, all done in solid oak, carved and pan-elled, the ceiling squared by beams of dark oak, each square bearing an escutcheon design. The walls away from the windowed eastern side bore large paintings of enormous dimensions depicting warlike scenes.
Canadian Corps is massing in Mons and organizing for the forward march to Eastern Belgium and Rhineland. Returning British prisoners of war arrive in town and pass thru every day now. They all wore black coarse uniforms, save a few wearing civies or Boche uniforms. They reports outbreaks of Hun soldiery in Brussels against their officers. Ger-man officers were here yesterday and today giving location of land mines and explaining locations of land mines and explaining organization of telephone service in all this back country.

Sun., Nov. 17:

A special thanksgiving service for Victory for the entire Cdn. Corps was held in Mons theatre at ten o'clock. Mr. Maxey and I took the Signal Coy.

---

19 Dumb Bells: "The Dumbells," formally the Canadian Army Third Division Concert Party, a popular army vaudeville act paid for and administered by the YMCA. The troupe continued to tour as civilians in peacetime throughout the 1920s.
20 La Brabançonne: The national anthem of Belgium.
21 Hôtel de Ville: Mons's Gothic city hall, dating from the fifteenth century.

representation.[22] The service was a failure and you couldn't hear much
for coughing. Men who have come through months and years of hell
don't want to be told that the outcome of it all is due to some outside
agency, a so-called Divine Providence.

The Hun has claimed the same Divine help all through and now
our padres claim it back in their favour. In the meantime, the best
men have won the victory with the help of tanks and Yanks and aeroplanes and the British navy, etc. Padres have conspicuously failed in
this war and only the few whose religion disappeared in their hu-
manity have made good. But they'll go back and claim all the glory
for themselves and *their* God in whom nobody believes. They never
touched men, only thought they did. A soldier's religion is beyond
their understanding.

Mon., Nov. 18:

Busy making arrangements for the move. A nun stopped me on the street
and asked me for a motor car to transport a flock of orphans across the
town to some new quarters. I got a lorry and had the job done – ten kids,
three sisters, and a pile of mattresses and kit. They surely were pleased
to be treated so. I think the sister was praying, for I saw her counting
her beads all the time she asked me and while waiting in the orderly
room until the lorry arrived. Her prayer was certainly answered and the
whole gang were very happy afterward.

Fri., Nov. 22:

A very fine day with an Indian summer mist in the air. Having the morning spare, I strolled about this historic town of Mons. It was here that
St. George is supposed to have killed the dragon. Every year they have
a public "jour de fête" during which the scene of the Saint mounted on
a charger and slaying the dragon is enacted in the Grande Place.

I went to the "Beffroi" first where are the chimes of the town.[23] It is
a massive square tower of stone built in an elevated park under which

---

22 Maxey: Lieutenant William Macdonald Maxey (1888–1954), born Scotland; attested
   Calgary, December 1915.
23 Beffroi: Mons Belfry (bell tower). The current structure dates to the late seventeenth
   century, replacing the earlier medieval structure on the same site.

is the reservoir of the town waterworks and ancient dungeons which I have not yet visited. This is the highest point in the town, Mons, "The Mountain". The Beffroi was built in 1410 by the Spaniards; it is 87 metres high and has 378 steps of stone by which you climb up to the chimes, thence by wooden stairs and ladders to the top from which a splendid view is had of the whole district in a 20 mile radius around Mons.

You can look down into the tiny streets and gardens and on to the roofs of houses from far above any other place or object in the town. The Germans had machine guns placed here and used the place as a post of observation from which they had telephonic communication with many places, like Maubeuge, the Gare de Mons, anti-aircraft batteries, etc.

Maubeuge is barely visible from here as it is some 30 miles distant.[24] I had no hope of seeing it because of the mist on the horizon, but the old guide in the park pointed out its exact direction. The Mons-Conde canal showed as a broad blue band reaching from the Railway Station straight away westward to disappear in the mist.

It was along there that the "Old Contemptibles" made their first stand in 1914, but from our position no sign of any damage was visible.[25]

The Railway Station appears to be undamaged, but the yards appear to have been heavily bombed and many buildings in the neighbourhood of the station are damaged. A train was in here from Brussels to take Belgian delegates up there, but there has been no train through yet from Valenciennes as the damage to the lines in that direction is very serious. We are doubtless being held up here until the break in railway communication can be repaired, so our railhead can follow us from Raismes, where it is now, forward as we advance.

I had a good look at the chimes, for you can climb all round among them. There are so many bells and they are so scattered about among the heavy timbered staging that I did not count them. The smallest bell is about eight inches in diameter, and the one I thought to be largest is 5' 10" in diameter with metal 8" or more thick. The weight of metal in the top of that tower is enormous, but the stone walls most of the way up are 6 to 8 feet thick and the staging that supports the bells is mostly of 12" to 16" squared oak beams.

---

24 Maubeuge: French town. Population in 1914 about 23,000.
25 Old Contemptibles: Nickname for the British Expeditionary Force, earned after the Kaiser allegedly referred to it as a "contemptible little army" in August 1914.

When you climb about among these dirty looking old bells, it seems impossible that they should produce such sweet-toned music as we hear in the streets below; but you have only to strike one to hear its clear sweet note.

Each bell has its own hammers which are connected with wires running to a small room where is a big wooden drum turned by a crank. The drum is fixed up to actuate the bell hammers just as a player piano is worked. The chimes can be played in this manner to a fixed tune as set on the cylinder, or can be played to any tune by the carilloneur who works with both hands and feet. The old caretaker down in the park told me that the present carilloneur is a 2nd prize Malines man and thought to be quite a wonderful artist. Besides ringing the hours each Sunday at noon, the old carilloneur plays for twenty minutes, and this is the time when every visitor to Mons should be present to hear the chimes.

After descending the tower, I went round to the church of St. Waudru and walked through it hurriedly.[26] There are many fine shrines to the different saints, some done in carved oak, some in marble of several colours. The principal local saints are St. George and St. Waudru. The stained glass in the large windows above and behind the altar is damaged by splinters from a bomb which fell in the street near the church.

For lunch we had some guests from the civilian friends of Maj. Campbell's: a M. et Mme. Jacquemont, a Mlle. Jacquemont and her brother, a Belgian officer on leave home for the first time since the beginning of the war; a Mlle. "Black-eyed Susan" and M. Maidon.

After lunch we had music and dancing, singing and carrying on till tea and five o'clock when the party broke up. It was the merriest party one could ever hope to attend. M. Maidon played the piano and sang, Mme. J. played dance music, and a Pte. Griffiths, a switchboard operator from Corps office, played and sang and danced. He used to run a music shop on Queen St. Toronto, and taught singing and dancing. He sang a soldier song of his own composition. M. Maidon is a very fine man, a real humanist, very musical, was on the International American Relief Commission and entertained the American representatives at his home throughout the war; in this way and by reading, has learned to speak English very well. M. Jacquemont has been in the German and British navies and is a kind of dark horse, speaks French and English perfectly. This party reminded

---

26 St. Waudru: Saint Waudru Collegiate Church, a late Gothic church dating to the mid-fifteenth century.

me of the ball in Brussels before Waterloo, described by Byron.[27] The Belgians have certainly shown their splendid loyalty and hospitality to us here in Mons.

Sat., Nov. 23:

Walked around town again this morning with Lt. Lawrence; visited the Church of St. Waudru and the Hotel de Ville and the Rly. Stn. Wanted to visit the dungeons connecting the Beffroi with the Church, but on enquiry found that both entrances are fallen in and impassable.

The oldest tablet covering a tomb in the church was dated 1580, but many in the floor have their inscriptions obliterated by the wear of passing feet. All inscriptions are in French, though many in the language as written in Montaigne's period showing its transition from Latin.[28]

At the railway stn. much damage has been done to the lines by the blowing up of the switchman's box and many of the sidings. Many of the charges placed by the Boche under the tracks have been dug up by our people and rendered harmless. Our railway troops are repairing the lines now and will soon have trains running in here from Valenciennes.

Mon., Nov. 25:

Visited Waterloo and Brussels in company with Maj. Campbell and Capt. Leeson. Went in the Sunbeam Car by Soignies and Tubize, then across to Waterloo village, but missed the battlefield which is a mile further south;[29] thence by Chaussée de Waterloo into Brussels, to Blvde. du Midi, and had lunch at Hotel de l'Espérance near Gare du Midi.

Here we picked up a Belgian Ofr. who showed us round the city. We went by Blde. Anspach, the Bourse, Grande Place, Eglise St. Gudule, Palais du Roi, Blde. Louise, Gare de Luxembourg, and return by Waterloo, Nivelles and Menage in order to take the Belgian Lieut. as near his home as possible, i.e. Binche, 14 kilometres east of Mons. Our trip was badly planned giving us only two hours in Brussels and the day was disagreeable.

---

27 Ball and Byron: A reference to the Duchess of Richmond's ball held on the eve of the Battle of Waterloo (1815), evoked in Byron's poem *Childe Harold's Pilgrimage*.

28 Montaigne: Michel de Montaigne (1533–1592), French writer and philosopher, noted in particular for his *Essais*.

29 Battlefield: Reference of the Battle of Waterloo, where Napoleon was finally defeated, 18 June 1815.

Sat. last was the fête day, when the King made his entry into the capital, and yesterday the celebrations continued, but today was quiet.[30] Yet the streets were full of people and there are very few soldiers to be seen, only the Belgian garrison, a few odd French and British in the place to look round. Khaki is a rarity and the people stop to look as each British soldier passes.

Every time we stopped the car, a crowd immediately gathered until it was soon difficult to start and get clear again. Some people were still exuberant enough to shout "Vivent les Anglais" but it was mostly just silent curiosity or perhaps admiration. Along the main roads between Mons and Brussels wherever our troops have passed are arches and bunting and flags or overhead banners with signs "Honneur aux Alliés" and many such greetings.

Wed., Nov. 27:

King Albert and the two princes visited Mons today in motor cars. I saw him as he entered the Government Buildings and again in the Grande Place. He and the elder Prince came out on the balcony of the Hotel de Ville to bow to the crowd.[31] The streets were packed and house fronts covered with people even to the eaves and some were on the roofs.

3rd Div. troops formed the Guard of Honour (Scotties in kilts) while pipers and another band attended. The cheering was lively but not very enthusiastic. There does not seem to be unanimous approval of a Kingship and I understand there is a strong party who wish to see a republic set up. But everyone admires King Albert; he certainly is a fine type of man in every sense.

Our first and second Divisions with Corps have gone eastward across the Meuse at Huy and are now in the neighbourhood of Spa on the German frontier. We third and fourth Divisions are remaining in Mons indefinitely, and have been attached to IV Corps of Fourth Army. Daily motor lorry excursions are being run to Brussels by all units. Apart from inspections, there is nothing to do.

Fri., Dec. 6:

Spent last Sun. and Mon. in Brussels with Capt. Leeson and LTs. Maxey, Bennet, and Gifford, and had a most enjoyable time. We are still resting

---

30 The King: Albert I of Belgium (1874–1934).
31 Elder son: Prince Leopold (1901–1983), who became King Leopold III in 1934.

in Mons though expected to be in Wavre or Namur long before now. G branch continue to amuse themselves by getting out operation orders and cancelling them next day. They've made me Education Ofr. for Signals, but there is little possible in the Khaki College line when we're on the QUI VIVE, expecting to move every day.[32]

Wed., Dec. 11:

Went to theatre last night with the niece of my hostess of the past month at 16 Rue du Parc, and a friend of hers. The niece is daughter-in-law to the owner of the big factory at Quiévrain which was used by the Boche as a munition factory until it was bombed, blown up and completely destroyed by our aviators some months ago. These people have much to tell of cruelties to British prisoners of war, how they were made to pull wagons and carts in place of horses, often with no boots or mere shreds of boots on their feet and their other clothing in tatters, half-starved and without adequate sleeping accommodation.

These civilians tried at every opportunity to give the prisoners food and clothing, but the Boche guards were very watchful to catch any signs of sympathy for their victims. Heavy fines were imposed on the civilians who were caught doing this and it brought additional cruelty to the prisoners or even death in some cases.

Marcel, daughter of M. Dufrasne of Jemappes, was repeatedly caught giving bread to English prisoners and her father had many fines to pay on her account. Finally she did two months in prison for the same offence.

I came on by lorry to La Louvière with Sgt. Wright, C-W set and equipment for an Advanced Div'l Report Centre which we established at the Railway Station at noon.[33] The people here gave us a warm welcome as they have had no troops stationed here before, only troops passing through and halting for a night or two.

I am staying at Hotel de la Station opposite the Gare and have the wireless set in an upstairs room. I thought it would be impossible to get a meal in town but I had a good supper for 7 francs for which you would pay 25 fr. in Brussels.

---

32 Khaki College: The Khaki University, established in 1917, was based at several locations in England and provided vocational education for Canadian servicemen.
33 La Louvière: Belgian industrial city, population in 1914 about 40,000.

Walked all round town in the p.m. but found nothing of interest, it was raining miserably, the church was closed, and not a theatre in town is open save Sat., Sun., and Mon. So I spent the evening chatting to the people in the hotel, or rather listening to conversations which I could follow fairly well, though my French is hardly fluent enough to make me want to say much. Excellent French is spoken here by everyone.

One man in the party had spent two months in prison in Charleroi in 1916 for forwarding letters, the correspondence between people here and their soldier relatives with the Belgian Army. There was a regular underground postal service which formed the only channel of correspondence through which families here might keep in touch with absent dear ones. Many of the people who assisted with this work were caught and punished from time to time, some got as much as two years imprisonment or heavy fines, but there were always new recruits to take their places, and the Hun never succeeded in stopping completely this service.

Another man present had paid 1,000 marks fine for some seeming trivial offence. I was shown a photo of a young fellow who had assisted Belgian male civilians in escaping via Holland to join the Belgian Army. They said he was too bold, took too many chances, for he was at last tracked down by the Boche and shot.

At the beginning of the war, the Boche blamed the civilians for sniping, and shot 480 (?) people, mostly young men of military age, having lined them up against a wall in a factory near the station, la Usine de M. Boel.[34]

The chap in charge of the telephone exchange by the Gare maintained communication with the English, giving them valuable information, for thirty-six hours after the Boche had captured the town and, as he thought, had put the telephone lines out of action. This in August, 1914. The hero escaped after that without incurring any suspicion on the part of the Huns, made his way to Holland, eventually joining the Belgian Army and is now back here on leave wearing a Belgian medal, which all agree he richly deserves.

Thurs., Dec. 12:

Raining and very disagreeable. Received word last night from Maj. Campbell to stay here at La Louvière until Friday before moving on to Nivelles.

---

34 Usine: The "factory" in this case is a steelworks established in the mid-nineteenth century by Belgian industrialist Gustave Böel.

At breakfast the lady of the house talked a full hour telling me all the sufferings she had gone through and heard of during the war. This town has been repeatedly bombed by our planes and much damage done to factories and railway lines.

She told of one place east of here where nine Boche mounted men were on the road when a British plane swooped down right upon them and machine gunned the party, killing all, both horses and men, riddling windows of houses on both sides of the road, though not one civilian was even injured.

In Charleroi, a relative of this lady saw a party of Allied prisoners of war passing in the street, all half-starved and in a pitiful condition. A little girl of nine stepped out and handed a Tommy some bread but the Boche guard saw the act and shot her dead. A Senegalese among the prisoners was so enraged at sight of this that he sprang upon the Hun with both hands on the fellow's throat to choke him.[35] But other Boches came up and beat the Senegalese to death with their rifles.

A M. Boel who owns one of the biggest factories in town, a steel mill and foundry, and has a fine big chateau, had his factory partially destroyed, the machinery taken to Germany, his chateau taken from him to be a Kommandantur HQ., he and his wife being deported to Germany.[36] They have only recently returned to their home here. Their two sons had escaped and joined the Belgian army to avenge their parents, and have just had their first leave home since the beginning.

Fri., Dec. 13:

Had supper at 7:30 last night at the home of the Prof. of French language and literature at the Ecole Moyenne. He has a nice home at #8 Rue Hocquet and a very charming little wife.

We had visited the school together during the afternoon when I met some of the other professeurs. The Boche had taken over the school and had used it as a hospital, so the classes were carried on in houses under considerable difficulty and inconvenience. The school furniture is now being put back in the classrooms and they are preparing to reopen the school on Saturday next.

---

35 Senegalese: Senegal was a French colony during the First World War. The Tirailleurs Senegalese was an infantry corps that served with the French Army. Some 200,000 served in all.

36 Kommandantur: A garrison post, in this instance of occupying forces.

The salary of this prof. is 225 francs a month which he contrasted at once with the salaries we get in Canada. I am afraid I increased their impression that Canada is a land of plenty when I told them what salaries teachers get there.[37]

School runs six days in the week here, but his average day comprises only three hours lecturing, the remainder of his time is mere supervision of studies. This is a boys' school and the girls' High School is in another building a quarter of a mile away. He says this is always the case in Belgium, boys and girls never being educated in the same school.

The building here is very fine, spacious with high ceilings and wide corridors, well lighted and well equipped, quite equal to the best I have ever seen in Canada, and conducted on similar lines to our modern city schools. This school has some 1,600 pupils normal attendance. Night classes are also conducted as an important feature.

We spent the evening at his home, during most of the time he related incidents of the war, most of which related to German atrocities, which were really so horrible as to numb the senses and render one incapable of appreciating them. Some relatives of these people live at Charleroi and witnessed the first inroads made by the Germans upon Belgian territory and some of the first atrocities.[38]

At Liège, 43,000 Germans were left dead on the field.[39] They stormed in mass formation and whole Battalions doing the goose step as they advanced, shouting "Sturmen, immer stormen" until they were shot away.[40] The Belgian artillery and machine guns were splendid and most effective. The Germans stormed five times and were beaten back every time.

Then they waited two days for the heavy Austrian howitzers to be brought up (which was done fifteen days before Austria was in a state of war with Belgium). A German officer sacrificed his life in order to locate the entrance to the principal fort, so as to direct effective fire upon it. He came over to the Belgians as a parlementaire carrying the white flag. He was marched under armed guard to the fort where General Leman had his post.[41] As he was entering the shaft leading to the casemate, he

---

37 Salaries: 225 francs was the equivalent of about 9 British pounds or 45 Canadian dollars. In 1914, a rural Saskatchewan teacher made about 65 dollars per month.

38 Charleroi: A Belgian industrial/mining town, population about 50,000 in 1914.

39 In the passage that follows, Miller recounts the Battle of Liège (5–16 August 1914), in which the German forces assaulted fortifications outside the Belgian city. German casualties were heavy but less than one-tenth of those recounted to Miller.

40 Stürmen, immer stormen: Roughly, "Attack, always attack."

41 Leman: Belgian General Gérard Leman (1851–1920), who commanded Belgian forts outside the city of Liège in 1914.

raised the white flag and waved it at arm's length, as a signal to Artillery Officers who were watching with powerful glasses from observation posts in the German line. The Belgian escort saw the treachery and bayoneted the Hun on the spot, but the harm was done and the enemy had the information he wanted. The bombardment reopened and soon a heavy shell fell directly in the shaft entrance, just inside the casemate, blowing up the magazine and destroying the fort. The few survivors refused to surrender and fought to the death among the shattered ruins. General Leman was found badly wounded and unconscious, was made prisoner and taken to Germany where he has been ever since up to the time of his release last month.

Mon., Dec. 16:

By lorry Nivelles to La Hulpe.

Tues., Dec. 17:

Burden and I went to live chez M. Van den Bulcke.[42]

Sat., Dec. 28:

Burden and I spent last night in Brussels with the family at 12 Rue de la Banque and returned this morning on foot from Boitsfort, having missed the train from Luxembourg.

Sun., Dec. 29:

Burden with transport left for Tournai.

Mon., Dec. 30:

I left with a lorry at 10:30 and arrived at Tournai at 4 pm, the other lorries of the convoy having bad luck. M. Thoumsin, a Belgian Arty Ofr., friend of the V.D. Bulckes, came with me on his way to Paris and we dined together in the hotel in the evening.

---

42 Burden: Walter Douglas Burden (1889–?), born England; attested Toronto, June 1916. Not Bert Allen *Burdon* of the 5th Battalion Signals (see entry 8 November 1915).

1919

Mon., Jan. 13:

To 7th Bde. at Estaimbourg to substitute for Peebles while on leave.[1]
To 24th Div. Show Tournai with French interpreter at night.

Tues., Jan. 14:

To Courtrai with French interpreter by train 10:48 and back at 3:18.

Mon., Jan. 20:

To Brussels Sat. and back today – "Au Revoir".

Mon., Jan. 27:

Return to Tournai.

Mon., Feb. 10:

Burden and I visited Brussels and La Hulpe Saturday morning and back
this evening – "Adieu".

---

1 Peebles: Lewis Raymond Peebles (1886–1947) of Nova Scotia; attested Winnipeg May
   1916. Served with 3rd Division Signals from November 1917.

Miller (bottom right) and the other officers of the 3rd Canadian Division Signals Corps pose for a picture in January 1919. Credit: William Rider-Rider, "Officers of the 3rd Canadian Division Signal Corps, January 1919." Department of National Defence/Library and Archives Canada/PA-003848.

Thurs., Feb. 13:

Main body of 3rd Div. Sigs. left Baisieux for Le Havre and Bramshott via Weymouth.

Fri., Feb. 14:

Lt. Burden and I with 70 men left Tournai on 1800 hrs. Leave train for Calais. Train of Caledonian Railway coaches including a cook van. Very comfortable trip via Lille, Armentieres, Bailleul, St. Omer.

Officers of the 3rd Canadian Division Signals Company in Tournai, Belgium, February 1919. On the reverse, Miller wrote:
– Back row left to right: Lea-Arty; Pryde-Arty; Sharpe-Arty; u/k 9th Bde. Inp.; Gibson-Transport & Q.M.; Rutherford-8th Bde. Inp.; Bennett-Div Sig. Master; Miller-Div. Wireless; Barbour-Div. Advt. Front row left to right: Maxey-Div. Lines; Capt. Robinson-Div. Paymaster; Maj. Leavitt-O.C.; Capt. Leeson-2nd in Cmd.; Burden-Transport. Absent: Peebles-7th Bde. Inp. Credit: Miller family collection.

Sat., Feb. 15:

Left Calais by 2 p.m. boat to Folkestone, arrive London about 6 p.m. Found room at 46 Grosvenor St. but eat at Cdn. Ofrs. Club at Chesterfield Gdns.[2]

---

2 Club: Providing meals and beds, the Canadian Officers' Club was established at Chesterfield Gardens in July 1918 by the Beyond the Seas Association, a philanthropic organization supporting overseas soldiers in the United Kingdom.

Miller's mess bill from Bramshott, found in his diary. Credit:
Miller family collection.

Mon., Feb. 24:

Left Waterloo Stn. 13:10 hrs. to Milford and to Camp. During trip to London (8 day leave) saw Cinderella (Pantomime) at Lyceum and Twelfth Night at Court Theatre.

Sat., Mar. 8:

Moved from Witley to Bramshott. I am in charge of fatigue party remaining behind. Took train Milford to Liphook.

Mon., Mar. 17:

S.S. *Olympic* loads at Southampton, taking Calgary, Ottawa, London, Halifax drafts from Signal Coy. Lieuts. Peebles and Maxey went with these drafts.

Wed., Mar. 19:

Left Camp 5:30 a.m. with drafts of Sig. Coy., 3rd Bde. C.E. Took train Liphook 7:20 a.m. via Reading, Oxford, Birmingham, Stafford, Crewe to Liverpool, arriving 5 p.m. Embarked 5:30 on S.S. *Cedric.*[3] Spent night in the Mersey.

Thurs., Mar. 20:

Weighed anchor and started 9 a.m. into Irish Sea in heavy fog. Going north of Ireland I understand.

BUCKINGHAM PALACE.

The Queen and I wish you God-speed, and a safe return to your homes and dear ones.

A grateful Mother Country is proud of your splendid services characterized by unsurpassed devotion and courage.

George R.I.

God-speed note from King George V. Credit: Miller family collection.

---

3 Cedric: RMS *Cedric*, a 20,000-ton White Star liner used as a troopship during the war. Launched in 1903, *Cedric* was for a brief time the largest ship in the world.

Afterword

So ends Leslie Miller's account of his service in the Canadian Expeditionary Force, on a rather perfunctory and yet somewhat wistful note. On 31 March 1919, the army discharged him in Toronto at the rank of lieutenant, four years and five months after he had enlisted. He was twenty-nine years old.

Over time, a pervasive and powerful mythology that the war had given birth to a new Canadian nation would emerge. By the time they celebrated their country's centenary in 1967, many Canadians took it for granted that the Canadian nation had been forged in the fire of the trenches and especially in the hard-won victory at Vimy Ridge.[1] But in 1919, Miller and tens of thousands of other veterans returned to a country rent by deep ethnic, regional, and class divisions. Beneath the veneer of patriotic consensus and enthusiasm, the war had exacerbated long pent-up social tensions. The fractures occurred along regional, class, and ethnic lines. Working people and farmers had seen the potential benefits of the wartime economic boom undercut by double-digit inflation that sent the cost of living soaring. Incessant strikes rather than patriotic cooperation had been the norm on the industrial front throughout the war, and the resumption of peace did not restore goodwill: massive strikes would grip Winnipeg and then Cape Breton in 1919 and 1920.[2]

---

1 On the gradual evolution of the belief that Canadian nationhood owed much to the victory at Vimy, see Tim Cook, *Vimy: The Battle and the Legend* (Toronto: Random House Canada, 2017).

2 On postwar Canada, see Tim Cook and J.L. Granatstein, eds., *Canada 1919: A Nation Shaped by War* (Vancouver: UBC Press, 2020).

Wartime jitters, intensified by real domestic disasters such as the Parliament Fire in February 1916 and the Halifax Explosion in December 1917, which killed over 2,000 people, rapidly transformed into paranoia and discrimination directed at particular groups, especially Canadians of German descent. Many Canadians, fearing spies and saboteurs everywhere, suspected and reported their neighbours, the embers of their suspicions fanned by outrageous rumours of enemy armies massing for invasion among allegedly hostile Irish and German immigrant communities in the United States.[3] Yet the hammer of domestic repression in Canada had fallen hardest on thousands of ethnic Ukrainians, whose families and communities were torn asunder in the government's nearly inexplicable decision to intern them as enemy aliens because they had been subjects of the Austro-Hungarian Empire.[4]

The most divisive issue of all had been conscription, and the political crisis precipitated by the Military Service Act, which authorized involuntary military service, had been the most severe in Canadian history.[5] A transparently corrupt election on the issue in 1917 resulted in a victory for pro-conscription forces, but opposition to the Act had been widespread, especially in Quebec, where violent anti-conscription riots had broken the Easter calm in Quebec City in April 1918. Despite enlistment rates that were probably higher than official figures showed, many French Canadians viewed conscription as a violation of the compact that had brought the country into being, and hypocrisy on the part of politicians who refused to defend French-language rights at home.[6] Meanwhile, a severe postwar recession left many veterans unemployed and disillusioned. To make matters worse, many were sick, stricken by the Spanish Flu, which spread like some modern version of a medieval plague across the globe. In Canada alone, the flu killed 50,000 people, nearly as many as had fallen in the war.[7] In a famous phrase, British

---

3 See Brock Millman, *Polarity, Patriotism, and Dissent in Great War Canada, 1914–1919* (Toronto: University of Toronto Press, 2016).

4 Bohdan S. Kordan, *Canada, the Great War, and the Enemy Alien Experience* (Montreal and Kingston: McGill-Queen's University Press, 2017).

5 On the crisis over the MSA, see Patrice Dutil and David MacKenzie, *Embattled Nation: Canada's Wartime Election of 1917* (Toronto: Dundurn, 2017).

6 Martin F. Auger, "On the Brink of Civil War: The Canadian Government and the Suppression of the 1918 Quebec Easter Riots," *Canadian Historical Review* 89, no. 4 (2008).

7 Mark Osborne Humphries, *The Last Plague: Spanish Influenza and the Politics of Public Health in Canada* (Toronto: University of Toronto Press, 2013).

Prime Minister David Lloyd George had promised it was his government's duty to make "a land fit for heroes." In this, he expressed a hope widely shared throughout the victorious nations: that the war had been fought to ensure a better world, where the expectation was not further sacrifice but a hard-earned share in a brighter future. But for many of those who returned that future was wrecked on the shoals of domestic division, economic chaos, and sickness.

If there was a unifying force in postwar Canada it was grief. Men such as Miller were "the lucky ones," as the saying went. Despite his lengthy service and several close brushes with death, Miller had come through the war in good health – although he had suffered the loss of hearing in one ear and his family recalls a wound to his leg which left him with a limp.[8] To give a sense of context, of the nearly half-million Canadians who had served overseas roughly sixty thousand had died or been killed. Tens of thousands of others had come home grievously wounded in body and in mind. For years the country remained in a state of mourning. With the great majority of the country's 65,000 war dead buried overseas, the cenotaphs built in nearly every city or town across Canada performed an important emotional role in the life of devastated communities. They were surrogate graves and the focal point of annual Remembrance Day services, services that were part of a process, as historian Jonathan Vance has argued, of providing consolation through commemoration.[9]

The nation may have descended into mourning, but life had to go on. After spending the summer of 1919 on the farm in Milliken, Miller resumed his studies at Victoria College at the University of Toronto in September. No one who came through the charnel house of the trenches was ever truly the same again, and no doubt the years he had served overseas had changed and perhaps even hardened his personality. Nonetheless, he seems to have returned to the life of a civilian student with alacrity. Once again, he earned outstanding grades, in part because he was able to deploy his now much-practised French and German in the classroom. In the 1919–20 academic year, he received

---

8 Patricia Sinclair, e-mail to the editor, 26 August 2021. No record of such a wound appears in Miller's service file.

9 The best study of the cultural response to the First World War in Canada remains Jonathan Vance's *Death So Noble: Memory, Meaning, and the First World War* (Vancouver: UBC Press, 1997.)

three distinguished awards, including the prestigious Regent's Prize for the best English essay, among whose recipients was Lester B. Pearson, the future prime minister of Canada and Nobel Prize laureate.[10] This reminder of Miller's talent for writing is further cause for regret that he never wrote a memoir of his own. There is no telling how far he might have gone academically – his younger brother Carman went on to earn a PhD in mathematics at the University of Toronto – but for the intrusion of fate. In January 1921, Miller was stricken with scarlet fever, a disease now largely forgotten but one that remained a dreaded killer in the 1920s. Seriously ill, he withdrew from the university. He never went back.[11]

After his recovery, Miller briefly returned to teaching in Saskatchewan, settling near Yorkton, but shortly thereafter came back to Ontario, enticed, perhaps, by a generous offer from his parents: money to help build a home and establish a farm on nearly 29 acres granted to him from the family farm. His father's sudden death in March 1924 thrust even greater responsibilities upon him, among them the task of helping to care for Carman, who was still in high school.[12] This probably ended any remaining prospect Miller had of completing his degree, if he still harboured such an ambition. In September 1926, Miller married his beloved Mary Isabel Fraser – Essie – a fellow teacher he had met in Stoughton before the war and with whom he had kept up correspondence while overseas.[13] Together they owned and operated the farm, growing fruits and vegetables, for four decades.

As war memorials and cenotaphs began to spring up across the country in the early postwar period, Miller created a memorial of a different kind. He had apparently returned from Europe with a souvenir befitting his enduring fascination with the natural world: dozens of acorns he had collected on the Western Front. These he planted on the family farm sometime in the spring or early summer of 1919. He subsequently dubbed the farm and woodlot that grew from his original plantings "the Vimy Oaks," or "Aux chênes de Vimy," an epithet he came to use in the heading of his correspondence.

---

10 University of Toronto Archives, A1989-0011/reel 65, Leslie Miller academic record.
11 University of Toronto Archives, A1989-0011/reel 65, Leslie Miller academic record.
12 "William Miller, Milliken," *The Globe*, 28 March 1924, 2.
13 "Marriages," *The Globe*, 8 September 1926.

The editor standing next to a "Vimy Oak" planted outside the
Visitor Education Centre at Canada's National Vimy Memorial in France.
Credit: Amy Shaw; Editor's collection.

Did the acorns really come from Vimy Ridge? Miller never mentioned
finding acorns at Vimy in his diary nor do his descendants recollect him
saying that he did. Indeed, Miller wrote very little at all about Vimy in his
diary. The famous Easter 1917 engagement passed in one of those curious and hard-to-explain lapses in his diary keeping. One rather fanciful
story concerning the discovery of the acorns, recounted nearly a century
later, holds that Miller gathered them from beneath a half-buried oak
on Vimy Ridge soon after the battle. No such account occurs in Miller's
diary, and acorns gathered in April 1917, even assuming any could be
found in the devastation immediately after the battle, probably would
not have been viable when planted two years later. This admittedly
charming fable, then, might best be understood as another of the many
emotive myths that the Battle of Vimy Ridge has given rise to over time.

But Miller almost certainly did collect the acorns on the Western Front, possibly in the autumn of 1918, and very possibly from somewhere on the long breadth of Vimy Ridge, as his service afforded him several opportunities to return to that sector.

Moreover, Miller's youthful nature notes, published in the Toronto *Globe,* as well as innumerable passages in his diary, reveal that he was above all else punctilious and exacting in his observations of the natural world. It would have been highly uncharacteristic for Miller to have dubbed his farm and the woodlot the "Vimy Oaks" if the acorns had not come from there. It is also unlikely that he simply chose the name in honour of the famous victory. Admittedly, the soldiers of the Canadian Corps recognized Vimy as an important victory at the time. The capture of the ridge had been one of the only bright spots in one of the darkest periods of the war for the Allies. But immediately after the war there was by no means a consensus that it had been the most important battle the Canadians had fought. Nor was the selection of Vimy Ridge as the site for sculptor Walter Allward's Canadian national war memorial automatic or uncontested. Only gradually, and certainly not prior to the unveiling of the memorial in 1936, did Vimy assume its position as Canada's pre-eminent battle of the First World War.[14] Some of Miller's "Vimy Oaks" stand today, on the property of a church in what is now Scarborough. In 2015, they became the source of an imaginative and ongoing commemorative project, involving the repatriation of acorns from Miller's original oaks to Vimy Ridge, as well as the planting of, to date, roughly a thousand descendant saplings at sites across Canada.

Leslie and Essie Miller sold their beloved Vimy Oaks in 1965. Leslie died on 29 December 1979 at Sunnybrook Veterans Hospital, Toronto, never having returned to the battlefields of his youth, never having returned to see the names of fallen comrades inscribed in cold and unmoving stone in the countless cemeteries and memorials to the missing in Belgium and France. Many of their names can be found on the base of the soaring Vimy Memorial, only a short distance from where the repatriated descendants of Vimy Oaks are growing near the visitor's centre at Vimy Ridge and in the newly dedicated memorial park. Just as the meaning of the First World War was debated by the generation that had fought it, so too did the centenary commemorations of the Battle of Vimy Ridge fail to escape controversy in 2017, as a new generation rushed forward

---

14 See Cook, *Vimy.*

to graft their own social concerns and impose their own meaning on the battle. So it should come as no surprise that the Vimy Oaks project involves controversies of its own. But it is fitting nonetheless that Miller's name will forever be associated with the project. At Vimy Ridge and sites across Canada, including, one hopes, the original woodlot, the oaks will stand and grow, perhaps for centuries, their branches reaching out across generations, a bridge between those who returned home and those who did not: not only a symbol, but part of life itself.

This logo, created by Dave O'Malley (Aerographics, Ottawa), symbolizes the repatriation of Lt. L.H. Miller's Vimy Oaks back to Vimy Ridge, creating a living memorial to all those who fought in the First World War.
Copyright: Patricia Sinclair

The Canadian Experience of War

General Editor: Kevin Spooner

George R. Lindsey (Edited by Matthew Wiseman), *The Selected Works of George R. Lindsey: Operational Research, Strategic Studies, and Canadian Defence in the Cold War*

Eric McGeer, *Varsity's Soldiers: The University of Toronto Contingent of the Canadian Officers' Training Corps, 1914–1968*

Terry Copp with Alexander Maavara, *Montreal at War, 1914–1918*

Leslie Howard Miller (Edited by Graham Broad), *Part of Life Itself: The War Diary of Lieutenant Leslie Howard Miller, CEF*

Printed and bound by CPI Group (UK) Ltd, Croydon, CR0 4YY

13/04/2025

14656517-0002